# Capitalism and the Media

And the money. Yeah, the money. The lifeblood, the oxygen of this wonderful civilization that we have built from the mud, the money, the corpuscles of life gushing around this nation, this world filling men and women all around with desire, quickening the ambition to own, and make, and trade, and profit, and build, and improve. I mean, great geysers of life, he willed. Of buildings, he made stand. Of ships, steel holes, amusements, newspapers, shows and films and life bloody complicated life! He made life happen.

Kendall Roy's eulogy to his father Logan Roy,
*Succession*, aired 23 May 2023

I underestimated the ability of a profit motive to make people do terrible things – to make companies do terrible things.

Former CEO of 21st Century Fox, James Murdoch,
*The Atlantic*, 14 February 2025

# Capitalism and the Media

Key Concepts for Understanding
Communications and Technology

Des Freedman

polity

First published in 2026 by Polity Press Ltd.

Polity Press Ltd.
65 Bridge Street
Cambridge CB2 1UR, UK

Polity Press Ltd.
111 River Street
Hoboken, NJ 07030, USA

ISBN-13: 978-1-5095-6530-6
ISBN-13: 978-1-5095-6531-3(pb)

A catalogue record for this book is available from the British Library.

Library of Congress Control Number: 2025948136

Typeset in 10.5 on 12 pt Plantin by
Cheshire Typesetting Ltd, Stockport, Cheshire
Printed and bound in Great Britain by Ashford Colour Ltd.

The publisher has used its best endeavours to ensure that the URLs for external websites referred to in this book are correct and active at the time of going to press. However, the publisher has no responsibility for the websites and can make no guarantee that a site will remain live or that the content is or will remain appropriate.

Every effort has been made to trace all copyright holders, but if any have been overlooked the publisher will be pleased to include any necessary credits in any subsequent reprint or edition.

For further information on Polity, visit our website:
politybooks.com

# Contents

# Acknowledgements

The origins of this project lie with an undergraduate class I taught at Goldsmiths for some 20 years. 'Media, Modernity and Social Thought' was usually greeted with reservations by more practice-minded students. By the end of the course, however, they had often incorporated the concepts we discussed into their creative work and energized me with their spirited debates. Massive thanks to all of them. And there are a lot . . .

The idea for this specific book lies in hugely enjoyable discussions with David Hesmondhalgh and Victor Pickard, both of whom are currently writing their own (and much more accomplished) books on capitalism and the media. Dave is likely to focus on culture and human flourishing, while Victor will be more preoccupied with non-capitalist media models and democracy. I'm not sure this book would have been written without their encouragement.

The book definitely wouldn't have been written without a Leverhulme Trust research fellowship for which I am extremely grateful. Additional thanks to Mary and Maddie at Polity for steering the book through production and to Jesse Armstrong for allowing me to use the wonderful quote from *Succession*.

Every academic leans on their colleagues and friends to complete a project like this and I don't know where I'd be without them. Chris Nineham, Feyzi Ismail, Kirsten Campbell, Paula Chakravartty, Sarah Banet-Weiser, Barbie Zelizer, Anamik Saha, Sydney Forde, Gavan Titley, Catherine Rottenberg, Marcela Pizarro, James Curran, Jo Litter, Graham Harwood and of course my *compañeros*, Gholam Khiabany, Milly Williamson and Natalie Fenton, who gave me such incredible feedback – you make all the difference.

It's been, to say the least, a challenging few years and, ultimately, I just want to thank Stanley, Dexter and Kirstie for their incredible love and patience. Kirstie is so important she gets two mentions.

# 1
## Capitalism Shouldn't Need an Introduction

***Overview*** This introductory chapter argues that while capitalism remains the dominant socio-economic system, it is insufficiently acknowledged or questioned in mainstream politics and culture. This applies as much to recent discussions of artificial intelligence as it does to the everyday operation of the media. Despite this, a growing anti-capitalist sentiment has emerged that has challenged this silence. The chapter provides a working definition of capitalism that sees it as a dynamic, complex, comprehensive and harmful set of social relations. Finally, it maps out the structure of the book which is organized around first identifying specific imperatives and features of capitalism and then considering their impact on various elements of our media and communications landscapes.

### Capitalism veiled and unveiled

Capitalism is the most powerful, creative and destructive social system the world has ever seen. It has saturated our environment at every level: it is the air we breathe and the water in which we swim (though both have been heavily polluted as a result of capitalism's insatiable appetite for growth); it provides the overarching reason for and underlying logic of much of our daily productive activity; it has simultaneously revolutionized and traumatized our planet; it has been vigorously celebrated and fiercely contested; it mutates constantly and yet it remains loyal to some core activities that include the privileging of private property, the pursuit of profit and the exchange of commodities under market relations.

In the light of centuries of both fascination with and resistance to capitalism, this book seeks to highlight capitalism as the central dynamic that shapes our lives and, in particular, that sets the conditions of existence for the spheres of entertainment, information and connection that absorb so much of our attention. Capitalist social relations have circumscribed the emergence of the media at every step: from pamphlets in the eighteenth century, newspapers in the nineteenth century, broadcasting in the twentieth century through to the online platforms of the twenty-first century. Media have always been products of capitalist development as well as vehicles for capitalist reproduction, whether we are talking about the commodity prices provided by the earliest gazettes, the televised rituals that have underscored nationalism and imperialism, the advertising that fuels consumerism, or the data that drive recommendation algorithms on our favourite streaming services.

Yet capitalism, as an identifiable concept and associated set of activities, is often relegated to the margins by mainstream political actors, business leaders, economists and commentators. Rarely do its core protagonists show any desire to turn the spotlight onto the more structural aspects of their own industries and practices and to trace back issues of funding, ownership, control and culture to a common source. Instead, despite providing the operating logic for everyday life across the globe, capitalism remains a spectral presence in the upper echelons of contemporary society, confined to the dark recesses of conventional economic courses and the odd primer from supranational organizations like the International Monetary Fund.

This is especially true for media and the technological developments with which they are intimately and increasingly associated. While the media landscape is littered, for example, with specialist financial publications, business correspondents and economics-focused podcasts, the content is mostly granular – dominated by stock market reports, investment tips, profit warnings and inflation figures – and fails to acknowledge the systemic roots of what are presented as disconnected phenomena. The British writer and environmental campaigner George Monbiot once asked, 'When did you last hear a critique of capitalism on the BBC? This is the system that dominates every aspect of our lives. Yet it seems to be off-limits at the BBC, and almost all other media. Seldom mentioned, never investigated, never criticised and never even properly explained' (Monbiot 2024).

Even those news sources most broadly associated with the world of finance and capitalism appear to be somewhat coy about its existence. The *Wall Street Journal*, for example, describes itself as 'the definitive source of news and information through the lens of business, finance, economics and money' while the *Economist* states that it has 'helped readers grasp the great drivers of change, from technology to geopolitics, finance and economics.' Japan's *Nikkei* presents itself as 'an indispensable tool in your pursuit of success in Asia – the center of global economic growth and innovation', while Bloomberg modestly claims that its customers 'rely on us to deliver accurate, real-time business and market-moving information that helps them make critical financial decisions'.[1] None of them refer to capitalism in their mission statements, even though reporting on it – indeed, servicing it – is part of their DNA and their actual business model. Capitalism, where it is mentioned in reporting, is often a descriptive afterthought, a variable among other variables (competing with human nature, the weather, technology and supposedly immutable economic principles), rather than a mobilizing concept that might bind together what are otherwise seen as discrete events.

This reluctance to foreground capitalism is especially evident in relation to mainstream analyses of technological innovations and media controversies. When did you last read that misinformation might not just be the product of 'bad actors' but the logical outcome of business models predicated on profit above all else? Why do news headlines still continue to cover 'extreme' weather events as individual occurrences and not the product of a climate crisis caused by an economic system that is addicted to fossil fuels? Why are the harms associated with overuse of social media viewed as the dysfunctions of individual psychologies and not connected to the 'winner takes all' structure of capitalist markets? Why is the blame for negative stereotypes around race, gender and religion frequently reserved only for 'backward' content producers and not linked to the structural inequities between social groups that have long existed in capitalism?

A recent example of this displacement can be seen in relation to 'common sense' ways of talking about artificial intelligence – or 'the biggest event in human history' as Professor Stuart Russell describes AI in his 2021 Reith Lectures on the BBC. Russell (2021) acknowledges the existence of 'profit-maximizing algorithms' and 'profit-neglecting externalities' but fails to connect them to any underlying political, economic or social system. Instead, AI appears to be, above all, the result of the application of 'human ingenuity' – not least the contribution of groundbreaking work done by people like Alan Turing and Arthur Samuel – and the innate affordances (and many challenges) of machine learning. There is a similar gap in Yuval Noah Harari's not-so *Brief History of Information Networks from the Stone Age to AI*, which blames not capitalism but a species-wide 'network problem' (2024: xiv) – a tendency for humans to collaborate with each other in large numbers which is based on deep-rooted myths – for our vulnerability to technologically related crises. The 2024 Nobel Prize-winning economist Daron Acemoglu provides a powerful corrective to the more outlandish predictions of AI's impact on productivity, but even his work is absorbed exclusively with specific macroeconomic developments and the 'architecture' of generative AI (Acemoglu 2024: 45). Capitalism – or indeed any structural socio-economic formation – is missing in action.

This absence is replicated in many of the popular guides to AI that you might see at the airport bookshop or on bestseller non-fiction lists. Here, 'technological innovation' is lauded as the key driver of AI as if it is somehow exempt from or immune to overarching economic laws and political choices. The influential futurist and entrepreneur Ray Kurzweil (2024) argues that AI is the result of an unstoppable technological journey towards 'the Singularity', the eventual integration of humans with unprecedented computing power. There are endless references to neurons but none to profits, labour or markets. Borg, Sinnott-Armstrong and Conitzer (2024), in their book on *Moral AI*, ask important questions like 'Can AI be safe?' and 'Can AI be fair?' without locating AI within the broader political and economic contexts that actually shape opportunities for and barriers to safety and fairness. Timandra Harkness (2024) claims that 'technology is not the problem', and yet she attributes the source of justified anxieties around breaches of privacy and extreme customization not to a social system but to individual failings, given that 'the problem might simply be *us*' (2024: x) and our need for relentless self-expression. Indeed, innovation itself can be seen as a largely individualized project such as when Margaret Mitchell, in her otherwise thoughtful and accessible introduction to the impact of AI, suggests that its origins can be dated to 'Two Months and Ten Men at Dartmouth [University]' (Mitchell 2019: x) – a common account of technological development where context is sacrificed for more biographical or microscopic detail.

Not everyone associated with AI at the highest level denies its links to capitalism. Sam Altman, the CEO of OpenAI, the company that developed ChatGPT, responded to an interview question in the business magazine *Fortune* on the tension between generating profits for investors and serving the public interest by saying that 'Capitalism is awesome. I love capitalism. Of all the bad systems the world has, it's the best one – or the least bad one we found so far. I hope we find a way better one' (quoted in Konrad and Cai 2023). Mustafa Suleyman, the co-founder of both DeepMind and Inflection AI and a highly influential industry voice, is also keen to explore 'ways to reconcile profit and social purpose' (Suleyman 2023: 255) and refers fleetingly to the 'distributed, global, capitalist system of unbridled power' in which AI sits (2023: 134). Yet the 'mega-system' (2023: 142) with which he is preoccupied in the book is technology itself and not at all a broader set of social relations that might underpin this. In the end, artificial intelligence – an innovation that will require trillions of dollars of investment, is based on the exploitation of global labour, depends on highly volatile markets for chips, rests on an extremely fragile environment for its power and is the subject of intense geopolitical competition – is all too often presented simply as the unstoppable outcome of the convergence between human acuity and computational power: the 'coming wave', as Suleyman's book is titled.

This reluctance to identify capitalism as both key technological and societal driver, let alone to criticize it and to explore its consequences at a structural level, extends as well to how the media classify themselves in their own accounts. The global Nexis news and information database shows that from 1981 until the time of writing, adjectives that privilege technological, temporal and mainstream liberal democratic political categories are far more likely to be

| Descriptor | Number of articles/broadcasts |
| --- | --- |
| 'social media' | 15.5 million |
| 'digital media' | 1.23 million |
| 'mass media' | 372,000 |
| 'mainstream media' | 347,000 |
| 'independent media' | 229,000 |
| 'traditional media' | 181,000 |
| 'public media' | 99,000 |
| 'free media' | 76,400 |
| 'liberal media' | 57,900 |
| 'corporate media' | 53,800 |
| 'conservative media' | 51,900 |
| 'right-wing media' | 35,100 |
| 'legacy media' | 23,900 |
| 'alternative media' | 20,700 |
| 'commercial media' | 15,200 |
| 'left-wing media' | 10,700 |
| 'capitalist media' | 597 |

(*Source*: Nexis database, July 2025)

deployed than ones that reference issues of power when describing specific types of media.

This means that audiences are likely to encounter a reference to 'social media' in the news nearly 26,000 times more often than to 'capitalist media', despite capitalism providing the underlying logic for the development and ongoing operation of social media. Audiences are 22 times more likely to see a mention of 'digital media' than they are to 'corporate media' even though corporate power is an important explanatory framework for understanding the operations and impacts of contemporary media and tech landscapes.

However, while one of the aims of this book is to challenge this obfuscation by reasserting the centrality of capitalism for media and society, it is, of course, not the case that there is some kind of *omertà* about the existence and status of capitalism in general. First, there is a growing and noisy anti-capitalist movement that seeks firmly to place societal dysfunctions and crises – including climate change, inequality, war, racism and hopelessness – at the door of a system that is wedded to reproducing harms more than it is able to generate benefits (Wright 2021). The willingness both to name and to criticize capitalism is widespread among ordinary people. A survey conducted in 34 countries found that only people in six – the United States, Poland, Czech Republic, Japan, Nigeria and South Korea – had a positive attitude towards capitalism: '[i]n most countries, anti-capitalist sentiment dominates' (Zitelmann 2023: 367). Among younger demographics, hostility to capitalism is even more pronounced, with only 40 per cent of 18–29 year old Americans reporting a positive impression of capitalism as distinct from 44 per cent who were more inclined to socialism (Pew Research Center 2022). When *Teen Vogue* publishes a hard-hitting explainer on capitalism that states that its critics see it 'as an inhuman, anti-democratic, unsustainable, deeply exploitative system that must be dismantled' (Kelly 2020), then something is going on under the surface.

For many on the receiving end – for young people with rising debts, for workers without sustainable work, for families without a family home, for communities under water because of a climate crisis spawned by our dependence on fossil fuels – capitalism is neither an abstract nor mythical entity but a very visible and visceral element of everyday life. This helps to explain the continuing refraction of anti-capitalist sentiment even into popular culture with the release in recent years of films such as *Sorry to Bother You* (2018), *Parasite* (2019), *The Menu* (2022) and *Triangle of Sadness* (2022), as well as television hits including *Succession* (2018–23), *The White Lotus*

(2021–25), *Severance* (2022–present), *Mr Bates vs the Post Office* (2024) and *Industry* (2021–24). I will return to the possibility of anti-capitalist expressions later in the book.

Second, capitalism is more likely to be acknowledged in news headlines as a meaningful term when the social and economic crises which, as we shall see, are a consistent part of its personality generate pressure that cannot be contained. In other words, there are times when even capitalists feel the need to talk publicly about the existence of capitalism. Such was the scale of the 2008 financial crisis, for example, that it was not possible to get away with simply blaming a handful of 'bad apples' or describing it as a 'minor correction'. Instead, when trillions of dollars were wiped off world stock markets, when millions of people lost their homes and when unemployment soared as a result of the systemic failure of markets and financial institutions, 'capitalism' – understood as a system as distinct from its discrete components – hit the headlines. References to 'capitalism' in news articles soared by 66 per cent in the period 2008–2010, as compared to 2005–2007,[2] as its staunchest advocates came out fighting to defend the ailing, though still prevailing, economic order. The *Times*, owned by the media mogul Rupert Murdoch, ran an editorial entitled 'Crisis and Capitalism', suggesting (somewhat counter-intuitively) that banks were the solution to the crisis (*Times* 2008) while the *Washington Post* ran an opinion piece by the conservative journalist Fareed Zakaria (2009), headlined 'The Return of Capitalism', which argued that the crash signified not so much a crisis of capitalism itself but of regulatory complacency. Zakaria concluded that capitalism would soon be 'rebalanced, reregulated and thus restored' and ideally, at least from the point of view of capitalists themselves, the term itself would retreat into the shadows once again.

Either way, capitalism, apparently dormant for so long, was finally back in the news and, as the left-wing American writer Nancy Fraser noted in 2014, it could not easily be disappeared once more. 'Capitalism is back! After decades in which the term could scarcely be found outside the writings of Marxist thinkers, commentators of varying stripes now worry openly about its sustainability, scholars from every school scramble to systematize criticisms of it, and activists throughout the world mobilize in opposition to its practices' (Fraser 2014: 55).

One example of this is the increasing number of critical books with capitalism firmly foregrounded in their titles that have appeared since 2008, including 'capitalist realism' (Fisher 2009), 'monopsony capitalism' (Kumar 2020), 'cannibal capitalism' (Fraser 2022), 'plastic capitalism' (Vanatta 2024), 'vulture capitalism' (Blakeley 2024) and 'extractive capitalism' (Khalili 2025). These have been complemented by titles that seek explicitly to assess the impact of digital innovations on contemporary societies, such as 'communicative capitalism' (Dean 2009), 'cool capitalism' (McGuigan 2009), 'cognitive capitalism' (Moulier-Boutang 2011), 'platform capitalism' (Srnicek 2016), 'surveillance capitalism' (Zuboff 2019), 'informational capitalism' (Cohen 2019), 'big data capitalism' (Fuchs 2019), 'chokepoint capitalism' (Giblin and Doctorow 2022) and 'AI capitalism' (Lindgren 2023). These examples of what David Hesmondhalgh (2026: 131) has called 'X-capitalism formulations'[3] often provide valuable insights into the consequences of recent technological developments but they are rarely primarily concerned with evaluating the extent to which these developments disrupt or intensify capitalist principles themselves. At times, the temptation to focus on what is new or different overrides the commitment systematically to identify the underlying and persistent features of capitalism that will shape how these innovations unravel and make themselves felt. Zuboff, for example, rarely refers to 'capitalism' in her work without using the respective conjoining term, suggesting that her priority lies, above all, with understanding surveillance as the engine of a radically new social order.

This emphasis on naming and exploring specific types of capitalism risks marginalizing its more durable characteristics and instead tends to fetishize the most valuable technological currency at any one time – whether that is cotton, oil, chips or data. According to this narrative, capitalist relations provide the scenery for fresh and dynamic innovations as if capitalism is utterly in thrall to surveillance or data and not the other way around. Handing agency to the technology as opposed to the social relations in which this technology was produced then generates the kinds of deterministic arguments we hear from futurologists and commentators whose impact I explore in the following chapter.

To be clear, this is certainly not the approach adopted by all 'X-capitalism' theorists. Srnicek, for example, pointedly locates technology companies as 'economic actors within a capitalist mode of production' (2016: 3) and contextualizes the rise of platforms in relation to a long-standing productivity crisis. Dencik and colleagues' work on data justice specifically links the emergence of datafication to broader economic and political shifts since the 1970s and argues that the 'rise of Big Tech is one that is intimately intertwined with the history of capitalism and capital's continued advancement in the wake of significant crises' (Dencik et al. 2022: 15). Julie Cohen, while preoccupied with the shift to a new 'informational' mode of capitalism, nevertheless acknowledges that this does not preclude a 'continuing orientation toward capitalist production, surplus extraction and accumulation' (Cohen 2019: 6), processes, as we shall see, that are at the heart of the DNA of capitalism.

Yet, for other theorists, the rules of capitalism as they have long existed are now being ripped up by the sheer exuberance and velocity of digital developments, and we are apparently witnessing a break with capitalist logic. Zuboff, for example, argues (2019: 53) that surveillance capitalism represents an '*unprecedented* formulation of capitalism' (my emphasis), and its ability to scrape and monetize every last bit of our personal data has generated a 'new form [that has] broken away from the norms and practices that define the history of capitalism' (Zuboff 2019: 13). The Greek economist and activist Yanis Varoufakis states that 'capitalism is now dead' (2023: 8) and that it has been replaced by a 'technofeudalism' based on the mutation of traditional capital into the exploitation of 'cloud capital'. On a similar note, McKenzie Wark speaks of a new 'vectoralist class' that has monopoly control of informational assets and digital supply chains such that we are witnessing a 'new mode of production. This is not capitalism any more' (Wark 2019: 5). The intangibility and elasticity of information demands that we think 'beyond' capitalism as a system that was predicated on ownership of material resources and confront instead terrifying new systems – whether 'vectoralism' or 'technofeudalism' – that are based on the extraction of surplus information.

Although coming from very different political perspectives, these positions chime with the work of the *Financial Times* columnist John Kay (2024), who also argues that ownership and circulation of physical assets is no longer decisive in a world of rentiers where economic value is dominated by corporate control of digital assets like patents, advertising and licensing. According to this logic, the intellectual property of Taylor Swift, the branding of top football clubs and the algorithms of our largest social media platforms are all far more valuable than products of the material economy, including the resource extraction and infrastructure development that makes all this possible. Yet, for Kay, 'the process I describe has very little to do with "capital" and nothing whatsoever with any struggle between capitalists and workers for control of the means of production' (2024: 7). Such a struggle belongs apparently to a distant past that was epitomized by hierarchical management structures and exploited labour and that is less relevant to what Kay sees as the 'relatively flat and participative' organizational culture of Apple, Amazon and Alphabet (Kay 2024: 3).

This book rejects the notion that we have moved beyond capitalism and, in particular, the claim that the prevalence of digital technologies and informational assets means that we should cast our attention towards other explanatory frameworks. Big Tech companies are just as tied into exploitation and hierarchy as their analogue predecessors, while the struggle between capital and labour remains just as relevant. We may be seeing the emergence of new business models, new sources of profitability and new pressure points in global trade, but these need to be located in relation, and not counterposed, to capitalist imperatives. The book attempts therefore to illustrate why an understanding of capitalism has been, and still remains, central for grasping the dynamics of society and media. It aims to provide a concise overview of the axial principles of capitalism, together with an assessment of some of the multiple ways in which media technologies and texts have both been constituted by and contributed to the reproduction of capitalist relations. Such an understanding is vital if we are to democratize media systems that have for so long been subject to – and corrupted by – capitalist imperatives.

## Defining capitalism

Much of this book is organized around these specific imperatives, but I want to make four more general points about how capitalism is understood before providing a working definition.

First, and most obviously, capitalism is frequently viewed as an *economic order* or, as Karl Marx puts it in the preface to *Capital* (1977 [1867]: 90, 92), as a 'mode of production' that underpins 'the economic formation of society'. Marx sought to examine in great detail what he describes as 'the economic law of motion of modern society' that includes the exploitation of labour that is capitalism's greatest source of value, the commodities that are its life blood and the compulsion to accumulate that is its Achilles heel. The German revolutionary Rosa Luxemburg writes of its need to expand as a 'coercive law, an economic condition of existence for the individual capitalist' (2003 [1913]: 12) while the Hungarian Marxist Georg Lukács claims that capitalism is 'the first system of production able to achieve a total economic penetration of society' (Lukács 1971 [1923]: 62). All see capitalism as a monstrous, chaotic and avaricious economic system that provides the material basis for the production and reproduction of everyday life.

Capitalists themselves also conceive of capitalism in economic terms but obviously in a much more benign and limited way – as a vehicle for the production, distribution and consumption of goods and services across the world. This is the 'common sense' definition that is adopted by its supporters, taught on mainstream economics courses and reproduced by untold business correspondents (at least where it is explicitly mentioned): that capitalism refers to a particularly productive way of organizing the 'natural' ebb and flow of economic transactions. According to the International Monetary Fund's in-house journal: 'Capitalism is often thought of as an economic system in which private actors own and control property in accord with their interest, and demand and supply freely set prices in markets in a way that can serve the best interests of society' (Jahan and Mahmud 2015: 44).

Capitalism, conceived in this way, is the institutional embodiment of the merging of a natural sense of self-interest with structural measures designed to stimulate wealth creation. As Adam Smith famously writes in *Wealth of Nations*, one of the earliest analyses of the 'commercial society' that we now describe as capitalism, '[i]t is not from the benevolence of the butcher, the brewer, or the baker, that we expect our dinner, but from their regard to their own interest' (Smith 2012 [1776]: 19). As mobilized through free and open markets, capitalism is seen to maximize the potential of unlimited exchange for both producers and consumers.

The beauty, for its advocates, is that this particular system of trade generates a series of externalities that are said to benefit populations the world over: increased life expectancy, greater freedom, improved literacy and reduced poverty, to name just a few. The fact that wealth remains so unequally distributed – for example, in 2022, the poorest 50 per cent of the world's population owned 1.7 per cent of all wealth[4] – and that capitalism's externalities also include environmental crisis, colonialism, war, authoritarianism and fascism does not seem to disturb its more evangelical supporters. As the Swedish libertarian Johan Norberg writes in his *Capitalist Manifesto*,[5] capitalism is an intrinsically democratizing, innovative and subversive economic model; in fact 'capitalism is not really about capital, it is about handing control of the economy from the top to billions of independent consumers, entrepreneurs and workers, and allowing them to make their own decisions about how they think it will improve their lives' (Norberg 2023: 16).

This book shares neither this wildly inaccurate picture of a benevolent, empowering and distributed economic order nor the conception of capitalism as a mere trading and pricing system – a convenient fiction for those who would like to restrict its scope to the numbers on a ledger or the data on a spreadsheet. Instead, capitalism is a far more expansive and ambitious concept that speaks to fundamental economic realities and yet also (and this is my second point) refers to the *social relations* that underscore these economic arrangements – to the power structures, institutions and forms of labour that allow one group of people, capitalists, to control the production and distribution of societal resources. Capitalism is a deeply and inextricably social phenomenon at the same time as it is intimately bound up with and driven by profound economic imperatives. Capital, as Marx and Engels state in the *Manifesto of the Communist Party* (1973 [1848]: 51), is both a 'collective product' and a 'social power' or, as Ellen Wood notes, 'a mode of production is not simply a technology but a social organization of productive activity; and a mode of exploitation is a relationship of power' (1995: 27).

This is a crucial point made by writers from very different backgrounds and indeed with markedly different perspectives on capitalism itself. Fernand Braudel, the prolific post-war French historian, argues that capitalism is a system of economic monopolization but also a 'political word' (1983: 237) that seeks to capture the workings of an entire society. 'The worst error of all', he writes (Braudel 1984: 623) is to suppose that capitalism is simply an '"economic system", whereas in fact it lives off the social order . . . it is and always has been a massive force, filling the horizon'. For classical sociologists like Weber, Durkheim and Simmel, capitalism furnished the environment in which they conducted their surveys of power, politics, ritual, rationalization and urbanization. The influential twentieth-century theorist of capitalist innovation Joseph Schumpeter notes that 'Marx defines capitalism sociologically, i.e., by the institution of private control over means of production' (Schumpeter 2010 [1942]: 17) and insists that only when the 'wild jumble of social life' is acknowledged do the 'ghostly concepts of economic theory begin to breathe' (2010 [1942]: 39). Fast forward nearly another century, and we find Nancy Fraser arguing that capitalism 'is best conceived as an institutionalized societal order' (2022: 19) that privileges profit seeking while cannibalizing the labour of those who make this happen both in directly productive labour and in what Fraser calls the 'extra-economic' spheres of social reproduction.

It's important to get the relationship between the economic and the social right. While narrow economistic definitions of capitalism fail to do justice to its expansive character – that it casts its shadow over the whole of society – definitions of capitalism that downplay its economic compulsions are equally counter-productive and idealist. Fraser may be right to argue (2022: 17) that 'Capitalism is Something Larger than an Economy' (as one of her subheadings is titled) and that 'boundary struggles' in the 'extra-economic' sphere are vital. That does not mean, however, that economic imperatives are subordinate features of the capitalist landscape or that there is a viable and autonomous sphere of social reproduction that is somehow independent of underlying economic factors. Indeed, as the radical political economist Nicholas Garnham argues, the 'necessary condition for a capitalist social formation is the existence of a more or less universal domination of social relations by the exchange relation, i.e. a market economy' (1990: 22). Neither capitalism nor society can be reduced to the act of exchange but neither can they be fully grasped without acknowledging the economic laws that prevail. Ellen Wood refers to these laws as the 'dictates of the capitalist market – its imperatives of competition, accumulation, profit-maximization, and increasing labour-productivity – [that] regulate not only all economic transactions but social relations in general' (Wood 2002a: 7).

My third point is that one of the consequences of these imperatives is that capitalism is a hugely *dynamic* system. It is constantly innovating, adapting, consolidating and expanding in order to satiate itself and to protect itself from the internal contradictions and external resistance that it generates. Like a patient suffering from akathisia, capitalism cannot afford to stand still. It needs constantly to recompose itself and to exploit new opportunities to achieve its underlying determination to stimulate accumulation and secure profits. In response to this constant reinvention, theorists tend to turn to top-level descriptions of capitalism – either temporal ones such as 'ages' and 'waves' of merchant capitalism, industrial capitalism, monopoly capitalism or neoliberal capitalism, Fordist or post-Fordist capitalism, or to the 'X-capitalism' frames mentioned previously that highlight information, knowledge and technology as key drivers – to capture this sense of change and development.

The danger of periodizing and classifying capitalism in this way is that, for example, data and information (or indeed cotton and electricity) come to be fetishized as virtually independent variables and as engines, in and of themselves, of economic change and social transformation. Instead of critically assessing technological innovations in relation to socio-economic contexts, there is the temptation to be dazzled by spectacular machines and killer apps and to obscure the more resilient factors – Wood's 'imperatives' – that not only shape the emergence of these technologies but also constrain the behaviour of capitalism at any one time. Capitalist social relations are, after all, predicated on the impulse for technological development aimed at increasing productivity and mitigating risks; that is precisely one of its ever-present characteristics and not a mere 'externality'. Change, in summary, is a constant feature of capitalism. When Mark Fisher describes capitalism as 'a monstrous, infinitely plastic entity, capable of metabolizing and absorbing anything with which it comes into contact' (2009: 36), he isn't suggesting that capitalism simply blows with the wind but rather that, by necessity, it learns to adapt to and to seek to exploit the new meteorological conditions which it helped to generate in the first place.[6]

Wark attacks this approach as evidence of the left's romantic notion that 'there is an eternal essence to Capital and that only its appearances change' (2019: 21). But this is precisely the issue: organizational forms, production techniques, mobilizing technologies and cultural norms do indeed change regularly, with enormous consequences for society. Transportation innovations, medical advances, the roll-out of electricity, the development of nuclear technology and the invention of the transistor have all, in very different ways, massively affected the lives and deaths of the world's population for many years. They have done so, however, in the shadow of a constantly mutating capitalism as opposed to one that has been innovated and informationalized out of existence. Despite Wark's argument that 'maybe the greatest trick of capitalism is to gull us into imagining that there is nothing but eternal capitalism' (2019: 22), capitalism is far from 'eternal'. This is, however, not because it has already been replaced by a new informational mode of production; nor will it wither away simply as a consequence of increased computational power or the fact that we spend more time online. The greatest threat to its survival (beyond environmental catastrophe) is not posed by artificial intelligence or the rise of a 'vectoral economy' but by organized resistance emerging out of its own internal contradictions as they affect global populations.

The persistence of this opposition leads to my fourth point: that capitalism is *harmful*. This is a system that consistently generates both enormous wealth and stark poverty; one that promises liberal democracy while simultaneously delivering authoritarian control; one that boasts of facilitating competition and choice and yet routinely produces monopolies and chokepoints; one that facilitates unprecedented technological breakthroughs and then imposes an exclusionary cost on them. As a result, throughout its history, capitalism has been repeatedly and fiercely resisted – whether we are talking about opposition to the land enclosures that marked its birth in the eighteenth century, the brutal working conditions and low pay that characterized its growth, the colonial conquests which expanded its markets and intensified its exploitation, or the structural unemployment and use of zero-hours contracts that have immiserated working people. These are not occasional drawbacks or technical faults that can be corrected with minor engine work but systematic harms that are related to capitalism's very operating principles.

The US sociologist Erik Olin Wright classifies these harms in his book, *Envisioning Real Utopias* (Wright 2010), in which he argues that capitalism:

- perpetuates suffering, especially through extensive exploitation of labour;
- blocks the means through which its benefits can be extended to all and therefore prevents human flourishing;
- fetishizes competition as a virtue which restricts individual freedom and undermines workplace autonomy;
- violates basic egalitarian principles of social justice;
- promotes inefficiency by under-producing public goods and stimulating the overconsumption of natural resources;
- privileges a shallow and alienating form of consumerism;
- leads to environmental destruction because of the constant pressure to increase profits no matter the cost;
- undermines ethical principles because of the domination of a commodity logic that mitigates against non-monetary values;
- fuels imperialism because of its underlying determination to extend markets to new places and to seek new sources of profit;
- corrodes community by undermining the mutualities and forms of solidarity that take place outside of exchange;
- negates democratic values because of private and unaccountable control of the economy.

While these are huge generalizations that need further corroboration and explanation, they nevertheless provide both a useful summary of the negative externalities associated with capitalism and a corrective to the unwarranted optimism of the dominant 'Business School approach' to free-market economics.

This book explores the ways in which media technologies and forms contribute to reinforcing many of these harms and to naturalizing the unequal distribution of resources across societies. As such, even though it draws on a wide range of theorists of capitalism with very different perspectives, it is *not* designed to be an impartial and non-judgemental account of our dominant social system and established modes of communication. Instead, it is part of a long, critical academic tradition of understanding capitalism as a deeply polarizing, profoundly troubled and yet highly complex system of thought and action. Indeed, as Jürgen Kocka notes (2016: 1), the reason for continuing to use the term 'capitalism', as opposed to its euphemisms like a 'market economy' or 'free enterprise', is precisely that it is often understood as 'a concept of critique: it is less a descriptive term than a critical one'.[7] This book is firmly based within that orbit; it adopts an *interested* perspective that is especially necessary given the deep crises that we are facing – of climate catastrophe, economic inequality, structural discrimination and the 'democratic delusions' (Fenton 2025) associated with digital communications – and the need to develop appropriate practical and theoretical responses.

In the light of these four contextual points about capitalism – that it is based on specific economic laws, that it refers to a particular set of social relations, that it has an irrepressible need to mutate and that it produces more harms than benefits – I want to propose the following working definition:

> **Capitalism is a highly dynamic and necessarily expansive socio-economic order based on private property relations and commodity exchange whose overarching priority is to secure profits, not to meet human needs.**

Other definitions are, of course, available. There are more neutral ones, such as James Fulcher's claim that capitalism is 'essentially the investment of money in the expectation of making a profit' (2015: 2) and Wright's notion that it refers to 'a particular way of organizing the economic activities of a society' (2010: 22), which are both admirably concise, if far too narrow. Then there are more partisan conceptions such as the International Monetary Fund's version referred to earlier that specifically equates market exchange with 'the best interests of society' or, alternatively, the one provided by left-wing economist Grace Blakeley (2024: 29) that capitalism is best defined as 'the divide between the people who own all the stuff required to produce commodities and those who are forced to sell their labour power to the capitalists to buy those commodities'. There is also the approach adopted by the Nobel economist Daron Acemoglu that definitions of capitalism are far too contradictory, misleading and ideological in their attempt to bind together such a radically different set of practices and rationalities that it is better simply 'to abandon this notion and concentrate on political and economic incentives forged by the broad complex of institutions' (Acemoglu 2017: 3).

## Capitalism is *the* variable

As I hope will already be obvious, this book has no intention of abandoning capitalism as a mobilizing concept. In fact, quite the opposite: one of its objectives is precisely to illustrate how capitalism – in all its complexity and diversity – provides us with the most rigorous and vital analytical framework for understanding what goes on in all corners of the globe, whether in the free-market heartlands of the United States, the 'welfare capitalism' of Northern Europe, the 'liberal capitalism' of Western Europe, the 'petro capitalism' of some countries in the Middle East, the 'state capitalism' of China, the 'authoritarian capitalism' of Russia and Hungary or the 'developing capitalism' of poorer countries in, for example, Africa, the Caribbean and Central America. In reality, these are mostly convenient labels that fail both to do justice to the specific organization of capitalism in these particular countries and regions *and* to capture the commonalities between how capitalism is exercised across borders and oceans. As Paul Bowles argues (2024: 2), 'Part of the challenge of understanding capitalism is therefore precisely that it is capable of exhibiting great variation across countries and through time and yet still retain the common elements that enable all its varieties, spatial and temporal, to be similar at root.'

There is also a broader methodological point to make here. In order to avoid accusations of reductiveness and to encourage interpretive approaches – around, for example, race, gender and geography – that were systematically marginalized for many years, there has been the temptation more recently to offer multiple perspectives on every event and to refute all notions of causality. It is as if no singular explanation can even start to do justice to the messy phenomena that we encounter and that all 'social facts' have such extensive and complicated genealogies that it would be nonsensical to 'impose' one overarching framework.

Yet why should this necessarily be the case if the category itself is sufficiently rich and diffuse and offers so many avenues for both critical and remedial work? Capitalism, unlike other explanatory systems, operates on the basis of fundamental economic laws that regulate the production and reproduction of daily life, that saturate the social, and that provide the inescapable infrastructure of material life. As such, capitalism is uniquely generative of social relations, pursuing its underlying ambitions across historical periods and operating in radically different circumstances from north to south and from east to west. This diversity leads some theorists to see capitalism more as an 'ideal type, a model that one uses even though one knows that it is not wholly identical with historical reality' (Kocka 2016: 23) or, as in the case of Erik Olin Wright, to talk of 'a wide variety of real-world capitalisms' (Wright 2010: 23) that deviate from some sort of pure iteration as expressed on the pages of Smith's *Wealth of Nations* or Marx's *Capital*.

Going against the grain of much academic literature, I understand 'capitalism' as a comprehensive and integrated set of social relations. David Coates suggests that both Smith and Marx, unlike the more specialized nature of contemporary scholarship on the topic, were 'committed to a holistic understanding of capitalism' (2016: 93). Certainly, this book adopts a methodological commitment to seeing capitalism not as an 'ideal type' that is refined in or adapts to specific circumstances but as a meaningful whole: an operating system that has its own rules even if it needs to be regularly updated. Indeed, why are we prepared to accept the logic of Windows, MacOS and Android as comprehensive (if monopolistic) operating systems that structure our interaction with the digital world but are more reluctant even to acknowledge capitalism as a similarly ubiquitous interface that mediates our access to everyday life?

This approach draws on Georg Lukács's notion of totality, the antidote to the fragmentation of society that appears natural under capitalist relations. Lukács believes that fragmentation is an 'illusion' (1971 [1923]: 12) and that individual components of a social order are meaningless without a more systematic understanding of how they cohere together as a whole.

> Only in this context which sees the isolated facts of social life as aspects of the historical process and integrates them into a *totality*, can knowledge of the facts hope to become knowledge of *reality*. This knowledge

starts from the simple (and to the capitalist world) pure, immediate, natural determinants . . . [and] progresses from them to the knowledge of the concrete totality, i.e. to the conceptual reproduction of reality. (Lukács 1971 [1923]: 8; italics in original)

In order to appreciate the contingent features of life – as Lukács notes, the 'determinants', whether they be technological, economic or social, that capitalists seek to endow with innate agency – it is necessary first to acknowledge the existence of the overarching structure which lends them meaning and purpose. Social relations may appear to be discrete and autonomous (and this book is especially interested in the means by which this occurs) but they are locked into what Lukács describes as a 'dynamic dialectical relationship with one another', which is part of an 'equally dynamic and dialectical whole' (1971 [1923]: 12–13).

Relating to capitalism as a 'totality' – as a singular entity precisely because of its diversity – has a further advantage in that it highlights its generative power in relation to other crucial areas of society. Capitalism's role in relation to, for example, slavery, colonialism, the family and the exploitation of the environment positions it as central to the ways in which we understand the nature and consequences of these phenomena. 'What all the talk about capitalism indicates, symptomatically,' argues Nancy Fraser (2022: 1), 'is a growing awareness that the heterogeneous ills – financial, economic, ecological, political, social – that surround us can be traced to a common root.' Capitalism, according to this perspective, offers a focal point of resistance to a multitude of sins including racism, oppression, poverty and environmental crisis precisely because it provides the underlying logic for the way in which these crimes have been spawned, operationalized and justified. The idea that there might be a common source of many of these problems does not at all indicate that they are somehow less serious than capitalism's headline economic failures but simply that they are intimately wrapped up with hundreds of years of capitalist social relations and that to resolve their harms will involve addressing capitalism's own systemic failures.

The analysis that follows in this book of the component parts of capitalism is therefore very much predicated on an understanding that we are dealing with an integrated system that seeks to hide its 'wholeness' (indeed its very existence, as we saw earlier with financial journalism) and instead to pretend that it is only the parts that count and not the sum. This involves processes of mystification and abstraction that place the media centre-stage as key vehicles through which real relations of power are obscured and fragmented. After all, what better institutions are there to naturalize 'common sense' assumptions about, for example, the desirability of competition, the efficacy of private property, the magic of markets, the fruits of liberal democracy and the separation of 'politics' and 'economics' than the broadcasters, streamers, journalists, editors, platform operators, programmers, advertisers, app developers and sponsors who collectively dominate the flow of information and communications across the globe? For all the focus on media and tech companies as 'attention merchants' (Wu 2017), they are also commodity traders in surface appearances where the 'forms of appearance are reproduced directly and spontaneously, as current and usual modes of thought' (Marx 1977 [1867]: 682). This is far from a conspiratorial operation, launched from what would have been smoke-filled rooms in previous years, but rather the utterly natural and logical consequence of capitalism's underlying imperatives and its major structural design flaw: the fact that it has far more losers than winners and that, somehow, this fact needs to be contained and normalized.

## What this book aims to do

The book seeks to provide a concise conceptual summary of key elements of capitalism's operating system and then to illustrate briefly how these are mobilized in and associated with both historical and contemporary trends in media and tech landscapes. It is, therefore, not a new social theory of media so much as an attempt to provide a critical vocabulary with which to grasp essential features of our information, entertainment and connection environments by linking them to a larger socio-economic order. It aims to provide a materialist analysis of broad issues (rather than specific policies and developments) – including media ownership, bias, misinformation, misrepresentation, commodification, celebrification, the dynamics of streaming, the role of public service media, and the environmental cost of contemporary communications – by locating them in a dialogue with a range of theories of capitalism. It draws heavily on both the tradition of critical political economy of the media (Garnham 1990; Mosco 2009; Murdock and Golding 1973) that recognizes capitalism as a vital contextual framework for evaluating and democratizing communications industries and practices, as well as contributions from economists, sociologists, technologists, political theorists and historians for whom capitalism was a distinct preoccupation. The book does not aim to provide a comprehensive literature review on every aspect of capitalism and social theory, nor the associated iterations in media and communications but instead to highlight some key texts and arguments that apply across different temporal, geographical and technological landscapes.

The first half of the book deals with what have often been seen as core, constitutive features of capitalism – such as private property, labour, class, exploitation and commodification – that tend to populate attempts to define it. The second half deals with more 'superstructural' issues which emerge from and are tangled up with the economic domain, for example, ideology, hegemony, the state, imperialism, oppression and globalization. While it is possible to view each chapter as free-standing without the need for prerequisites, my earlier argument about seeing capitalism as a totality would suggest that each chapter provides only a glimpse of the interconnected aspects of a much bigger system. Indeed, each chapter can only provide a partial analysis, given that capitalism is not formed of discrete units. For example, it is virtually impossible to talk about commodification without talking about labour, just as it makes little sense to separate colonialism from the wider pursuit of accumulation or to analyse the state without talking of its ambition to protect private property. Nevertheless, each chapter is designed to offer an overview of headline features of capitalism, together with their presence across selected media examples.

My hope is that, by the end of the book, readers will agree with me that capitalism provides a uniquely valuable critical frame for analysing contemporary media and communications landscapes and, crucially, understanding that its failures and harms will generate the momentum to seek a radically different way of organizing society.

# 2
# Technology and Revolution

***Overview*** Capitalism is often seen (even by some of its greatest critics) as a 'revolutionary' system based on sustained and unprecedented technological innovation, not least in relation to media and communications. This chapter explores capitalism's compulsion to innovate and discusses the significance of Joseph Schumpeter's work on the role of innovation and the entrepreneur. It then draws on Raymond Williams's critique of technological determinism to assess the nature and extent of the 'digital revolution'.

## Capitalism as the outcome of social revolution

Capitalism is a revolutionary system. That is to say, capitalism emerged out of a revolutionary transformation of the feudal social relations that dominated until the eighteenth century. This revolution is often seen in primarily technological terms – in relation to the diffusion of increasingly sophisticated and productive instruments that led apparently inexorably towards an industrialized society. Yet the revolution was not simply the result of technological breakthroughs and entrepreneurial zeal but the consequence of a clash between a ruling order that was not able and willing to change and a rising capitalist class that was desperate to exploit new 'conditions of possibility' (Wood 2002a: x). Capitalism was not the automatic product of a series of innovations that increased productivity and stimulated exchange, nor was it the inevitable outcome of a competitive and creative 'human nature' as conceived by Adam Smith in his *Wealth of Nations* (Smith 2012 [1776]). Instead, capitalism was unleashed by the successful, epoch-changing struggle led by an emerging class – the 'bourgeoisie' – that wanted to take advantage of new social property relations and a highly specialized division of labour. Technological innovation was not the cause but the effect of this struggle.

On the other hand, capitalism is no longer a revolutionary system. It lost many years ago its insurgent energy and its determination to defeat forces of conservatism. It has become precisely the atrophied ruling order it sought once to overthrow: one dominated by excessive caution, glaring inequality, permanent crisis and a deep irrationality (the most obvious example of which is capital's continuing investment in fossil fuels, which is endangering its own sustainability). Yet, curiously enough, we are constantly told that we live in 'revolutionary' times mainly because of digital technologies that threaten both to improve and disrupt every corner of our lives. In recent years alone, commentators have identified a 'third industrial revolution' (Rifkin 2011) generated by a combination of internet technology and renewable energy, superseded by a 'fourth industrial revolution' (Schwab 2017) driven by supercomputing and biotechnology, and now a 'fifth industrial revolution' (Sodergren 2023) fuelled by artificial intelligence. Thanks to an interconnected series of developments – including blockchain, robotics, quantum computing and increased processing power – the digital has, it seems, been particularly vigorous in fostering a series of 'revolutions' in many areas of capitalist society. This leads me to ask two interrelated questions: in what ways is capitalism revolutionary and why are technological developments so often dubbed as revolutionary?

Capitalism's most famous critics, Karl Marx and Frederick Engels, were in no doubt about the revolutionary status of capitalist society when they were writing in the middle of the nineteenth century. Opposed to pre-Enlightenment mysticism and in thrall to new productive possibilities, the new capitalist class was in the business of producing miracles on earth. As they write in the *Communist Manifesto*, 'The bourgeoisie, historically, has played a most revolutionary part . . . It has accomplished wonders far surpassing Egyptian pyramids, Roman aqueducts, and Gothic cathedrals' (1973 [1848]: 35–6). It achieved this through the systematic exploitation of emerging technological forces through new social relations of production that offered, as we shall explore in later chapters, unprecedented opportunities for exchange and accumulation.

The bourgeoisie, during its rule of scarce one hundred years, has created more massive and more colossal productive forces than have all preceding generations together. Subjection of nature's forces to man, machinery, application of chemistry to industry and agriculture, steam-navigation, railways, electric telegraphs, clearing of whole continents for cultivation, canalisation of rivers, whole populations conjured out of the ground – what earlier century had even a presentiment that such productive forces slumbered in the lap of social labour? (Marx and Engels 1973 [1848]: 39)

The question posed by Marx and Engels is rhetorical: it would not have been possible to conceive of such a situation in earlier centuries because the preconditions for this 'colossal' form of productive activity did not exist. The crude division of labour, the inefficient organization of property and the broad distribution of populations that were common to feudalism precluded this kind of energy and innovation. But when the enclosure of land in eighteenth-century England produced greater concentrations of propertyless agricultural labourers and a political order willing to sanction the economic activity of formally sovereign individuals, it then became possible to imagine such an enormous historical shift. For Wood, the 'revolutionizing of productive forces *presupposed* a transformation of property relations and a change in the form of exploitation that created a historically unique need to improve the productivity of labour' (2002a: 26). The 'ceaselessly revolutionary techniques of modern production', as Lukács calls them (1971 [1923]: 97), reflected capitalism's structural imperative to drive forward as much as the earlier 'objectively relatively stable, traditional craft production' (1971 [1923]: 97) expressed the more conservative tendencies of a dying feudalism.

This was a social revolution in which technology was mobilized and which, in turn, offered opportunities for technological development to deepen and intensify the revolution. The British historian Eric Hobsbawm describes events in Western Europe from 1789 to 1848 as a 'dual revolution' with both a political and an industrial character: the 'triumph not of "industry" as such, but of *capitalist* industry; not of liberty and equality in general, but of *middle class* or "*bourgeois*" *liberal* society' (1964: 17; emphasis in original). The US and French revolutions of the late eighteenth century were the harbingers of new republican political orders which also fuelled unprecedented opportunities for economic expansion in both scale and scope. This 'dual revolution' involved, therefore, not just new tools and new leaders but entirely different relations of power from those that had gone before. As Hobsbawm notes, 'The gods and kings of the past were

powerless before the businessmen and steam-engines of the present'
(1964: 73).

## Technological innovation and the capitalist entrepreneur

The problem is that many subsequent theorists of capitalism have
become all too fixated simply on the 'businessmen and steam-
engines' associated with capitalism – in other words, simply on the
people and the technologies as opposed to the system's underlying
social relations. For the economist Joseph Schumpeter, whose 1942
book *Capitalism, Socialism and Democracy* remains influential today
(particularly with Silicon Valley investors and Big Tech moguls),
this translates into a focus on the entrepreneurs and the innovative
technologies that he argues constitute the beating heart of capitalism.
Schumpeter spends the first part of the book challenging Marx's
analytical framework, accusing him of a reductive approach which
blames capitalism for all social ills. Where they have common ground,
however, is that Schumpeter agrees entirely about capitalism's dynamism and its inability to stand still:

> capitalist economy is not and cannot be stationary. Nor is it merely
> expanding in a steady manner. It is incessantly being revolutionized
> from within by new enterprise, i.e., by the intrusion of new commodi-
> ties or new methods of production or new commercial opportunities
> into the industrial structure as it exists at any moment. Any existing
> structures and all the conditions of doing business are always in a
> process of change. (Schumpeter 2010 [1942]: 27)

The key figure in this process of continuous flux, however, is not the
capitalist nor the worker but a separate figure, the entrepreneur, who
provides the ongoing spark for productive innovation. Schumpeter
argues that Marx lacks 'an adequate theory of enterprise' and notes
'his failure to distinguish the entrepreneur from the capitalist'
(Schumpeter 2010 [1942]: 28). Capitalists may control the sphere of
economic activity, but the role of the entrepreneur is even more vital:
'to reform or revolutionize the pattern of production by exploiting an
invention or, more generally, an untried technological possibility for
producing a new commodity or producing an old one in a new way,
by opening up a new source of supply of materials or a new outlet for
products, by reorganizing an industry and so on' (2010 [1942]: 117).
The main attribute of entrepreneurs for Schumpeter is that,
through technology, they are able to shrug off conservative tenden-

cies and to *transform* the situation in which they find themselves. It is this kind of activity that generates the '"prosperities" that revolutionize the economic organism' (2010 [1942]: 117) and on which, he insists, capitalists are utterly dependent. This is quite different to the conception of innovation pursued by Marx who identifies it as a strategic orientation by capitalists themselves to develop technology in order to foster accumulation, stimulate competition and intensify the exploitation of labour. 'The machine', argues Marx in *Capital* (1977 [1867]: 492), 'is a means for producing surplus-value' for capitalists – an engine of profits – and not an instrument for enriching society more generally.

Schumpeter, however, sees the individuals who most effectively exploit the possibilities of technological development to secure economic progress as the most decisive actors in contemporary society – not least because they are best placed to rescue capitalism from its own self-destructive tendencies of monopolization, bureaucratization and sclerosis. They provide the inspiration for the repair work that Schumpeter famously describes as 'creative destruction' (discussed further in chapter 6): the ongoing and repeated purges within capitalism where, as a result of innovation, weaker capitals are destroyed and more dynamic ones rise in their place to galvanize the system once more. Actually, Schumpeter, writing in the middle of the last century, was already quite despondent about capitalism's ability to maintain its dynamism; he argues that 'innovation itself is being reduced to routine' (2010 [1942]: 117) and that repeated cycles of 'creative destruction' would not be enough to save capitalism itself from collapse. Influenced by Max Weber's notion of 'disenchantment' (2013: 139), which is itself the result of capitalism's high level of rationalization, Schumpeter writes that the 'romance of earlier commercial adventure is rapidly wearing away because so many things can be strictly calculated that had of old to be visualized in a flash of genius' (Schumpeter 2010 [1942]: 117–18).

Today's innovation gurus, however, have little appetite for this kind of caution and simply ignore Schumpeter's warning about capitalism's unsustainability. Instead, we hear frequently about the huge value to society of innovation and the central role of entrepreneurs. This is driven, as Mariana Mazzucato (2015) argues, by a series of myths: for example, that small, nimble companies are necessarily more productive than large firms, that patents are inherently redistributive, that investment is best served by less 'red tape' and, most significantly, that the public sector is intrinsically less innovative and productive than the private sector. This latter belief has fuelled the idea that today's true revolutionaries are the corporate programmers, data scientists and engineers who disrupt existing markets and force us to imagine new ways of being and doing – exemplified by billionaires and tech moguls like Apple's Steve Jobs, Microsoft's Bill Gates, Tesla/SpaceX's Elon Musk or OpenAI's Sam Altman. Indeed, innovation, together with the technologies with which it is associated, has become fetishized as an autonomous area of productive activity with its own philosophy, academic programmes and professional practices. These developments both conflate competing conceptions of what constitutes a revolution and misunderstand the status of technology in capitalist societies.

## Definitions of revolution

There are two quite distinctive ways to understand revolution. The first, as previously sketched out in relation to the emergence of capitalism, is associated with underlying structural social change. As the US political scientist Theda Skocpol argues (1979: 4), social revolution refers to the 'rapid, basic transformation of a society's state and class structures, accompanied and in part accomplished through popular revolts from below' – the ability to turn the world 'upside down', as the historian Christopher Hill once described the English revolution (Hill 1984). While this conception focuses on political and social rupture, there is a second definition that focuses more on individual change and physical motion (as in wheels turning and records spinning and where turntable speeds are measured in terms of 'revolutions per minute'). As the *Cambridge Dictionary* puts it, revolution refers to 'a big change or improvement in the way that someone works or looks, or in the way that people do a particular activity',[1] a definition that points to less dramatic although still significant instances of behavioural and perceptual change.

The British cultural theorist Raymond Williams suggests that, compared to the more expansive, political definition of revolution, it can 'seem curious to read of "a revolution in shopping habits" or of the "revolution in transport"' (1983: 273). For Williams, this is an example of 'the language of publicity' and a way of talking about 'some "dynamic" new product' (1983: 273–4) rather than about fundamental social change. Reflecting on the rise of broadcasting, for example, he suggests that, 'The transistor revolution might seem a loose or trivial phrase to someone who has taken the full weight of the sense of social revolution, and a technological or second industrial revolution might seem merely polemical or distracting descriptions. Yet the history of the word supports each kind of use' (1983: 274). Williams is making the point here that there is a world of difference between a social revolution and the invention and roll-out of new products and even new industries. Using the former to describe the latter is a 'polemical' strategy designed to serve particular capitalist interests (and to 'distract' more critical approaches).

In this context, while the 'digital revolution' speaks to changes in, for example, processing and computational power that have facilitated radically new forms of production, distribution and consumption, it has not fundamentally altered the status of private property, the need for accumulation or fact of exploitation (as I shall explore in later chapters). To speak of a 'digital revolution' begs a series of questions: in what ways has a new 'informational' mode of production gener- ated social relations that are distinct from those that preceded it, and to what extent has it facilitated the transfer of power not within elite groups but to other social groups who have remained largely marginalized and disempowered? In other words, to what extent has power in a 'digital revolution' meaningfully shifted from control of both resources and decision-making by a tiny and powerful minority to control by the majority of citizens?

Marx himself did write about industries 'revolutionized' by tech- nological innovation, but his point was that capitalism itself was defined by its compulsion to innovate as distinct from earlier social formations, not that innovation itself generated revolutionary trans- formations. As he puts it in *Capital*, 'Modern industry never views or treats the existing form of a production process as the definitive one. Its technical basis is therefore revolutionary, whereas all earlier modes of production were essentially conservative' (1977 [1867]: 617). In other words, specific aspects of the production process may regularly be 'revolutionized', but this should not suggest that the balance of power within that process, let alone within society more broadly, has changed.

Today's digital entrepreneurs, however, insist that algorithms and AI have shifted goalposts to such a degree that the language of 'power shifts' and 'revolution' is entirely appropriate. For Mustafa Suleyman, the 'coming wave' of AI will 'force a set of tectonic shifts in power . . . This will create vast new enterprises, buttress authoritarianism yet also empower groups and movements to live outside traditional social structures' (2023: 17). Taylor Lorenz opens her book on the 'creator economy' and the role of influencers by stating that:

This is a book about a revolution. Like most revolutions, this one has done less than some of its vanguards promised and more than anyone predicted. It has radically upended how we've understood and interacted with our world. It has demolished traditional barriers and empowered millions who were previously marginalized. It has created vast new sectors of our economy while devastating legacy institutions. (Lorenz 2023a: 1)

This is a vast exaggeration of the degree of popular empowerment and system transformation that has taken place as a result of online innovation. The digital world contains many of the same concentrations of power, organizing principles, inequalities, contradictions and social problems as its analogue predecessor, despite the enormous possibilities that have been opened up. The one 'legacy institution' that has clearly not been devastated is of course capitalism itself, a fact actually acknowledged by Lorenz in an interview when her book was published: 'I think a lot of the root problems here are related to capitalism, and the desire to put shareholder profit above a generation's mental health. What we have is this hyper-capitalist tech landscape where we have very few platforms – Meta and Google – that dominate everything. They're not accountable, and they don't give a shit about the negative consequences' (Lorenz 2023b). In other words, the 'revolutionary' impact of social media on mental health and individual identity that Lorenz writes about stems from (and is contained within) residual practices of capitalism.

Digital technologies have clearly affected the lives and possibilities of their users in many enduring and complex ways, but to describe them as facilitating fundamental social change (whether positive *or* negative) is to equip them with a kind of transformative power that needs detailed empirical and analytical interrogation before we reach for the now-familiar vocabulary of 'revolution' that is increasingly detached from its more radical associations. Technology is a contingent feature of capitalist society and not a fixed property. As the Nobel economist Daron Acemoglu warned in a Goldman Sachs investment report on AI, 'Technological innovation has undoubtedly meaningfully impacted nearly every facet of our lives. But that impact is not a law of nature. It depends on the types of technologies that we invent and how we use them' (quoted in Goldman Sachs 2024: 5).

## Technological determinism and capitalism

This determination to endow technologies with revolutionary agency and impact pre-dates social media and has always been part of the very genealogy of technological innovation (Marvin 1988). Tom Standage's book on *The Victorian Internet* is clear on this point.

> In the 1880s, advocates of electricity claimed it would eliminate the drudgery of manual work and create a world of abundance and peace. In the first decade of the 20th century, aircraft inspired similar flights of fancy: Rapid intercontinental travel would, it was claimed, eliminate international misunderstandings. Similarly television was expected to improve education, reduce social isolation and enhance democracy. Nuclear power was supposed to usher in an age of plenty where electricity would be 'too cheap to meter'. The optimistic claims now being made about the Internet are merely the most recent examples in a tradition of technological utopianism that goes back to the first transatlantic telegraph cables, 150 years ago. (Standage 1998: 197)

As Standage suggests, this 'hype' now flourishes in the digital age. Consider, for example, Esther Dyson, one of the leading pioneers of the online world and a founding member of ICANN, the organization that assigns domain names. In her book *Release 2.0*, written in the early days of the Web, she writes that the internet 'will change all of our lives. It will suck power away from central governments, mass media and big business' (Dyson 1997: 6). The British AI entrepreneur Nigel Toon makes a series of similar claims about artificial intelligence in his book *How AI Thinks*: that it 'will let us solve problems we previously found impossible' (2024: 4), 'will transform our lives' (2024: 4), 'will transform drug discovery and make treatments accessible to all' (2024: 183) and 'will improve efficiency in the workplace taking over dangerous or repetitive tasks and freeing us to focus on more creative activities' (2024: 191). The key word in these statements is 'will': the certainty that these things are destined to take place because of the intrinsically transformative potential of the digital and irrespective of any countervailing economic pressures, regulatory decision-making or consumer resistance.

These 'revolutionary' accounts of technology and innovation are premised on a set of *deterministic* discourses. They are everyday examples of a technological determinism that remains a very powerful force in contemporary conversations about the digital and that describes a situation where a new technology emerges and necessarily changes the world into which it is introduced. As Raymond Williams puts it, technological determinism refers to the belief in 'a new society, a new phase of history, being created – "brought about" – by this or that new technology: the steam-engine, the automobile, the atomic bomb' (Williams 1974: 9). This approach both to innovation and technology marginalizes other political and economic contexts and, crucially, leaves insufficient room for human agency. Just as social revolutions refer to a highly volatile process – as the Italian theorist Enzo Traverso puts it (2021: 16), of 'history breathing in and out' that requires analysis of 'their hesitations, ambiguities, misleading paths and withdrawals' – technology itself needs to be understood in more complex and contextual terms.

Williams argues that technology is 'always, in a full sense, social' (1981: 227) and distinguishes between *technique* and *technical invention* – the application and development of particular skills in laboratories, workshops or perhaps Silicon Valley basements – and the social institution of the *technology*. He is more interested in the process by which a technical invention becomes an 'available technology', in other words, the decisions about which inventions to develop, invest in and manufacture, than he is about the potential capacities of any particular technology. Far from a technique unravelling along its own internal logic, it is the behaviour of real individuals in particular historical circumstances that shapes the transformation of a potential innovation into an available technology. As the historian Lynn White Jr puts it in relation to medieval technologies (1964: 28), 'a new device merely opens a door; it does not compel one to enter.'

For Williams, technology refers not to a fixed entity (no matter how powerful) but to a *relationship*: it is 'necessarily in complex and variable connection with other social relations and institutions' (1981: 227). For example, Williams argues that broadcasting – a hugely disruptive technology – was not invented in a single flash of inspiration or indeed in a single place (despite the road signs near where I live in the United Kingdom saying that 'radio was invented here'). Instead, broadcasting was developed during an extended process of technical experimentation. What was crucial in this process and what organized these experiments into an available technology was the desire for a medium that would complement the contradictory experience of new forms of urban life in the West in the 1930s, based simultaneously on increased mobility and social atomization. Williams famously describes radio and television as forms of 'mobile privatisation' (1974: 26): they offered the possibility of extending people's horizons, of stimulating their curiosity, of providing them with news from 'outside', but they did so by focusing on the family home as the centre of this communicative process. Crucially, Williams links this to shifts in the social organization of capitalism from the 1920s onwards: increased centralization of production and decision-making, and therefore a loss of control over one's daily life, results in growing investment in the private domain. Broadcasting proved to be a suitable technology to link the private with the public and, in so doing, helped to change the definition of both. These are the sorts of issues that we still need to ask about the world nearly a century later.

Williams also argued that there is no predictable identity to or single function of communication technologies. Instead, the eventual outcome of the process of innovation is related to the preferences of human actors and not the affordances of machines. Consider the case of radio that, back in the 1920s, was the subject of competing models in its early development, either as a 'phone booth of the air' or as a 'newspaper of the air' (Sawhney 1996). In other words, how radio developed was not in any sense predetermined: it could either be a precursor to CB radio in terms of point-to-point communication (and very useful to the sailors and navies across the globe) or it could be an instrument that could transmit a single message to millions of people. The eventual outcome of broadcasting (as opposed to narrowcasting) was due less to technological factors than the lobbying of the main US telephone company, AT&T, to keep the 'common carrier' telephone network to itself and to make sure that radio developed on different lines.

That radio developed according to a certain logic that is now seen as obvious is partly due to the allure of a determinism that is seen as 'common sense' by governments and technology companies when, actually, it is the result of a strategy pursued by dominant groups in order to secure an acceptance of their institutional models for particular innovations. Precisely because competing models are technically possible, corporations are forced to attempt to convince investors, regulators and the public that the opposite is true: that there are no alternative paths and that resistance is futile because technological development is preordained. Technological determinism, therefore, is a discursive means of highlighting novelty, naturalizing innovation and paving the way for structural and regulatory changes that are then seen to be necessary. For example, Williams claims that back in the 1980s, cable and satellite technologies were represented as 'socially new' and 'essentially paranational' (1985: 139) phenomena which provided a technical, rather than a political, justification for deregulating and privatizing the media as called for by private media interests. According to this logic, governments were left with no option but to liberalize what had up to that point been highly regulated markets if they were to see the benefits of these new technologies.

The deployment of any innovation is far from a natural or inevitable process but one that takes place in specific technological, cultural, social and economic circumstances. This simple point is all the more important today when we are surrounded by claims about the revolutionary potential of digital technologies. Indeed, according to more sceptical voices, like the anthropologist David Graeber, even the internet has yet to demonstrate its truly revolutionary credentials.

> The Internet is a remarkable innovation, but all we are talking about is a super-fast and globally accessible combination of library, post office, and mail-order catalogue. Had the Internet been described to a science fiction aficionado in the fifties and sixties and touted as the most dramatic technological achievement since his time, his reaction would have been disappointment. *Fifty years and this is the best our scientists managed to come up with??* (Graeber 2012; italics in original)

Perhaps AI will not be a 'disappointment' and will usher in the groundbreaking changes (whether positive or negative in this case) that its more apocalyptic analysts believe to be the case. Whatever happens, however, there is little sign so far that it will be able to shrug off the processes of commodification, concentration, data capture and accumulation that are endemic to all capitalist developments and that have historically rewarded a small group of investors and entrepreneurs over the vast army of workers and users who continue to generate the revenue necessary to sustain even an innovation as 'revolutionary' as artificial intelligence.

## Conclusion

Capitalism itself was the result of a revolutionary transformation of society that marked the end of feudal relations and the emergence of a dynamic socio-economic order that both depended on and required constant technological innovation. Repeated claims of an unfolding 'digital revolution', however, illustrate a narrow preoccupation with technological development that marginalizes broader capitalist imperatives and privileges a deterministic account of social change that largely evacuates issues of agency and power. Artificial intelligence may well change the world, but it is indisputable that the world is going to change AI.

# 3
## Private Property and Enclosure

***Overview*** Capitalism is based on the forcible creation of private property relations achieved in part by circumscribing previously public or common spaces. The chapter highlights the capitalist fetish for private property and discusses the wave of privatizations that has taken place since the 1970s. It then considers how private property has been consolidated inside the media and discusses the various barriers, moats and 'walled gardens' that characterize the enclosure of contemporary digital landscapes.

### The creation of private property

Capitalism is unthinkable without a significant degree of society's assets being held by private individuals, companies and trusts supported by legal protection to secure these proprietary relations. Private property is seen by its advocates, such as the English philosopher John Locke, as a 'natural right' along with life and liberty, and a fundamental tenet of a 'free' economic system that allows individuals to both acquire and possess goods that are not held in common. It is alleged that it is more efficient than common ownership because it incentivizes individual actors and offers a vital check on the power of unaccountable state apparatuses. It is as if owning a house, a car, a ranch or a business of your own automatically provides you with a productive identity and offers you immediate protection from public-sector bureaucrats who do not have your interests at heart. As Friedrich Hayek writes in his celebration of free-market economics, *The Road to Serfdom* (1944: 78), 'the system of private property is the most important guarantee of freedom, not only for those who own property, but scarcely less for those who do not.' Access to private property, according to this logic, generates social and economic benefits for all those who are exposed to it and is promoted as a default position of all 'competitive societies'.

There is a basic problem, however, in that private property did not come about spontaneously or naturally. Instead, as John Bellamy Foster and colleagues state (Bellamy Foster, Clark and Holleman 2021: 1), it 'requires as its basis enclosure and exclusion' – a violent, centuries-long process that involved the historic expropriation of common resources and their transfer into private hands. In other words, the transformation of private property into an organizing principle for wider society was rolled out as a precursor to capitalism. It was then subject to all sorts of post hoc rationalizations, legal instruments and everyday expressions – including in recent years the plethora of property shows on television from *Property Ladder* (2001–9) to *Relocation, Relocation* (2003–present) and from *Buying Beverly Hills* (2002–4) to *Selling Sunset* (2019–present) – to lend it the immutable and benevolent character that its advocates have long associated it with.

Marx argues that capitalism as a dominant system emerges following a process of 'primitive accumulation' that took place in England from the fifteenth century and that involved forcing farmers and peasants off the land they had been living on for centuries. Silvia Federici highlights the persecution of witches and the development of a 'new sexual division of labour' (2004: 12) as essential to primitive accumulation, while the historian Peter Linebaugh argues that the sixteenth century in particular marked not just the beginning of the Atlantic slave trade and the prison but of 'modern capitalism' itself. Accompanied by comprehensive land redistribution and the dissolution of the monasteries, this period saw 'the first great phase of the English enclosure movement: the privatization of England had begun' (Linebaugh 2008: 47). Comparing it to the role that original sin plays in theology, Marx suggests that primitive accumulation facilitated the 'dissolution' of feudal society (Marx 1977 [1867]: 875) by imposing new property relations via the 'expropriation of the agricultural population from the soil' and, later, the '"clearing of estates", i.e. the sweeping of human beings off them' (1977 [1867]: 889). Marx describes this process of 'the theft of the common lands . . . and its transformation into modern private property' as a kind of 'ruthless terrorism' (1977 [1867]: 895) and devotes a whole chapter in *Capital* to the state's 'Bloody Legislation against the Expropriated'. The acceleration of private property, according to this perspective, is not organic and harmless but deliberate and brutal, 'accomplished by means of the most merciless barbarism, and under the stimulus of the most infamous, the most sordid, the most petty and most odious of passions' (1977 [1867]: 928).

Marx was by no means the only critic of the consequences of a society based on the enclosure and exploitation of what was formerly common land. The Enlightenment philosopher Jean-Jacques Rousseau warned a century before Marx that exclusive ownership of common resources would lead to division and conflict:

> What crimes, wars, murders, what miseries and horrors would the human race have been spared had someone pulled up the stakes or filled in the ditch and cried out to his fellow men, 'Do not listen to this imposter. You are lost if you forget that the fruits of the earth belong to all and the earth to no one!' (Rousseau 1987 [1755]: 60)

Adam Smith, meanwhile, accused the new owners of private land of 'indolence' (2012 [1776]: 256) and accused an emerging rentier class of distorting the free market he was so keen to see.

> As soon as the land of any country has all become private property, the landlords, like all other men, love to reap where they never sowed, and demand a rent even for its natural produce. The wood of the forest, the grass of the field, and all the natural fruits of the earth, which, when land was in common, cost the labourer only the trouble of gathering them, come, even to him, to have an additional price fixed upon them. (Smith 2012 [1776]: 52)

Yet it is Marx, and writers in the Marxist tradition, who have most energetically and consistently highlighted the invidious effects of the capitalist fetish for private property. While viewing it as a precondition for a radically new division of labour (that I discuss in the next chapter), Marx highlights the profound alienation of the dispossessed not simply from the land but from relationships that previously would have had a more communal character. The domination of private property means that something is especially valued under capitalism only when it is not shared: 'Private property has made us so stupid and one-sided that an object is only *ours* when we have it – when it exists for us as capital, or when it is directly possessed, eaten, drunk, worn, inhabited, etc.' (2009 [1844]: 106). Capitalism, in other words, privileges precisely those goods and services that have a proprietorial and exclusive character. Just as I discussed in the previous chapter the (false) claim that innovation is an asset exclusive to the private sector, capitalism seeks to endow private property with a sheen that is absent from assets held in common. This remains as true today as it was when Marx was writing, despite the growth of open-source software, cooperative enterprises and the digital commons (Fenton 2025), let alone 'sharing' platforms like homeexchange.com, Turo and Tulerie, which allow for peer-to-peer borrowing of homes, cars and clothing respectively (although all three are private companies which significantly dilutes their status as viable alternatives to proprietorial enterprises).

Of course, this fetish for private property exists not only in relation to physical objects but also to the ability to control *access* to goods, services and ways of life. For Ellen Wood, writing about the origins of capitalism, 'enclosure meant not simply a physical fencing of land but the extinction of common and customary use rights on which many people depended for their livelihood' (2002a: 108). This relates to C. B. Macpherson's notion that property is based on the notion of *rights* and not *things*: either the right of publics not to be excluded from 'the use or benefit of something' *or* for the right of property holders to exclude publics from this very same use (1978: 4–5). Property, according to this perspective, is therefore a relational, not simply a tangible, phenomenon and very much connected to the ability to shape the control and distribution of resources – in other words, to the exercise of power.

Macpherson suggests that the equation of property with objects as opposed to rights emerged only under capitalism through the market exchange of commodities (see chapter 5) where capital itself came to be seen as the embodiment of property. Yet he also identifies a transformation in the last century that is particularly relevant to the topic of this book: that property is increasingly being defined – in a nod to its pre-capitalist roots – as 'a right to a revenue rather than a right to a specific material thing' (1978: 8). The difference in the twentieth and twenty-first centuries is that the revenue accrued from private property is likely to be generated not simply by ownership of land[1] but additionally by control of assets like intellectual property, data and licensing – the 'rentierism' discussed in chapter 7 – that are central to media and tech landscapes.

## Privatization: the new enclosure movement

Meanwhile, the drive to change common resources into exclusively private ones has only intensified in the last 50 years as part of a renewed process of enclosure and expropriation that the Marxist geographer David Harvey describes as 'accumulation by dispossession' (Harvey 2005). This is part of a broader attempt to rescue capitalism from its doldrums in the 1970s by pursuing what have come to be seen as 'neoliberal' reforms: the implantation of market logic into every area of social and economic life and the attempted removal of all obstacles to profit. This includes attacks on trade unions and welfare rights, deregulation of financial markets and, crucially, the selling off of public assets across the globe. Harvey argues that this privatization constitutes the 'cutting-edge of accumulation by dispossession' (2005: 157), a 'mantra' that saw the disposal of whole swathes of the public sector as part of a 'new round of "enclosure of the commons"' (2005: 158). In the United Kingdom, this included the privatization of sectors such as social housing, gas, electricity, transportation and telecommunications – a 'redistribution of assets that increasingly favoured the upper rather than the lower classes' (2005: 159).

Privatization was 'sold' by its advocates as a means of improving economic efficiency, shifting assets to the allegedly more dynamic private sector and generating much-needed income. Poorer countries, however, were often required by transnational actors like the World Bank and the International Monetary Fund to dispose of state assets as a condition of receiving additional financial support as a part of broader 'social adjustment' programmes. According to World Bank figures, nearly 6,000 state-owned enterprises in 80 countries (including more than 2,000 in developing countries) were sold off in the 1980s alone (Kikeri, Nellis and Shirley 1992: 1–2). In the following decade, the IMF boasted of the huge 'proceeds' from privatization (Davis et al. 2000: 5): in Argentina (1990–1995), nearly US$23 billion was generated, amounting to 2% of GDP; in Kazakhstan (1993–1998), there were some US$6 billion of 'proceeds', 5.5% of GDP; and in Hungary (1991–1998), nearly US$12 billion of assets were sold off (4% of GDP). One of the most contested cases of privatization took place in Bolivia where water was among the US$863 million of assets that were sold off between 1995 and 1998 (4.2% of GDP), leading to the Cochabamba Water War as whole sections of the Bolivian population protested against the unaffordable price rises associated with privatization and organized a hugely effective social movement (Finnegan 2002).[2] According to the Indian novelist and activist Arundhati Roy, reflecting on the dispossession of millions of agricultural labourers in India in the 1990s, the sale of public assets to private companies 'is a process of barbaric dispossession on a scale that has no parallel in history' (quoted in Harvey 2005: 161).

Although there are now simply fewer state assets to be sold off, the appetite for privatization and its status as both marker and enforcer of a vigorous capitalism remains strong. For example, the far-right libertarian candidate for the Argentinian presidential election in 2023, Javier Milei, campaigned successfully (at times holding a chainsaw) on a programme of cuts to public spending, the introduction of payments for some services that used to be provided for free and a wave of privatizations (Criales 2023). Similarly, former defence minister Prabowo Subianto championed privatization throughout his successful presidential election campaign in Indonesia in 2024: 'I don't see for instance why we [the government] need to be present in every sector of the economy . . . now we must allow private sectors to be more and more dominant' (quoted in Suroyo and Sulaiman 2024). The 'fact' of private property, together with the active process by which common resources are enclosed and transformed into assets controlled by a minority – the privatization described by Linebaugh (2008: 310) as the 'relinquishing of what belonged to all to the enjoyment of a few and called enterprise' – are far from the exclusive preserve of far-right politicians and transnational institutions. Indeed, as we shall now explore, private property has been central to the dynamics of media and communications industries in both analogue and digital times.

## Establishing private property in media

Private property has long played a dual role in relation to media: as engine of capital accumulation and influence and as protector from unwarranted state control. Private media ownership is as old as capitalism itself precisely because its earliest instruments – the gazettes, newsletters and broadsheets that carried information about commodity prices and military adventures from the sixteenth century on – helped to cement the power of an emerging mercantile class and its growth, over centuries, into a new ruling class. From the outset, media were both capitalized themselves and purposefully operating in the service of capitalism's expansion. The historian Paul Starr notes the dependence of this nascent media on capital: 'Publishing was associated with capitalism in part because the industry itself was a prime instance of capitalist development. It took considerable capital to finance not only the equipment in a shop but also the paper and other costs of production' (Starr 2004: 26). Yet news-papers, as they came to be, were forced to operate in the orbit of states that had little interest in granting them full autonomy and instead subjected them to a series of measures – including censor-ship, licensing and taxation – that undermined their independence. Privately owned media, therefore, were seen as a democratic force and a bulwark against the state at the same time that they were always entangled with the power of home states that had a strategic orien-tation on how to 'manage' emerging media and communications technologies.

This contradictory relationship explains the uneven patterns of private ownership and changes of ownership structure that have marked media and communications sectors over time. This is effec-tively because the state – as I examine further in chapter 10 – has long reserved the right to decide what specific form of ownership would best serve its interests, a decision subject to multiple political, eco-nomic and demographic considerations. For example, the US federal government decided not to invest in the development of telegraphy in the 1840s and to leave the industry in the hands of private capital in order to maximize its commercial potential. European countries, more preoccupied with security concerns, viewed the telegraph as a political, rather than a commercial, device and kept it in state hands while the UK state bought out private companies and took control of the telegraph system in 1870, 'convinced that rather than conflicting with their economic principles, nationalization of the telegraph was another species of free-trade legislation' (Starr 2004: 177).

There are many other examples of such contingent decisions over the public/private nature of media property. This includes the nationalization of the British Broadcasting Company, composed of private radio manufacturers, and its transformation in 1927 into the British Broadcasting Corporation (BBC); the sell-off of the formerly state-owned French public service broadcaster TF1 in 1987 as an expression of the then president's commitment to neoliberalism; the wholesale privatization of newspapers following the collapse of communism and introduction of capitalism in Eastern Europe after 1989, a process that may have involved a change in ownership but nevertheless revealed 'a marked continuity at the level of social struc-ture' (Sparks 1998: 109); the privatization in 1995 of NSFNET, the internet's backbone originally overseen by the US National Science Foundation; and the promise by the incoming far-right president Javier Milei in 2024 to privatize all public media outlets in Argentina, a commitment that has stalled at the time of writing.

Another mechanism for consolidating private property within the media is through the emergence of intellectual property regimes and, in particular, the use of copyright as a double-edged sword: both an incentive to produce content by protecting the livelihoods of content creators and a means of securing this content as the exclusive asset of the copyright holder (that is increasingly likely to be a corporate entity). Typically, for capitalism, an instrument that was initially promised to reward the creative outputs of private individuals has been consolidated – through the passing of a series of laws and international treaties – into a mechanism that is dominated by large corporations and that further embeds private property relations into creative processes. For Nicholas Garnham (1990: 40), copyright is a strategic reaction on the part of property owners to attach an exchange value to cultural outputs – 'an attempt to commoditize information by turning the author into a commodity' – rather than an incentive for further creative labour.

Nevertheless, while the status of media property is often contested and certainly not predetermined, private property generally remains the default ownership structure of the media under capitalism, and its logic and imperatives are increasingly evident in a whole series of organizational and strategic manoeuvres that are reshaping digital landscapes. These are only the latest form of 'enclosure' of what might previously have been seen, and safeguarded, as public spaces.

## Fences, moats and walled gardens

In 1996, John Perry Barlow, co-founder of the Electronic Freedom Foundation, issued his stirring 'Declaration on the Independence of Cyberspace'. Warning government (in general) to stay out of a domain in which, he argued, it has neither mandate nor business, he also insisted that '[y]our legal concepts of property, expression, identity, movement, and context do not apply to us. They are all based on matter, and there is no matter here' (Barlow 1996). Not only has it become increasingly obvious that there is plenty of 'matter' in the online world – including everything from the minerals extracted to power our smartphones to the huge data centres warming the planet – but it is also clear that capitalist property relations certainly do apply to digital landscapes[3] which are increasingly enclosed by a series of fences, moats and walled gardens designed to secure private control of online spaces and to shrink the digital commons.

Julie Cohen argues that enclosure or, as she also describes it, 'propertization' (2019: 15), is vital to the creation of 'informational capitalism' and the exploitation of the data on which it is based. Just as land was fenced off, populations displaced and legal entities created to protect the rights of the emerging capitalist class centuries ago, the enclosure of 'intangible resources' is now necessary to secure an updated mode of capitalist development based on 'digital enclosure' (Andrejevic 2007). Although the focus on information might suggest a break with previous iterations of capitalism, Cohen warns against technological determinism and highlights the 'continuing orientation towards capitalist production, surplus extraction and accumulation' (2019: 6) in the significant expansion of intellectual property that has taken place with new trademark, patent and branding regimes facilitated by digital processes. She describes the transformation of what was previously a relatively open internet infrastructure into a network of private operators in which 'platform providers work to define both collected data and algorithmic logics as zones of exclusivity' (2019: 44). This process of 'de facto appropriation and enclosure' (2019: 25) far exceeds the pace of the legal frameworks established to normalize these acts and establishes the underlying logic for the 'land grabs' we see in the media and tech sectors today.

One of the earliest structures to enclose the free flow of media in the online world was the paywalls erected by newspaper companies grappling with a disastrous collapse in advertising, readers and therefore long-term profitability. The strategy was pursued initially by specialist business news outlets like the *Wall Street Journal* and the *Financial Times* who, in 1997 and 2001 respectively, launched experiments whereby some content was placed behind paywalls in order to test out readers' appetite to pay for news delivered digitally. By 2022, some 41 per cent of news websites had some kind of paywall in operation, with most opting for 'freemium' or 'hybrid/dynamic' models based on a combination of articles that are freely available and those that readers have to pay for (Piechota 2023). By 2024, the *New York Times* was able to boast of more than US$1 billion in annual digital subscriptions from some 10 million subscribers (Tobitt 2024) – a sure sign that the internet's early promise of free and open access to information had foundered on the harsh realities and structural imperatives of contemporary capitalism.

At one level, paywalls are an entirely predictable strategic response to a capitalist business model in turmoil, but they are not without negative consequences in that they are likely to serve wealthier, niche audiences above less wealthy, generalist ones and unlikely fully to replenish the revenue lost to digital rivals. Pickard and Williams (2014) suggest that the growth of paywalls is an understandable, if short-sighted, response to an increasingly severe journalism crisis: both a much-needed new source of revenue to pay reporters' wages and a much less welcome source of anxieties about the very mission of news. 'Arguably, paywalls defy the internet principle of openness; they disenfranchise people unable to afford the digital subscription cost; they further inscribe commercial values into newsgathering processes; and, by extension, they may further constrict the scope of voices and viewpoints in the press and in our national discussions' (Pickard and Williams 2014: 207). Paywalls may rescue some of the largest outlets, but without a more imaginative approach to sustainability that recognizes the societal, and not just financial, value of news, elements of the existing news ecosystem – particularly local and not-for-profit ventures – will remain very much at risk (see chapter 14 for a further discussion of the journalism crisis).

Paywalls are, therefore, the most likely outcome of digital news landscapes that are focused on generating profit and that, in the absence of publicly funded alternatives, are subject to thoroughgoing segmentation into private fiefdoms. Where public service news media do exist, they are constantly forced to defend themselves against accusations of inefficiency and bureaucracy from advocates of privatization. From former prime minister Margaret Thatcher in the 1980s to the free-market think tank the Institute of Economic Affairs more recently (Booth 2020), some of the most bullish British capitalists have regularly called for a subscription model to 'liberate' the BBC from what they see as the 'tyranny' of public funding and public ownership. The problem is that a subscription model, the preferred tool of today's digital news providers, is likely to obliterate one of the BBC's stated core remits to cater to all audiences, irrespective of geography and background, and, instead, to replace the principle of 'universality' with one focused on serving the 'particular' interests of those who can best afford to pay. Privatization and subscription funding of public service news media would do little to address their existing deficits concerning accountability and independence (discussed further in chapter 10) but would certainly entrench the further enclosure of the media landscape.

Paywalls, however, are far from the only mechanism that is being used to concentrate private property relations inside the media. Instead, we can see a handful of 'walled gardens' – effectively digital 'one-stop shops' – that preside over specific sectors of the online universe. Amazon has built a fortress for shopping, Apple for entertainment, Meta for connection, Spotify for streaming and PlayStation for gaming. These are closed ecosystems that exploit the logic of 'network effects' – the idea that a site is exponentially more valuable when a large number of people use its services – to keep users within these 'gated communities' and stop them going to rivals for similar services. Nick Srnicek argues that the enclosure of large ecosystems is one of the key strategic imperatives of what he describes as 'platform capitalism', the latest attempt to monetize an emerging resource (in this case data) and, in so doing, to revitalize capitalism itself. This involves attempts to 'tie users and data to the platform by locking them in through various measures: dependency on a service, inability to use alternatives, or lack of data portability' (Srnicek 2016: 110).

For example, Amazon entices customers to its 'garden' by providing a loss-making service like Prime that promises entertainment as well as free and speedy delivery of the earthly goods that customers will most likely have both searched for and ordered on its own platform. With some 40 per cent of the US online retail market – an enormous concentration of power – Amazon is a digital fiefdom that sets the parameters for retail transactions and stifles possibilities for exchanges that lie outside its walls. Similarly, although Apple's App Store was originally developed simply as a way of selling more iPhones and iPads,[4] it soon became clear that this would be an extremely lucrative business, with Apple both dictating the terms of entry for apps and preventing Apple users from downloading apps from any other source. This was at the heart of the decision in March 2024 by the US Department of Justice to sue Apple for 'exclusionary behaviour', not least for its anti-competitive gatekeeping of the App Store that includes prioritizing its own services and keeping out the 'Super Apps' which would, according to one Apple insider quoted in the DoJ's suit, 'let the barbarians in at the gate' (Palma and Acton 2024).

Indeed, one of the most effective ways of keeping out the 'barbarians' (for which read 'competitors') at the same time as keeping users within the walls is to build a 'moat' around the business. Drawing on the words of the billionaire investor Warren Buffett that his preferred companies were 'economic castles protected by unbreachable moats', Rebecca Giblin and Cory Doctorow argue that this is precisely what underscores today's 'chokepoint capitalism': the ability to construct barriers to 'lock in users, lock in suppliers, make markets hostile to new entrants, and, ultimately, use the lack of choice to force workers and suppliers to accept unsustainably low prices' (Giblin and Doctorow 2022: 142). Giblin and Doctorow highlight examples of anti-competitive acts of enclosure (which I discuss further in relation to monopoly and monopsony in chapter 6), including Amazon's control of books, Google and Facebook's domination of online advertising and Live Nation's hegemony over live music. They argue that the largest tech companies have positioned themselves as all-powerful intermediaries between buyers and sellers – audiences and content creators – who dictate the terms of trade and make their billions through their exclusive ability to manage this relationship. Where Apple, for example, had started off simply making money from selling hardware, through its control of the App Store 'it was [now] making money as ferryman: the only one that could cross the river between buyers and sellers' (Giblin and Doctorow 2022: 113). Mark Zuckerberg, the CEO of Meta, has admitted that he wants the company to 'use M&A [mergers and acquisitions] to build a competitive moat around us on mobile and ads' (quoted in Palma and Murphy 2025).

Enclosure, therefore, generates a series of 'harms' – both democratic, as Pickard and Williams demonstrate in relation to putting news behind paywalls, and economic, as Giblin and Doctorow argue in relation to Big Tech's anti-competitive chokehold on different sections of the media and creative industries more generally. Hesmondhalgh and colleagues (2023) add to this discussion by exploring the implications of the 'propertization' of online music and the rise of streaming platforms. From a situation in which the internet initially facilitated forms of peer-to-peer downloading through services like Napster and BitTorrent, intense lobbying by rights holders to secure favourable copyright protection, the prosecution of illegal downloaders and the 'tethering' (Zittrain 2009) of content to specific technologies once again re-established the rule of private property. According to Hesmondhalgh and colleagues, this process involved the 'incorporation' of music into a capitalist logic based on an 'infrastructure designed to ensure security and seamlessness, rather than the generativity, interactivity and open-ness envisaged by an earlier generation of internet enthusiasts' (Hesmondhalgh et al. 2023: 304). At the same time as offering unparalleled and immediate access to back catalogues of recorded music, platforms also 'operated as the main means by which the democratising and emancipatory possibilities afforded by the (always partial) commons-based openness of internet infrastructure were eroded or "closed down"' (2023: 304).

## Conclusion

Enclosure thoroughly (and often violently) restructured the economic and social geography of feudal societies as a condition of capitalist development; digital enclosure is now once again reasserting the primacy and desirability of private property as it further embeds itself inside contemporary media and technological landscapes. While there remain important examples of public ownership and state control of communications, private property relations are intensifying their grip with the emergence of chokepoints, paywalls and closed ecosystems, with little transparency or accountability to users. The 'walled gardens' established by Amazon, Apple, Meta and Spotify are twenty-first-century digital fiefdoms that generate huge benefits for owners and shareholders but produce a series of economic and democratic harms for wider society.

# 4

# Labour, Exploitation and Class

**Overview**  Capitalism has fostered a distinctive form of 'free labour' that is the source of both economic value and high levels of exploitation. This chapter assesses the central role of labour in capitalist societies and explores the continuing relevance of class, as a specific form of social stratification, in both industrial and 'post-industrial' contexts. In particular, it evaluates recent debates on the exploitation of labour – from user-generated content to the roles that drive AI – and argues that wage labour still plays a central role in digital landscapes just as class continues to be the central marker of stratified media systems.

## The emergence and exploitation of 'free labour'

Along with water and oxygen, labour – not cotton, oil or data – is the essential ingredient for sustaining all forms of human life: the ability to transform the environment to generate the resources necessary for everyday existence. This can be physical, in terms of the skills required to produce the food we eat and the shelters we build, or intellectual, in terms of the ideas and symbols with which we communicate. Our ability to labour – to work consciously, creatively and collaboratively – is a distinctive human characteristic and, for Adam Smith, perhaps the most precious asset of all: 'The property which every man has in his own labour, as it is the original foundation of all other property, so it is the most sacred and inviolable' (Smith 2012 [1776]: 127). Yet capitalism has transformed labour in two dramatic ways: first, through the development of a highly specialized division of labour that paved the way for a vastly more efficient mode of production and, second, through establishing a system in which people could sell their labour 'freely', in other words, without being subject to visible coercion.

Smith starts his account of the new 'commercial society' of the eighteenth century by focusing on the unprecedented dynamism of the labourers and the productivity of the manufacturing process. 'The greatest improvements in the productive powers of labour, and the greater part of the skill, dexterity and judgment, with which it is anywhere directed, or applied, seem to have been the effects of the division of labour' (2012 [1776]: 9). According to Smith, a more rationalized, commercial system of production would allow 10 workers to produce, for example, 48,000 pins in one day, whereas working separately – as was the trend in more primitive social arrangements – they would have been hard pressed to make even one in that time (2012 [1776]: 10). The same logic applies today when, for example, thousands of Taiwanese workers collectively produce the millions of Nvidia graphics processing units (GPUs) that fire up the AI 'revolution'.

Smith was convinced that, treated properly and without unfair restrictions on trade, an interdependent commercial system reliant on efficient forms of labour would benefit the public good. But he also noted something else that was distinctive about labour: not that it was some kind of innately 'noble' activity but that it provided the source of wealth in society. 'It was not by gold or by silver, but by labour, that all the wealth of the world was originally purchased; and its value for those who possess it, and who want to exchange it for some new productions, is precisely equal to the quantity of labour which it can enable them to purchase or command' (2012 [1776]: 35).

Labour is, therefore, the main source of the value of the transactions that take place in society – except that there is a problem: how do you quantify this value, given that there is an 'abstract' quality to labour that there is not in the 48,000 pins produced daily by pin-makers? Smith's answer is that this is where money comes in: as a tangible and calculable proxy for the labour that is necessary to produce the essentials of life. 'The butcher seldom carries his beef or his mutton to the baker or the brewer, in order to exchange them for bread or for beer; but he carries them to the market, where he exchanges them for money, and afterwards exchanges that money for bread and for beer' (2012 [1776]: 36). This is the prelude for a lengthy discussion in *The Wealth of Nations* on 'the real and nominal price of commodities', which is precisely the version of Adam Smith that has been adopted in countless economics courses and repeated by neoliberal business commentators: the search for the perfect pricing mechanism and the most efficient fiscal rules to enable the maximum number of transactions in a competitive market.

Marx, however, takes this discussion of the value of labour in a completely different direction. While sharing Smith's conception of labour as the foundation of wealth, he argues that labour is not innocently transformed into money but, under capitalism, is exploited and appropriated by those who buy it – the capitalists. For Marx, it is not just that labour generates the commodities that circulate in society but that labour itself – 'the worker's own life-activity, the manifestation of his own life' (1978 [1849]: 19) – becomes a commodity (with life-changing consequences that I explore further in the next chapter). In particular, he argues that labour has a 'twofold character': it refers both to the *abstract* capacity of humans to work that he describes as 'labour-power', as well as the 'expenditure of human labour-power in a particular form and with a definite aim' (1977 [1867]: 137). This distinction between 'abstract' and 'concrete' labour is essential in understanding that, while particular forms of labour will change dramatically over time – whether from 'material' to 'immaterial' forms of labour (Lazzarato 1976) or from 'secure' to 'precarious' employment (Standing 2011) – labour power itself remains the underlying commodity and overarching source of value as measured in the time spent on productive activity.[1] 'Labour-power', as Marx puts it (1978 [1849]: 18), 'is a commodity, neither more nor less than sugar. The former is measured by the clock, the latter by the scales', a phenomenon (of time in relation to output) that remains true whether applied to pin-making, GPU production or data annotation.

Marx also insists that ordinary people have little choice *but* to sell their labour power if they are to earn the money needed to survive. As Marx puts it, 'the possessor of labour-power, instead of being able to sell commodities in which labour has been objectified, must rather be compelled to offer for sale as a commodity that very labour-power that exists only in his living body' (1977 [1867]: 272). There is a strong element of compulsion here: wage labourers are, of course, free *not* to sell their labour power and therefore free *not* to have the money to acquire somewhere to live, food to eat and clothes to wear, but this is indeed a very limited kind of freedom where exercising your right not to work has such dramatic consequences. Selling your labour power, therefore, is a necessary and, according to a nineteenth-century weaver quoted in the socialist historian E. P. Thompson's fantastic book on *The Making of the English Working Class* (Thompson 1963: 297), urgent task: 'Labour is always something carried to market by those who have nothing else to keep or to sell and who, therefore, must part with it immediately.'

Separated both from the land and from the fruits of their labour, Marx argues that 'free workers', as he describes them, are 'free from, unencumbered by, any means of production of their own' (Marx 1977 [1867]: 874). Because they lack control of anything else, they are 'free' only to sell themselves 'piecemeal' (1978 [1849]: 20) in order to bring home the pay cheque they need to survive and which is the ultimate outcome of their labour. They are 'free' only in so far as they may get to choose the identity of their employer but not the conditions under which their employment takes place; they are 'free' to look for another job but then to risk a period of unemployment; they are 'free' to work 'flexibly' but are likely to face a toll in the shape of lower wages and reduced benefits; they are 'free' to retrain in the hope of finding more rewarding labour but cannot be assured that such a job will be available.

Crucially, another feature of the labour of the 'free worker' is that a portion of their labour is provided to their employer for 'free' – the portion of their labour time that is realized by the employer as profits and for which they are not compensated. This is the basis of the *exploitation* that for Marxist theorists forms one of the great imperatives of capitalism: to short-change the 'free labourer' in order to generate the surplus labour appropriated exclusively by the employer as profit. For advocates of capitalism, this is a just reward and a necessary incentive for capital to bear the risks of running a business; for working people, this is a form of theft and it enraged Marx, who describes capital as 'dead labour which, vampire-like, lives only by sucking living labour, and lives the more, the more labour it sucks' (1977 [1867]: 342).

Exploitation (much like the 'alienation' discussed in the next chapter) is a term that is often used loosely – viewed in this case as a familiar feature of contemporary capitalist life that refers to the tendency of the powerful to 'take advantage' of the vulnerable. But Marx uses the term in a far more precise way: as a fundamental characteristic of the way in which capital both diminishes and regulates wage labour to its advantage. Olin Wright (1997: 10) very helpfully outlines the three main criteria that are specific to capitalist exploitation: first, there is a causal relationship between the 'welfare of exploiters' and the 'material deprivations of the exploited'; second, the exploited are systematically deprived of access to and control over productive resources; and finally (and crucially), exploitation refers to the 'appropriation of the fruits of labor . . . by those who control the relevant productive resources'. Exploitation certainly does take place in a number of other spheres – for example, in relation to sexual violence and the trafficking of migrants – but capitalism's *systematic* drive to realize surplus value through the robbery of 'free labour' is worth bearing in mind when reflecting on more recent debates on the 'exploitation' of digital users that I discuss later in this chapter.

The final point on this aspect of exploitation is that it is not illegal (unlike sexual violence and trafficking) but, indeed, the very basis of capitalist enterprise. 'Only in capitalism', argues Ellen Wood, 'is the dominant mode of appropriation based on the complete dispossession of direct producers, who (unlike chattel slaves) are legally free and whose surplus labour is appropriated by purely "economic" means' (2002a: 96). The exploitation that is at the heart of the productive process remains largely hidden, breaking out only when the relationship between capital and labour becomes so demonstrably unequal that the status quo cannot continue – as in the case of industrial disputes over falling pay or concerns over health and safety. However, in 'normal' circumstances, when antagonisms remain beneath the surface, Marx's famous words in *Capital* remain relevant: 'The silent[2] compulsion of economic relations sets the seal on the domination of the capitalist over the worker. Direct extra-economic force is of course still used, but only in exceptional cases. In the ordinary run of things, the labourer can be left to the "natural laws of production"' (Marx 1977 [1867]: 899) – precisely the 'imperatives' to, for example, privatize assets, maximize profits and increase labour exploitation which are at the heart of this book.

## Class: 'the collective social expression of the fact of exploitation'

One of those 'natural laws' is that, according to Marx and Engels, there is an ongoing conflict in capitalism between two contending classes, defined by their position in relation to the production process: a group of people who, as we have seen, are compelled to sell their labour, and a ruling elite who control productive resources. This applies to the manufacturing of pins in the eighteenth century as much as it does to the production of GPUs in the twenty-first century; it speaks to the production of material goods just as it does to the creation and distribution of information and media; it relates to the labour carried out both in classic industrial contexts as well as more recent platform environments. Of course, the division of labour has become far more complex since the mid-nineteenth century (Savage 2015) and yet, while there are other intermediate classes – for example the middle class and a lower-middle class 'petit bourgeoisie' – their futures are ultimately decided by the struggle and changing balance of forces between capital and labour as opposed to their own 'independent' course of action.

Marx and Engels argue that while class is not a phenomenon specific to capitalism, the new economic system emerging in their time had nevertheless 'simplified the class antagonisms. Society as a whole is more and more splitting up into two great hostile camps, into two great classes directly facing each other: Bourgeoisie [the ruling class] and Proletariat [the working class]' (Marx and Engels 1973 [1848]: 33). Where there used to be a 'complicated arrangement of society into various orders, a manifold gradation of social rank' (1973 [1848]: 33), capitalism's operating system flattened these distinctions in relentless pursuit of the exploitation of 'free labour' which leads to a new, if highly volatile and, at times, combative, class structure.

Class, according to this understanding, is an objective social relation that classifies individuals according to whether they are 'exploited' or 'exploiter', as described earlier in this chapter. For the Marxist historian, Geoffrey de Ste Croix, class refers to 'the collective social expression of the fact of exploitation, the way in which exploitation is embodied in a social structure' (1981: 43). Even Schumpeter, despite his profound differences with Marx, acknowledges the significance of an approach to stratification that is predicated on 'the ownership, or the exclusion from ownership, of means of production such as factory buildings, machinery, raw materials and the consumers' goods that enter in the workman's budget' (Schumpeter 2010 [1942]: 14). Class, for Schumpeter, is not a question of individual perception or labelling but an outcome of the division of labour in society: social classes, he argues, 'are not the creatures of the classifying observer but live entities that exist as such' (2010 [1942]: 12) and provide powerful incentives for collective action based on class position.

Yet there is a popular current today that does see class in far more subjective terms: as a descriptive indication of, for example, dress, accent and background but also as an identity that can be owned or shrugged off by the individual concerned. Polls regularly ask citizens to describe their 'class orientation', while there are plenty of online quizzes designed to assist people in locating their class position by answering questions about their occupation, consumption habits,

leisure activities and preferred holiday destinations.[3] While occupation is a slightly more reliable indicator of class than whether you fly
with a low-budget airline, it nevertheless shifts the emphasis from an
objective assessment of labour-market power to a question of social
status. According to the sociologist Mike Savage (2015: 35), focusing
on an occupational measure of class 'was actually a way of making
for cultural judgements about the ranking and social importance
of jobs. They subtly hinted at the moral worth of different kinds of
jobs and therefore the respectability that flowed from them.' Savage
concludes that this reflects an 'elitist concern to demarcate and map
the boundary of respectability' (2015: 36), rather than an attempt
to illuminate the unequal distribution of wealth and power in any
society.

One of the inspirations for a less economically determined approach
to social stratification is another engaged critic of Marx, the social
theorist Max Weber. Weber agreed with Marx about the economic
roots of class in capitalist societies but had a more pluralistic understanding of stratification more broadly. Weber speaks not of class per
se but of multiple 'class situations', defined as the opportunities (or
lack of) to maintain standards of living and 'personal life experiences'
(2013: 181) that are based on income rather than a relationship to
production. Famously, Weber also notes the significance of status
as a marker of social standing where 'status groups' are cross-class
formations shaped by the 'social estimation of honor' and reinforced
by 'special styles of life' (2013: 193) revolving around, for example,
fashion and social networks. So while classes are organized on the
basis of the acquisition of goods, status is related to consumption in
a situation in which 'class distinctions are linked in the most varied
ways with status distinctions' (2013: 187).

This more fluid understanding of stratification was adopted and
updated by Pierre Bourdieu in his influential book *Distinction*, in
which he identifies both cultural and social capital – as the embodiment and mobilization of certain types of tastes and dispositions – as
central variables in the composition of class societies. According to
Bourdieu (1984: 106), social class

> is not defined by a property (not even the most determinant one, such
> as the volume and composition of capital) nor by a collection of proper-
> ties (of sex, age, social origin, ethnic origin) . . . nor even by a chain of
> properties strung out from a fundamental property (position in the rela-
> tions of production) in a relation of cause and effect, conditioner and
> conditioned; but by the structure of relations between *all* the pertinent
> properties. (Bourdieu 1984: 106; emphasis added)

This lends an especially important role to the media as institutions that specialize in the circulation of symbolic capital and thus in the reproduction of capitalism more generally, even though it takes class away from its specific orientation on the relations of production. This is a tension – between a conception of class that is directly related to conditions of exploitation versus a more amorphous definition that sees class performed across much broader patterns of activity – that becomes especially clear in discussions of digital labour and of the kinds of exploitation that take place on platforms and in AI models.

## The exploitation of 'digital labour'

Labour has been central to recent debates concerning the growth of generative AI, but it is not the labour *of* AI but the labour to be displaced *by* AI that dominates policy and media discussions, along with speculations of a (utopian or dystopian) robot-dominated future. In other words, it is not the labour needed to extract the minerals, assemble the chips, scrape the data or build and protect the storage centres that provides the basis for AI but its impact on specific roles and careers that is the object of attention. The latter focus, after all, offers much more spectacular headlines, such as Elon Musk's revelation that, thanks to AI, there 'will come a point where no job is needed' and that 'you can have a job if you want a job . . . but AI will be able to do everything' (quoted in Gross and Murphy 2023). When the think tank the Institute for Public Policy Research (IPPR) published a report on the significant but uneven impact of AI on sectoral employment, concluding that 'we do not expect there to be an immediate "job apocalypse"' (IPPR 2024: 11), the *Guardian* responded with a headline: 'AI "Apocalypse" Could Take Away almost 8m Jobs in UK, Says Report' (Partington 2024). This is at odds with the rather more sober tone of the research which suggests that secretarial work, data entry, marketing and copywriting are the specific areas that are most at risk. The report outlines a range of scenarios for what might happen both to employment and overall economic prospects and, in an implicit critique of technological determinism, insists that 'there is no one predetermined path for how AI implementation will play out' (IPPR 2024: 7).

A significant amount of investor and policymaker attention is also focused on AI's contribution to raising the general productivity of labour. If businesses are to invest the trillions of dollars needed fully to take advantage of AI-related innovations (Goldman

Sachs 2024), a major incentive will be required, and productivity growth – operationalized as the intensification of the exploitation of labour using large language models – is at the heart of this. The inter-governmental Organisation for Economic Co-operation and Development (OECD) devoted its entire 2023 *Employment Outlook* report to the challenges and opportunities presented by AI, including the prospect of cost savings and productivity gains offered by AI: 'Firms do not hide the fact that one of their main motivations to invest in AI is to improve worker performance (i.e. productivity) and reduce staff costs' (OECD 2023: 96). Even though it finds little evidence thus far of major increases in productivity – dampening down some of the more overblown claims about an AI 'revolution' – the OECD nevertheless recognizes the need for what it calls 'social dialogue' – in other words, negotiations between employers and workers' organizations – as the roll-out of AI gathers pace. If the Nobel Prize-winning economist Daron Acemoglu is correct in his assessment that 'AI will not reduce inequality' and will instead 'further expand the gap between capital and labor income as a whole' (2024: 6), then collective bargaining is going to feature prominently in any forthcoming AI-related industrial relations landscape. This is likely to be an uneven, if crucial, development because, as the OECD itself acknowledges (2024: 227), 'AI-based surveillance of workers generates information asymmetries' – for example, where AI is used systematically to monitor and discipline workers or where new working conditions facilitated by AI are simply imposed – that will weaken their ability to confront their employers.

The public and policymaking emphasis on jobs and productivity and the lack of attention paid to the labour that actually fuels AI reinforce the marginalization of socio-economic approaches to AI that I referred to in the opening chapter of this book. This form of labour may not dominate parliamentary debates and media headlines but large language models, digital platforms and cloud computing would not exist without the labour performed by a growing number of workers across the world. 'While the public is distracted by the specter of non-existent sentient machines', argue AI researchers Williams, Miceli and Gebru (2022), 'an army of precarized workers stands behind the supposed accomplishments of artificial intelligence systems today'. This refers not to the contribution of tech companies in Silicon Valley or investment banks in New York but to an international working class that includes content moderators in Kenya, data labellers in Venezuela, data annotators in Argentina, miners in eastern Congo, chip makers in Vietnam and Web scrapers in India.

This is exploited labour in the 'classic' sense – in that transnational corporations pay wages to workers who are formally free to accept or refuse employment and whose labour directly generates surplus value for the firm. Conditions of employment may change radically from country to country and firm to firm – some are permanent jobs while others are temporary; some accrue benefits while others are utterly precarious – but the underlying social relations remain familiar to the picture of exploitation spelled out earlier, as well as to colonial patterns that I discuss later in chapter 11.

James Muldoon and colleagues (2024), in *Feeding the Machine*, identify a series of very different roles in the AI labour chain, including the annotator, engineer, technician, artist, investor and operator. What is particularly useful about this approach is that, as well as making visible the often-hidden layers of labour, they treat AI not as a shiny and prefigured technology but as the outcome of a range of different material and social processes with specific contexts and histories. AI is an 'extraction machine' that 'draws in critical inputs of capital, power, natural resources, human labour, data and collective intelligence and transforms these into statistical predictions which AI companies, in turn, transform into profits' (2024: 8). AI organizes the outputs of human intelligence, creativity and labour and trains its algorithms to perform a series of tasks that are only later – in other words, only as a result of its data – represented as impacting labour, even though its entire DNA runs on the basis of the initial exploitation of labour power.

The exploitation of concrete labour at the heart of artificial intelligence may help to shed some light on recent debates on what has been described as the 'free labour' carried out by users as they search the Web, post on Facebook, buy goods on Amazon or download music on Spotify. Tiziana Terranova was one of the first theorists to highlight the significance of the data freely provided by users in the early days of the internet. 'Simultaneously voluntarily given and unwaged, enjoyed and exploited' argues Terranova (2000: 33), 'free labor on the Net includes the activity of building websites, modifying software packages, reading and participating in mailing lists, and building virtual spaces on MUDs and MOOs.' These multi-user domains and open-source communities hark back to a more open online environment in which individuals willingly collaborated, often without immediate financial considerations or indeed remuneration; this was 'free labour' because it expressed the creative initiative of decentralized users. However, given the subsequent intensive commercialization of the internet (McChesney 2013) and the use of this 'freely given' data to generate profits – mostly through advertising – for emerging online companies, the status of this labour assumed a new character. For theorists like Arvidsson (2005) and Fuchs (2011), user-generated content has now become a key resource to be appropriated and exploited by corporate actors. Posting to TikTok or uploading to YouTube positions the user in a subordinate position in a commercial transaction. According to Fuchs (2011: 299), 'the users are exploited – they produce digital content for free in non-wage labour relationships.' This exploitation of user-generated content, whether in the form of comments, likes, videos, photographs or searches, mines the precious resource – data – that underpins the business logic of the 'surveillance capitalism' that Shoshana Zuboff describes as the 'default model of informational capitalism on the web' (2019: 92). It represents a new form of extraction that intensifies capitalism's vampiric tendencies and that, according to Zuboff, hands over our very humanity to the scraping tools that yield a 'behavioral surplus' that is accrued by firms like Google and Meta (and that I discuss further in chapter 7).

There is, of course, little doubt that Big Tech profits hugely from appropriating the content and attention of its users and that there are significant and unresolved problems around harms, privacy, ethics and ownership. Yet it is not at all clear that this constitutes a form of exploitation, at least not in relation to the definition of 'free labour' discussed earlier in this chapter that relates to the *compulsion* to work and the subsequent exploitation of wage labour by employers in order to secure a surplus. This remains the case even in a situation in which a tiny minority of influencers do derive income from their social media activity. Terranova is quite clear that, for her, 'free labour . . . is not necessarily exploited labour' (2000: 48), whereas for Marx, this was precisely his understanding – that 'free labour' relates to the experience of wage labour and its exposure to subsequent disciplinary measures designed to drive down costs and increase profits for capital.

Some theorists, however, continue to argue that new technological innovations generate radically new divisions of labour whether in the shape of Zuboff's 'surveillance capitalism' (Zuboff 2019) or McKenzie Wark's 'vectoralism' (Wark 2019) or, in some cases, a return to the past, as with Jodi Dean's concept of 'neofeudalism' (Dean 2025) and Yanis Varoufakis's notion of 'technofeudalism' (Varoufakis 2023). For the latter, developments in cloud computing and AI have returned us to an almost pre-capitalist mode of production where twenty-first-century peasants are performing unpaid but highly profitable labour for digital barons. 'The true revolution cloud capital has inflicted on humanity is the conversion of billions of us into willing cloud serfs volunteering to labour for nothing to reproduce cloud capital for the benefit of its owners' (Varoufakis 2023: 79). Varoufakis suggests that technofeudalism has not entirely done away with wage labour but that this generates a diminishing proportion of the wealth and power that is monopolized by today's tech giants on the backs, or rather from the fingers, of a new hyper-exploited population of digital serfs.

Whether user-generated content constitutes a new form of exploitation is not a mere semantic issue but a question of where power and productivity lie in capitalist production: with disaggregated, atomized users uploading videos and playlists for fun or with workers who are formally 'free' but, in reality, compelled to sell the labour which turns the raw material of data into profits for their employer. In order to distinguish between formal 'labour' and what might be viewed as 'pleasure', Ursula Huws suggests that we have to consider the extent to which a specific activity 'is carried out voluntarily or by coercion, under the direction of another person or organisation' (Huws 2013: 94). Social media activity, for example, more closely resembles Huws's notion of 'consumption work', a form of unpaid though productive labour that 'because it does not generate income directly for the worker . . . has to be treated differently from paid labour in relation to its contribution to subsistence' (2013: 96). This is also the position adopted by Srnicek, who insists that user-created data are not the result of formally 'free labour' (2016: 55): 'In examining the activities of users online, it is hard to make the case that what they do is labour, properly speaking. Beyond the intuitive hesitation to think that messaging friends is labour, any idea of socially necessary labour time – the implicit standard against which production processes are set – is lacking'.[4] That, in turn, means that the usual disciplinary techniques to maximize profits – increasing productivity, extending the working day, outsourcing production – are not immediately available, even though platform owners regularly provide incentives for users to stay online for longer or to upload more content.

The point is that while the economic value of an individual raw material may change – whether it is cotton or coal, oil or data – the underlying patterns of labour exploitation as mapped out in this chapter are more durable and more persistent. They relate not to a specific product or service but to the imperatives to which both capitalists and workers are attached. Indeed, the very concept of 'digital labour' is potentially misleading; the activities it describes –

whether moderating social media posts, scraping data for AI models or designing new cloud-based systems (let alone the social media activity whose relationship to work is far more problematic) – simply refer to labour in digital, as opposed to, for example, cotton, fields. This is not an understanding of labour power that is subject to entirely new imperatives but is instead attached to new raw materials and new labouring techniques. It would, therefore, be more useful if theorists were to move on from speaking of a discrete 'digital labour' and to consider the ways in which exploitation and propertization continue to be inscribed into all forms of production, including within the creative and media industries (Mirrlees 2025).

This is an urgent issue both for content creators and for those organizations who own their intellectual property when it comes to developing generative AI and its more advanced cousin, artificial general intelligence (AGI). Given that AI is ultimately based on the mining of historic content, the securing of this data to train emerging large language models is a critical objective, albeit one fraught with problems. For example, there was a spate of lawsuits in 2023 and 2024 by artists, newspapers and music labels claiming copyright infringement by AI companies of creative works. This included actions by the *New York Times* (*NYT*) against OpenAI (part owned by Microsoft) and by Universal, Warner and Sony Music against the music generator platforms Suno and Udio. Accusations of exploitation feature in both cases. The *NYT* described OpenAI as 'a multi-billion-dollar-for-profit business built in large part on the unlicensed exploitation of copyrighted works' (Pope 2024), while the music companies alleged 'mass infringement of copyrighted sound recordings copied and exploited without permission by two multi-million-dollar music generation services' (Tencer 2024).

The exploitation referred to in these cases is closer to the 'classic' definition offered by Marx in that the AI companies are directly profiting from appropriating the fruits of monetized labour – whether contracted in the case of *NYT* journalists or self-employed in the case of musicians. Given that both the *NYT* and the music labels are very unreliable intermediaries for journalists and musicians respectively – precisely because they are also implicated in exploiting the labour they claim they are now trying to protect (Kreps 2015; Pope 2024) – this is an issue that is unlikely to disappear any time soon. Indeed, the most effective way to tackle this form of exploitation is likely not to be corporate legal action but (what is often presented as) old-fashioned industrial action, as exemplified by the gains achieved by Hollywood writers and actors in their lengthy strikes in 2023.

According to *Wired*, the disputes, which saw the achievement of 'guard rails' against the displacement of labour by AI as well as significant increases in benefits, 'ended up setting a tone for how labor movements in the future could push back against encroaching automation' (Watercutter 2023).

## Class: marker of a stratified media system

That actors and writers could have spent months on a picket line also suggests that class interests and class struggle are very much alive in twenty-first-century capitalism and pertain to labour organized in the private, as well as the public, sector. Indeed, class continues to function as a central marker of stratification both 'behind the camera' and 'on screen' across the media industries. It delineates employment patterns that privilege opportunities for the most advantaged (and limit those for the poorest) sections of the population and generates highly unequal structures of representation and consumption. So, for example, a 2020 report on employment in the UK creative industries found evidence of what the authors describe as 'widespread and persistent class imbalances' (Carey et al. 2020: 2), with the wealthiest more than twice as likely to be employed in creative industries, 'shaping what goes on stage, page and screen' (2020: 2). People from working-class backgrounds are significantly under-represented in a range of creative roles occupying just 15% of jobs in advertising, 16% of film, broadcasting and video, 13% of publishing and 12% in music, performing and visual arts (2020: 12). The researchers conclude that working-class people in the creative industries also 'tend to experience less autonomy than their privileged peers, particularly over job tasks, task order or work hours' (2020: 17) – in other words, they face relatively higher rates of exploitation than their more privileged counterparts.

Class-based disparities are equally, if not more, entrenched in journalism, a field which used to be more accessible to those without high-level personal networks, postgraduate qualifications and wealthy parents. Research carried out for the National Council for the Training of Journalists reveals that 67% of British journalists have a parent from the wealthiest socio-economic categories, with only 9% having a parent in the poorest categories (Spilsbury 2024: 32). This confirms earlier research carried out by the Sutton Trust which found that 44% of newspaper columnists, 43% of top editors and broadcasters and 29% of BBC executives were privately educated, as compared to 7% of the general UK population (Sutton Trust 2019: 37). Additionally, approximately 39% of this group studied at either Oxford or Cambridge University as compared to less than 1% of the UK population (2019: 37). That a profession so closely associated with the performance of democracy is drawn from such a narrow and privileged base is deeply concerning and is bound to shape the agendas and frames that dominate journalism. This is not simply a question of individual bias or professional failings but the result of a systemic asymmetry of opportunity and reward in which class – along with other characteristics such as race and gender that I explore in chapter 12 – plays a central role.

This unequal distribution of voice 'behind the camera' has implications for the representation of diverse communities on screen as well. The leading British playwright James Graham devoted his MacTaggart Lecture at the 2024 Edinburgh Television Festival to the crisis of working-class employment and representation in broadcasting. Referring to recent data showing that only 8 per cent of those working in television were from working-class backgrounds, Graham highlighted the disappearance of 'the arenas, the platforms and training grounds that particularly working-class voices built their muscles in' – from arts education in school to cutbacks in the single-drama television format (Graham 2024). In particular, he warned about the impact of purging working-class experience from the screen at a time of economic uncertainty for the poorest sections of the population whose lives are rarely acknowledged in full. 'If you see a person, or a character, who looks like you or sounds like you on screen, whose experience or dilemmas, or joy, reflects your own . . . you feel more seen. There is a catharsis here, for audiences. A validation' (Graham 2024). This sense of exclusion is also borne out by audience research carried out by the communications regulator Ofcom in relation to BBC content. The research demonstrates that working-class audiences in particular feel under-represented and that 'the complexity of ordinary life – encompassing people's struggles and difficulties but also their joys and successes – was generally absent from BBC content' (Ofcom 2023: 22). Where working-class lives were represented, this content 'tended to focus on extreme stereotypes, for example emphasizing criminality, drink and drug cultures, and financial hardship' (2023: 22), best exemplified by programmes like *Little Britain* (2003–5) and *Benefits Street* (2014–15) in the United Kingdom and *Here Comes Honey Boo Boo* (2012–14) and *My Big Fat American Gypsy Wedding* (2012–18) in the United States.

Class, and the division of labour with which it is associated, is therefore crucial in reproducing the power relations, routines and consumption patterns of the media and wider creative industries. While it is significant that a majority of the UK population identifies as 'working class',[5] class – understood as an objective indicator of social position in the production process – also continues to shape everything from the opportunity to find a job in the media to the conditions of employment and from the structure of media markets (where the ability to attract the wealthiest consumers still retains a premium) to the behaviour of media audiences. Referring to television in the 1980s, the political economist Nicholas Garnham spoke of the 'class determination of cultural consumption' that was related to the unequal amounts of time, disposable income and dispositions available to different groups (1990: 124). There is little reason to believe that those factors have meaningfully diminished in contemporary circumstances.

## Conclusion

In today's far more fragmented and volatile media and tech landscapes, class division and the 'fact' of exploitation are just as central to the productive activities of the AI companies, platforms, streamers, broadcasters and journalists who operate under capitalism as they were previously. 'Free labour', in which workers are compelled to sell their labour in order to survive, remains critical to the operation of both 'old media' and 'Big Tech'. As such, the whole concept of a distinctive form of 'digital labour' is potentially misleading and counter-productive. As Malcolm Harris argues in a critical account of 'technofeudalism', in which he challenges claims that data extraction constitutes a new mode of production beyond wage labour (Harris 2022), 'Big Tech's trash-collecting algorithms . . . can eat data scraps, but we can't. And that's how you know that this is still capitalism: Tomorrow we have to go find work.'

# 5
# Commodification and Marketization

*Overview* This chapter explores the rise and impact of a market system predicated on the 'free' exchange of commodities. While some theorists, including Adam Smith and Milton Friedman, see markets as essentially 'natural' and desirable spaces of human activity, critics of capitalism highlight the unequal power relations that underpin their construction and operation. The chapter considers the consequences of the 'commodity fetishism' that critics, for example Karl Marx and Georg Lukács, see as a defining feature of capitalism and explores both the scale of and the limits to commodification by discussing examples from celebrity culture, branding and contemporary journalism.

## Brought to market

For thousands of years, buying and selling has taken place in dedicated marketplaces – from the agoras of ancient Greece and great bazaars of the Islamic world (Koehler 2014) to the annual MIPTV television festival in Cannes and the digital financial exchanges of the twenty-first century. These spaces facilitate the everyday economic transactions that sustain complex societies, yet they also speak to something beyond the directly economic. For Adam Smith, the existence of markets reflects 'a certain propensity in human nature . . . to truck, barter, and exchange one thing for another' (Smith 2012 [1776]: 18). In fact, this is not only natural but also a distinctly *human* activity given that, according to Smith, dogs, for example, never engage in contractual negotiations to secure their favourite objects. 'Nobody ever saw a dog make a fair and deliberate exchange of one bone for another with another dog. Nobody ever saw one animal by its gestures and natural cries signify to another, this is mine, that is yours; I am willing to give this for that' (2012 [1776]: 18). Given that buying and selling appear to be essentially human patterns of behaviour, Smith welcomed the rapid development of the division of labour that facilitated the emergence of 'commercial society' precisely because it expanded the possibilities for market exchange beyond the limited interactions that took place in earlier societies.

Smith's *Wealth of Nations* is littered with phrases about goods being 'brought to market' as if this is a spontaneous and unmediated process that matches buyers and sellers along agreed 'market rates' as long as there are no artificial distortions imposed on these exchanges. For Smith, a fully functioning market depends on people having 'perfect liberty' (2012 [1776]: 60) in which to operate – for example, they need to be free from undue government interventions or not distracted by ill-advised colonial ventures. Citizens need instead to be left alone to conduct their business, guided above all by Smith's famous conception of an 'invisible hand' (2012 [1776]: 445) presiding over commercial transactions that acts to leverage individual self-interest in order to benefit society as a whole. This is the basic rule that animates the vision of a capitalist free market: 'By pursuing his own interest, he [the economic actor] frequently promotes that of the society more effectually than when he really intends to promote it' (2012 [1776]: 445). The market, according to this conception, provides the perfect space in which freely competing individuals can come together to meet the needs of all.

For critics like the economist Ha-Joon Chang, a truly free market is more of a dream than an empirical reality. 'The free market', he writes (2011: 1), 'doesn't exist. Every market has some rules and boundaries that restrict freedom of choice.' Smith's 'invisible hand' guiding the operation of any market is inevitably subject to a range of regulatory frameworks, legal requirements and institutional choices. Markets do not burst spontaneously into life but are constructed both materially (as above) and ideologically – in part through the news, entertainment and professional discourses that dominate public culture. Yet, as Stuart Hall notes (2011: 716), 'This does not mean that markets are simply manufactured fictions. Indeed, they are only too real! They are "false" because they offer partial explanations as an account of whole processes.' The claim that markets are either 'free' or the result of natural inclinations serves to conceal their underlying dynamics and support mechanisms and obscures the very real and unequal power relations on which markets are based.

The notion that 'free' markets are intrinsically efficient, democratic and human structures has long featured in mainstream economic discourse including, famously, in the work of the influential conservative economist Milton Friedman. Markets may have a very old history, but it is only under 'competitive capitalism' – what Friedman describes as a 'free private enterprise exchange economy' (2002 [1962]: 13) – that a full market logic can be unleashed and inefficient feudal modes of exchange superseded. For Friedman, markets are decentralized structures and a 'direct component of freedom' (2002 [1962]: 12) because no one is, or at least should be, forced into taking part in a transaction they are not comfortable with. In fact, markets *prevent* coercion because there is always another seller to deal with, another brand to buy, another job to go to or another demographic to target. Markets, he insists, are also impersonal and politically neutral: 'No one who buys bread knows whether the wheat from which it is made was grown by a Communist or a Republican, by a constitutionalist or a fascist' (2002 [1962]: 21). They are the ultimate expression of the separation of politics and economics because, at least according to Friedman, markets don't care about the colour of your skin or your voting intention but simply about what is productive and profitable. People operating in markets are motivated simply by securing a return on their investments and not by the distractions of politics or ideology: 'The suppliers of paper', he writes (2002 [1962]: 18), 'are as willing to sell it to the *Daily Worker* as to the *Wall Street Journal*.'

The separation of politics and economics as distinct zones of human activity is central to capitalist ideology: that while economics is based on certain immutable laws, for example, around the need to match supply and demand and the self-balancing tendencies of capitalist markets, politics is necessarily a more messy and partisan process. In his book, *The Great Transformation* (Polanyi 2001 [1944]), the economic sociologist Karl Polanyi challenges this notion of a clear division between the political and the economic. The 'propensity to barter' that Adam Smith had argued was a fundamental human trait was, according to Polanyi, a marginal aspect of economic life until the Industrial Revolution when commodity exchange came to dominate all aspects of economic, as well as non-economic, pursuits. Under capitalism, the market becomes a defining feature of society: 'Instead of economy being embedded in social relations, social relations are embedded in the economic system. The vital importance of the economic factor to the existence of society precludes any other result' (Polanyi 2001 [1944]: 60). Far from being straightforward and transparent, the market is rather a constitutive – or in Ellen

Wood's terms, a compulsive (2002a: 7) – social relation that satu-rates capitalist societies. The market is far from a neutral, natural or merely 'technical' mechanism but an instrument of social control that is fundamental to capitalism.

Yet Friedman's notion that the market is simply a 'technical device' (Friedman 1990: 55) to facilitate the distribution of goods remains a powerful component of capitalist common sense. Indeed, one of the 'pillars' of capitalism, as the International Monetary Fund (IMF) puts it, is the existence of a 'market mechanism that deter-mines prices in a decentralized manner through interactions between buyers and sellers' (Jahan and Mahmud 2015: 44). While the IMF acknowledges the existence of market imperfections and the dangers of inequality, it nevertheless treats market exchange as an entirely natural process and as the most effective way to organize economic activity. Conceived in this way, the market is not a tool of power but an ultimately benign element of any capitalist society, and its logic applies, as Friedman makes clear, to a free market in ideas just as it does to a free market in goods and services (Friedman 2002 [1962]: 114). Little wonder, then, that Friedman's work was one of the central inspirations for what came to be known as *neoliberalism*, a more recent iteration of capitalism – appearing at the end of the 1970s – that highlights the intensive application of market discipline to all areas of human activity.

At one level, neoliberalism refers simply to a set of practices that are already familiar to the DNA of capitalism, including privatiza-tion, deregulation of labour markets and commodification. Its very name suggests that it is, at its root, an updated form of the classical liberal commitment to the market that was promoted by Adam Smith two hundred years earlier. Neoliberalism, however, emerged in spe-cific circumstances following the deep economic crises across the western world in the 1970s that saw falls in productivity and profits; it was simultaneously an economic paradigm that sought to extend free trade across nation-states and to challenge protectionist tariffs, as well as 'a *political* project to re-establish the conditions for capital accumulation and to restore the power of economic elites' (Harvey 2005: 19; emphasis in original). This was not an inevitable economic development but a purposeful political enterprise. As such, it was less laissez-faire and more *dirigiste*: an elite intervention or, as Wendy Brown puts it, a new 'political rationality' (2015: 36). In the early 1980s, the governments of Ronald Reagan and Margaret Thatcher in the United States and the United Kingdom respectively attempted to put neoliberal tenets into practice by introducing measures to reduce public spending, break the power of organized labour and celebrate the creative vigour of market relations. These initiatives were complemented by the rise in influence of supranational institutions like the International Monetary Fund, the World Bank and the World Trade Organization, as well as international trade agreements, including the TRIPS agreement on intellectual property and the General Agreement on Trade in Services. All of these bodies were predicated on a belief that free trade and market values would incentivize productive activity and stimulate economies that had fallen on hard times.

The unique contribution of neoliberalism, however, lay not in developing radically new tools of capitalist accumulation but in attempting to extend market mechanisms to the provision of *all* public goods and services – in other words, much as Polanyi had suggested, in embedding the market well beyond economic transactions and in every aspect of society. It wasn't enough only to deregulate, for example, financial markets and labour laws but also to seek to enshrine market principles inside institutions that were not previously focused specifically on profit making, such as health services, public broadcasting, public transport and party politics (Leys 2001). By the end of the twentieth century, neoliberalism had assumed a zeitgeist status, fuelling market transformations of politics, economy and society, enraging those opposed to its impact on increasing inequality and legitimizing the 'greed is good' philosophy that underpinned Oliver Stone's 1987 film *Wall Street*. It simultaneously nourished a new obsession with entrepreneurship and innovation and drove an anti-capitalist politics that identified market fundamentalism as the main enemy. It was, as a *Guardian* 'Long Read' once put it, 'the idea that swallowed the world' (Metcalf 2017).

Yet neoliberalism was always a vulnerable project. While neoliberal ideas certainly did permeate established political, economic and cultural elites, 'rarely, however, has it come near to dominating popular consciousness' (Nineham 2023: 136) in terms of winning support for enshrining the market in areas like health and education. Harvey notes a 'creative tension' (2005: 19) between the utopian aspects of a fully fledged neoliberalism and the far more pragmatic practices of 'neoliberalization' – in other words, the concrete attempts to restructure institutions and industries along market principles – that have flourished across the globe in the last fifty years. Indeed, neoliberalism itself has floundered and virtually crashed in recent years – rocked by the impact of a 2008 global financial crisis that was caused by its obsession with unleashing market forces at all costs (Crouch 2011) and undermined by the later advance of protectionist governments and the use of tariffs as a central economic tool. According to some business commentators, we are witnessing a 'zeitgeist shift' and the re-emergence of a type of 'patriotic' or state capitalism, as evidenced by the US government's partial nationalization of chipmaker Intel in 2025 (Tett 2025). As such, neoliberalism's uncritical celebration of a market logic that it sees as relevant to *all* human endeavours is perhaps best understood not in relation to a relatively recent period of human history but as rooted in a much older capitalist trait: its fetish of commodities.

## The commodity and commodity fetishism

Commodity fetishism would not be a problem if commodities were the simple objects – and commodity exchange the transparent process – that capitalists themselves proclaim them to be. Marx, however, starts *Capital* with a lengthy analysis of why this isn't the case. For Marx, a commodity is 'first of all, an external object, a thing which through its qualities satisfies human needs of whatever kind' (Marx 1977 [1867]: 125). However, one of the distinguishing features of capitalism is that it values the things we produce through our own labour not particularly in terms of their usefulness but in terms of their ability to be exchanged in a free market – to put it simply, not for their 'use value' but for their 'exchange value'. Diamonds, which have little social purpose but require intense amounts of labour to extract, are extremely valuable, while staples like flour or rice, on which billions of people depend, are far less valuable. In essence, a commodity is a phenomenon that acquires value when it is exchanged and, as Marx puts it, exchange value is 'the necessary mode of expression, or form of appearance, of value' (1977 [1867]: 128) of capitalist commodity production. The commodity, therefore, is not a minor player but a constitutive element of capitalism.

Indeed, many Marxists identify the production and circulation of commodities as the definitive feature of capitalism. 'The problem of commodities', writes Georg Lukács (1971 [1923]: 83), 'must not be considered in isolation or even regarded as the central problem in economics, but as the central, structural problem of capitalist society in all its aspects'. Franz Jakubowski echoes this point, arguing that under capitalism, 'social wealth appears as a vast collection of commodities. The commodity is therefore the root phenomenon of the capitalist economy and also of its ideological superstructure'

(1976: 87–8). This is why Marx refers regularly to the fact that while a commodity appears initially to be a quite straightforward thing – 'an object with a dual character, possessing both use-value and exchange-value' (Marx 1977 [1867]: 131) – it is, in reality, far more elusive, 'a very strange thing, abounding in metaphysical subtleties and theological niceties' (1977 [1867]: 163). Commodity production refers not simply to an economic but also a deeply ideological process in which, as I discuss in chapter 8, the world is mystified and defamiliarized. The key reason for this is that the value of the labour – whether intellectual or physical – required to produce all commodities is transferred under market relations from the labourer to the products of their labour. Yet a key way in which capitalism sustains itself, according to Marx, is that this process appears to be entirely logical and natural even though, as we saw in chapter 4, it is *labour* that produces all wealth.

This contradiction emerges out of a very specific problem: the fact that, under capitalism, we are alienated from our own labour, and that which ought to belong to us – that is central to our very being – is instead taken from us. Just as building workers are rarely able to afford to buy the properties they build, or car workers the high-end cars for which their labour is still central, or miners the precious minerals they extract, neither are media workers able to control their own creative outputs when it is often publishing companies that own the copyright or AI companies who use the content to train their models. This alienation is particularly clear, for example, in relation to a long history of musicians objecting to the use of their content by politicians they oppose – most prominently in the case of Donald Trump, who has been sued by several artists for unauthorized use of protected works (McCarrick 2024). In this situation, labour appears as external to the worker – as if they are just an appendage to the machine and not the source of value – precisely because their labour power is bought and sold just like any other commodity in the marketplace.

This alienation is expressed most clearly in what Marx calls *commodity fetishism*, a concept that describes the worship of objects made by humans but then endowed with some sort of magical status. Under capitalism, a table, for example, is not just a table:

The form of wood, for instance, is altered, if a table is made out of it. Nevertheless the table continues to be wood, an ordinary, sensuous thing. But as soon as it emerges as a commodity, it changes into a thing which transcends sensuousness. It not only stands with its feet on the ground but, in relation to all other commodities, it stands on its head, and evolves out of its wooden brain grotesque ideas, far more

wonderful than if it were to begin dancing of its own free will. (Marx
1977 [1867]: 163–4)

Marx argues that objects of production appear to workers as something outside of them, external and strange to them, even though
it is their labour that has produced them. Instead of reflecting real
social relations, labour appears to them as relations between objects
– between things and not between people. So everyday goods lose
their familiarity and, through market relations, become mysterious;
they acquire a strange kind of power. We start to worship commodities but are also encouraged to accept the argument that the free
market – where goods and labour are turned into commodities – is
the common-sense way of organizing production.

The wonder of capitalism is that it is able to intimate that the value
of the table lies not with the labour that produced it but with the table
itself, which now appears to have an objective character, independent
of and separated from the social relations under which it was created.
It is not simply that we overvalue commodities – whether it is the
latest iPhone, the hottest trainers or an Instagrammable meal – but
that, in the act of doing so, we undervalue ourselves. In other words,
we give life to – we animate – external objects and, in so doing,
diminish our own creative power. This is what Marx described as
'commodity fetishism', a form of disempowerment captured perfectly by Michael Taussig when he argues that fetishism 'denotes
the attribution of life, autonomy, power, and even dominance to
otherwise inanimate objects and presupposes the draining of these
qualities from the human actors who bestow the attribution' (Taussig
1980: 31). Commodity fetishism therefore involves the projection
of mystery, beauty and awe to objects that workers' own labour
has produced while at the same time concealing the fact that it
was human labour that produced these objects. Under commodity
production, argues Marx, 'a definite social relation between men
... assumes, in their eyes, the fantastic form of a relation between
things' (1977 [1867]: 165), thus obscuring the material social relations of commodity production. This does not mean that fetishism
automatically generates an enduring 'false consciousness' but instead
that it generates a distorted picture of the world that hides the very
real experiences of exploitation and alienation suffered by workers
under capitalism.

There are four consequences of commodity fetishism that are worth
briefly considering. First, fetishism legitimizes the whole process of
commodification. What happens, according to Taussig, is that 'an

ether of naturalness conceals and enshrouds human social organization' (Taussig 1980: 32). The beauty of the market, for capitalists at
least, is that it makes the valuing of objects above ordinary social relations seem so normal and an example of 'common sense'. How could
we do things otherwise? Why would we want to change something so
'fantastic' as a consumer society predicated on the mass circulation
of commodities? Fetishism is a crucial ingredient in the securing of
consent to marketized social relations.

Second, when we focus on external objects at the expense of
privileging our own agency, we run the risk of decontextualizing
social relations: as I have already suggested, the meaning comes to
lie in the 'thing' itself as opposed to the circumstances in which it
was produced or in relation to the network of relationships between
the producers. What is then lost is not simply the context of social
interactions but the prospect of a 'totality' from which it is possible to
assess and react coherently to events as they happen. 'The social division of labour creates a series of special sub-spheres, not only in the
economy but in the whole of social life and thought. They develop
their own autonomous sets of laws. As a result of specialisation, each
individual sphere develops according to the logic of its own specific
object' (Jakubowski 1976: 95). As a result of fetishization, social
life – stripped of any overarching dynamic – becomes increasingly
fragmented without consistent patterns of behaviour or underlying
continuities.

This connects to the third consequence: the objectification of social
life or, to put it a little more crudely, the 'thingification' of social relations more generally. Georg Lukács was rather more elegant when
he talked of the phenomenon of reification: the act of characterizing
relations between people as 'thing-like'. He argued that under conditions of market exchange, social relationships acquire 'a "phantom
objectivity", an autonomy that seems so strictly rational and all-
embracing as to conceal every trace of its fundamental nature: the
relation between people' (Lukács 1971 [1923]: 83). Under capitalism, commodity fetishism leads to the experience of reification in
which individuals are atomized and their relationships rationalized,
precisely as Weber had warned some years earlier in relation to capitalism's bureaucratic logic which leads only to 'disenchantment' and
the disappearance of 'ultimate and sublime values' from public life
(2013: 155).

Reification, therefore, is a consequence of a commodified society
in which individuals lose a sense of their collective power and identity, further increasing their disempowerment. Reification is not an

experience that is unique to capitalism, but its impacts are uniquely disastrous, given the scale and intensity of commodity fetishism in capitalist market relations; only under capitalism is it possible for 'the commodity structure to penetrate society in all its aspects and to remould it in its own image' (Lukács 1971 [1923]: 85).

The fourth, and related, consequence is that, through fetishism, the dynamics of the social world are mystified and made 'spectral'. Social processes and interactions start to have a ghost-like appearance and seem to have a life of their own that is independent of their creators and participants. For Jakubowski, it is in 'capitalist commodity production alone that the false appearance is a general phenomenon' (1971: 90), leading to the reification of social relations and the systematic distortion of the lens through which we view the world around us, a process in which the media are intimately involved. Similarly, Lefebvre (1968: 47) argues that the 'commodity form possesses the peculiar capacity of concealing its own essence and origin from the human beings who live with it and by it. The form is fetishized. It appears to be a thing endowed with boundless powers.' Commodity fetishism, in summary, naturalizes market exchange, displaces value from labour onto the products of labour, disempowers us and clouds the real social relations that shape our lives.

## Is there life beyond commodification?

An important question then arises: to what extent is the commodity genuinely 'endowed with boundless powers' or are there limits to its scope and energy? Lukács's notion that commodity fetishism penetrates *throughout* capitalist society as 'the universal category of society' (1971 [1923]: 86) and Meszaros's analysis of the 'universal extension of "saleability" (i.e. the transformation of everything into commodity' (1975: 35) have been criticized for exaggerating the grip of commodification on everyday life. What about spaces – for example within the family, culture and local communities – that are not so easily or immediately subject to the commodity form and exchanged in a market? Is it really the case that everything has a price and that we are as alienated at home as we are at work? Can we really talk about mutual aid, voluntary work and public goods as sharing the same commodity characteristics as for-profit production?

Nancy Fraser rejects the idea that we live in a fully commodified world. Confronting Lukács directly, she argues that, even in capitalist society, there is not a 'single all-pervasive logic of reification'

(2014: 67) and points to the existence of different kinds of values operating in capitalist life. She highlights the caring and affective forms of labour that take place 'outside the market, in households, neighbourhoods and a host of public institutions, including schools and childcare centres' (2014: 61) and that are not therefore subject to the same disciplinary force as *direct* economic activities. Borrowing from Marx's own concept, she identifies the 'hidden abodes' of social reproduction that make possible the more visible activities that take place in the capitalist market but that, in themselves, are not organized around commodity exchange. According to Fraser, 'these non-commodified zones do not simply mirror the commodity logic but embody distinctive normative and ontological grammars of their own' (2014: 66). This includes the 'boundary struggles over gender domination, ecology, imperialism and democracy' (2014: 72) that are as important as more traditional class conflict. Marketized and non-marketized spheres of activity are therefore mutually reinforcing and inseparable.

Fraser's argument is a powerful critique of economic determinism and political fatalism – and a hugely important reminder that anti-capitalist resistance can take many forms – but it also misrepresents the traditional Marxist position. First, Marx doesn't argue that literally everything is a commodity under capitalism. As he writes in *Capital*, a 'thing can be a use-value without being a[n exchange]-value ... Air, virgin soil, natural meadows, unplanted forests, etc, fall into this category. A thing can be useful, and a product of human labour, without being a commodity' (1977 [1867]: 131). The point, however, is that capitalism's expansive impulse is to draw things – whether they are 'natural' or manufactured – into the exchange process with the result, therefore, that nothing is safe from its drive to commodify. This is precisely the logic of neoliberalization: to extend the commodity process into areas of human life – including education, public health and sexuality – that appeared to be relatively insulated from market imperatives but have been increasingly restructured to accommodate commodity logic.[1] Fraser is well aware of this and indeed warns against romanticizing non-market spheres as being somehow '"outside" capitalism and as inherently opposed to it' (2014: 69). Yet her argument about the mutual dependence of economic and 'non-economic' domains suggests an equivalence of power that overlooks the central and constitutive role of what she nevertheless describes as the 'core economic practices associated with capital accumulation' (2014: 69). It is not that class struggles are intrinsically more important than ones in the political or reproductive spheres but it is a reminder that, because reification is a process that emerges at the point of production and threatens to spread across all social relations, capitalism is at its most vulnerable in relation to directly productive labour.

Second, there is a significant difference between pointing out the expansive logics of reification and commodification and writing off the possibilities of resisting these processes. As we shall see in the next section, it is true that the insatiable appetite of commodification led some theorists virtually to abandon hope, and Fraser is quite right to focus on the heterogeneity and vitality of anti-capitalist struggles. However, this is certainly not true of Lukács, whose great contribution was to identify the fissures and contradictions in reification whereby, through class struggle, the worker is able to become aware that their labour has been commodified. For Lukács, this results in a growing self-consciousness and an ability to move beyond 'immediate' circumstances in order to engage in more holistic forms of struggle against commodified social relations. Only through the experience gained through struggle does it become possible 'to recognise the fetish character of *every commodity* based on the commodity character of labour power' (Lukács 1971 [1923]: 169; emphasis in original) and to sow the seeds of a challenge to reification as a whole. Commodification may be an intense and ubiquitous tendency in capitalist society, but it is never irresistible.

## The commodification of culture

Media, communications and cultural industries are primarily, as Graham Murdock and Peter Golding once put it, 'industrial and commercial organizations which produce and distribute commodities' (1973: 206). As with any sector of the capitalist economy, they are subject to the imperatives of reification and commodification which funnel creative energies towards the realization, above all, of exchange value. This is an extremely uneven process, given that there is a significant difference between someone singing alone in a shower and the commercial exploitation of their voice via copyright, between member-led community journalism and Fox News, or between a non-profit venture like Wikipedia and the ferociously market-oriented practices of the biggest tech companies. Yet the lone singer, the community news site and Wikipedia do not exist, as Fraser was quoted above, 'outside' capitalism, nor are they fully insulated from its logic. The direction of travel is very much towards the integration of media and communications into commodity exchange systems.

Yet this is far from a straightforward process, as cultural outputs more closely resemble 'public goods' than traditional commodities. 'The problem with cultural and information goods', argues Nicholas Garnham (1990: 28), 'is that, because their use value is almost limitless (they cannot be destroyed or consumed by use) it is extremely difficult to attach an exchange value to them.' Unlike eating an apple (which disappears after consumption), one person's viewing of a video does not prevent another person from viewing the same video and, of course, it costs virtually nothing to distribute the video to additional audiences who can enjoy it without diminishing its value to the first viewer. The non-rivalrous and non-excludable characteristics of media goods mean that corporations are forced to devise a range of strategies – including subscription mechanisms, paywalls and intellectual property restrictions – which exploit the value of the content and transform public goods into private commodities. These are strategies designed to mitigate the obvious risks of investing heavily in culture: a domain that is particularly vulnerable to changing and unpredictable public tastes (see Hesmondhalgh 2026).

Yet, despite the complexities of the cultural commodity, more areas of mediated interaction than ever before have been brought directly into the orbit of the market in recent years – examples include the neoliberal disciplining of public broadcasting (Freedman 2008), the privatization of the internet's infrastructure (Holt 2024), the development of hybrid revenue-generation models and the rampant financialization of the media sector more generally (deWaard 2024). Venture capitalists are investing heavily in the communications and technology sectors while many social media companies now operate on the basis of a business model that depends on the commodification and exploitation of personal data in a way that is contiguous with, and not a break from, traditional models of capitalism (Srnicek 2016).[2]

Vincent Mosco sees commodification as 'the entry point from which to begin to theorize the political economy of communication' (2009: 156). He highlights the media commodity in relation to three areas – content, audiences and labour – but argues that most attention is paid to the commodification of content precisely because of its ideological consequences. For Mosco (2009: 134), 'Communication is taken to be a special and particularly powerful commodity because, in addition to its ability to produce surplus value (thereby behaving like all other commodities), it contains symbols and images whose meaning helps to shape consciousness.' This is also what absorbed the Frankfurt School theorists Theodor Adorno and Max Horkheimer in their assessment of the consciousness-lowering impact of the 'culture industry' in the 1930s. Adorno, in particular, leans very heavily on Marx's notion of commodity fetishism in his famous 1938 essay on 'the fetish character in music' (Adorno 2001), in which he argues that the real 'secret of success' in the commercial popular music industry of Tin Pan Alley had less to do with aesthetic judgement than the more objective fact of 'what one pays in the market for the product' (2001: 38). Appreciation of music has been reified to such an extent that the 'consumer is really worshipping the money that he himself has paid for the ticket to the Toscanini concert' as distinct from the music itself.[3] This is a mysterious process in which the listener feels that they have an 'immediate' and direct relationship to cultural goods but, in reality, are simply being enticed into a world of commodities and encouraged to think that this is completely natural. 'The appearance of immediacy', he concludes (2001: 38), 'is as strong as the compulsion of exchange value is inexorable.'

Adorno and Horkheimer write very powerfully about the 'pseudo-individualization' and homogeneity that dominate capitalist cultural production in their highly influential essay, 'Enlightenment as Mass Deception' (in Adorno and Horkheimer 2002 [1947]). However, they also treat commodification as an absolute process which flattens any distinction between use and exchange value and extinguishes the possibility of challenging commodity logic. Mass culture, they argue, 'is so completely subject to the law of exchange that it is no longer exchanged; it is so blindly equated with use that it can no longer be used' (2002 [1947]: 131). This collapse of use value into exchange value is problematic for two major reasons. First, because individuals are effectively written off – 'tolerated only as far as their wholehearted identity with the universal is beyond question' (2002 [1947]: 124) – and, second, because it evacuates the tension between use and exchange value which Marx placed at the centre of commodity relations. Adorno and Horkheimer's 'perception of the populace as passive, atomized and sutured into consumer capitalism, due to alienation and separation from the collective', writes Milly Williamson (2016: 9), 'only presents one side (although an important one) of the relations of production under capitalism which are, at their heart, contradictory' – a point I return to in chapter 14.

Adorno and Horkheimer's assertion that all culture is effectively just a form of advertising resonates with the later assertion by the Canadian political economist Dallas Smythe (1977) that the main commodity produced by commercial media is the audience – packaged and sold to advertisers as a vital element of capitalist reproduction. Smythe describes the focus on the ideological dimension of media as an idealist preoccupation with '*superficial* appearances' (1977: 2; emphasis in original) which hides the fact that media content is simply an 'inducement (gift, bribe or "free lunch") to recruit potential members of the audience and to maintain their loyal attention' (1977: 5). At one level, this is a persuasive argument given the fact, for example, that radio programming was often an afterthought to what was seen as the more important need to sell broadcast receivers in the 1920s or in the light of Netflix's more recent business model (assessed further in chapter 7) where content is merely a 'means to an end' – in other words, simply a mechanism to acquire and maintain ever greater numbers of subscribers (Tavlin 2025). Yet, for all the value of Smythe's analysis of how commodification knits media corporations and audiences into the wider capitalist economy, it treats audiences as essentially passive victims of the media's social engineering: 'The prime purpose of the mass media complex is to produce people in audiences who work at learning the theory and practice of consumership for civilian goods' (Smythe 1977: 20). Nicholas Garnham's response to this was to accuse Smythe of failing to recognize the contested nature of the commodity form, describing his argument as an 'extreme reductionist theory' that evacuates any notion of struggle and contradiction (1990: 29).[4]

Milly Williamson places this sense of contradiction at the heart of her analysis (Williamson 2016) of the interconnections between capitalism and celebrity. While notions of fame pre-date market society, the modern celebrity – whether an influencer or an 'ordinary' person catapulted into the limelight via reality television – is an expression of the desire for individuality and autonomy at precisely the same time that they are thoroughly integrated into, and a promoter of, the wider commodity process. As Williamson puts it, celebrity is 'a sign of the dominance of the commodity form and the idea of culture for profit, and yet it speaks to desires and cultural values outside of the logic of the economic – if it did not, it would have no economic value' (2016: 21). Celebrification hints, therefore, both at the immersion of the individual into the commodity process and its opposite: that 'the human can never be fully contained by the self-as-commodity' (2016: 163).

Celebrity endorsers and labels also feature prominently in Naomi Klein's *No Logo* (Klein 2005 [1999]), the bestselling and searing indictment of the rise of marketing, advertising and, in particular, branding across a capitalist society dominated by transnational corporations. Klein provides powerful examples of commodity fetishism in a context in which the tussle between use and exchange value has seen the growing prominence of the latter in terms of privileging the *identity* of goods and services. Harking back to Marx's notion of the 'metaphysical subtleties' of the commodity, Klein argues that in the neoliberal marketplace: 'the product always takes a back seat to the real product, the brand, and the selling of the brand [has] acquired an extra component that can only be described as spiritual. Advertising is about hawking product. Branding, in its truest and most advanced incarnations, is about corporate transcendence' (Klein 2005 [1999]: 21).

Commodity fetishism fuels a culture in which highly desirable consumer products aim to fulfil symbolic and spiritual needs as well as material ones and in which branding offers an affective stimulus to the danger of underconsumption. It underpins a marketplace that proclaims itself to be a vibrant and accommodating space that satisfies consumers simply on the basis that it provides branded competition: McDonalds versus Burger King, Nike versus Reebok, Apple versus Samsung, or Tesla versus Polestar.

In reality, branding serves to hide the material relations that undergird the circulation of commodities, not least the sweatshop labour and horrific working conditions in the factories and fields that actually produce the shiny objects. This is far from a cosmopolitan vision of a frictionless capitalism but a commodity system based in particular on the exploitation of workers in the Global South: 'The travels of Nike sneakers have been traced back to the abusive sweatshops of Vietnam, Barbie's little outfits back to the child labourers of Sumatra, Starbucks' lattes to the sun-scorched coffee fields of Guatemala, and Shell's oil back to the polluted and impoverished villages of the Niger Delta' (Klein 2005 [1999]: xviii). At one level, Klein's point – that branding aims to mystify social relations, naturalize consumption and teach us how to be 'good consumers' – is not that different to Smythe's argument about the aim of the commercial media system. Yet Klein sees branding as a highly contested phenomenon which has already generated significant opposition both in the South and the North. In response, the book not only identifies simply the logic and reach of branding but highlights examples of resistance to the rule of the brands: the anti-marketing campaigns, culture jamming and anti-corporate activism – in other words, opposition to commodity fetishism as a whole – that emerged across the globe at the same time as the book was published.

## The reification of journalism

Commodification is often discussed simply in terms of its focus on exchange value and an ensuing emphasis on (and often glorification of) consumption. But Marx, as we saw earlier, notes that commodity fetishism leads to both 'a personification of the thing and a reification of the person' (quoted in Saito 2023: 149) – a reminder that, under capitalism, workers are alienated from their own labour power and subject to highly rationalized, bureaucratic routines and objectives. A complex division of labour in which tasks are specialized and workers atomized therefore applies not just to the assembly line but also to the production of less tangible products such as news and information. For Lukács, this specialization – whether applied to the factory floor, the Uber Eats driver's car or the newsroom – reproduces only a fragmented and partial view of the world that hides the more systemic connections of capitalist life. Rather surprisingly, he argues that this reified consciousness applies not only to working people but also – in fact, *in particular* – to mainstream journalists who have an 'abstract' and detached relationship to their stories. Following in the line of other professionals forced to adopt a 'specific type of bureaucratic "conscientiousness" and impartiality' (1971 [1923]: 99), Lukács claims that the 'journalist's "lack of convictions", the prostitution of his experiences and beliefs, is comprehensible only as the apogee of capitalist reification' (1971 [1923]: 100).

Liberal journalism is predicated, of course, on independence of thought and the separation between the 'church and state' of editorial and advertising. Yet this is precisely what drives Lukács to describe journalism as a clear example of what happens when commodity fetishism penetrates even the most 'sacred' spaces: 'The more deeply reification penetrates into the soul of the man who sells his achievement as a commodity, the more deceptive appearances are (as in the case of journalism)' (1971 [1923]: 172). This brutal assessment of the difference between rhetoric and reality also means that journalism, diminished by its reified status, is unable either to portray a true picture of the dynamics of capitalist society (even if it wanted to do so) or to sustain its preferred narrative of heroic reporters holding power to account. Journalists, like other 'bureaucratic' professionals, are deeply compromised by reified social relations: 'What appear as irreducible human characteristics which, as such, defy all attempts at commodification, turn out to be all too commodifiable in journalism, and the basis for the thoroughgoing rationalization of the cultural sphere' (Hall 2011: 125).

This notion that journalism necessarily reflects wider decon-textualized and fragmented social relations is similar to Raymond Williams's well-known analysis of 'flow' in broadcast news bulletins in *Television: Technology and Cultural Form* (Williams 1974). He finds that advertising-dominated US news programmes are particularly disjointed with no effort to trace connections between the different elements of the broadcast, for example when the lead and final story about false claims within drug advertising is interspersed with commercials for aspirin or when a trailer for a western movie immediately precedes a news story about a stand-off between Native Americans and Justice Department officials. Williams argues that the newscast is characterized by a 'sense of hurried blur' and that 'the flow of hurried items establishes a sense of the world: of surprising and miscellaneous events coming in, tumbling over each other, from all sides' (1974: 116).

Yet the world is not dominated by 'miscellaneous events' and random occurrences but by actions that do have meaningful histories and connections. While journalism studies focuses on the growing risks of audience fragmentation caused by digital proliferation and its impact on sustaining shared conversations and reaching political consensus (Fletcher and Neilsen 2017), there is a danger of ignoring a deeper problem: the fragmentation of consciousness itself in what Lukács calls 'carefully segregated partial systems' such as journalism (1971 [1923]: 98). This means that underlying trends, associations and contexts are flattened in journalism's myopic obsession with the present and its yearning for 'clarity' over complexity – so that, for example, national debt is often (wrongly) treated simply as household debt (Inman 2024) and infrastructure tragedies (like bridge collapses and apartment block fires) are routinely blamed on individual failings and not linked to wider socio-economic conditions (Barling 2019). The former newspaper editor Harold Evans stumbled across the truth when he railed against widespread institutional obfuscation following the 2008 financial crash: 'Fog everywhere. Fog online and in print, fog exhaled in television studios where time is anyway too short for truth' (Evans 2017: 3–4). Whether in relation to a linear television news bulletin or a social media news feed, the reification of journalism means that the world is frequently chopped up into discrete parcels of information which seem to have no bearing on each other and which hide any systematic interconnections.

This is particularly evident in relation to mainstream journalism about Israel's war on Gaza. There is a long history of reporting on Israel and Gaza in a way that marginalizes history and context and, all too often, offers a perspective from the safest (and permissible) vantage point in Jerusalem or Tel Aviv. An internal report into the BBC's coverage of Israel and Palestine that was commissioned by the Corporation's then governors in 2006 clearly identified this loss of memory as a problem. Noting that many viewers found its coverage confusing, the report states that given 'how little history or context is routinely offered, it is easy to understand their bewilderment' (BBC 2006: 3). The report also criticizes journalists' 'failure to convey adequately the disparity in the Israeli and Palestinian experience, reflecting the fact that one side is in control and the other lives under occupation' (2006: 7). This points to an asymmetry that was glaring in mainstream journalism's identification of 7 October 2023 as the starting point of a conflict that – for Palestinians certainly – can be dated to the Nakba of 1948.

A comprehensive analysis of mainstream reporting of the war carried out by the Centre for Media Monitoring (CfMM) found evidence of this historical amnesia.

> Much of the news coverage of 7 October 2023 refers to Hamas's attacks on Southern Israel as ground zero with guests or commentators who try and explain the 75-year-old occupation of Palestine being accused by some presenters and columnists as justifying the attacks. Ignoring the context and history, especially the recent history of 'occupied' Gaza which has been under an Israeli blockade since 2005, is favourable to an Israeli narrative which has constantly promoted the attacks on Gaza and in the West Bank as a war between light and darkness. (Hanif 2024: 9)

The CfMM examined 25,000 online articles for four weeks after 7 October 2023 and found that more than three-quarters framed the conflict as an 'Israel–Hamas war' with only 24 per cent of stories that mentioned Israel, Hamas or Gaza referring to either 'Palestine' or 'Palestinian' (2024: 24). The media's spotlight on a single date – no matter how understandable – means that they are both unable fully to explore the meaning of this event in relation to previous events and implicated in a very partial reading of a long-standing conflict. 'Our view', conclude the CfMM (Hanif 2024: 34), 'is that whilst news outlets can (and perhaps should) focus on a specific incident at the time it occurs, when it is part of a broader news story that continues over many weeks and months, it is unreasonable . . . to simply take the Israeli perspective, and not provide the relevant context.' While there are significant ideological reasons for taking this position (that I explore in chapter 8), it is also the case that the reified labour of journalists renders them unable to perform the 'truth-telling' role with which they like to be associated.

## Conclusion

Markets are far from the innocent or natural spheres of activity that they are often claimed to be. The commodity fetishism on which they are predicated alienates workers from their own labour and distorts what is seen as valuable in capitalist society. One of the great strengths of Marx's analysis was his insistence that, however durable and comprehensive commodity production may be, capitalism is nevertheless riddled with crises and contradictions that simultaneously render it unstable and partial. Fetishism suggests mystery and transcendence but it is, at the same time, opaque and destructive. In highlighting the process by which the worker – whether engaged in manual or creative production – cedes control over the systems that they would otherwise expect to shape, an understanding of fetishism can also suggest a way forward. 'The task before us', argues Taussig (1980: 5–6), is 'to liberate ourselves from the fetishism and phantom objectivity with which society obscures itself [and] to take issue with the ether of naturalness that confuses and disguises social relations'. This refers to the concrete actions – in relation to, for example, the collective organization of newsrooms, the pursuit of non-profit journalism models and the struggles against concentrated ownership that I discuss in the next chapter – that are necessary to challenge the mysterious allure of markets with which the media are intimately involved.

# 6

# Competition and Monopoly

***Overview*** This chapter explores the extent to which capitalism
has generated vigorous competition as well as the throttling of
competition through oligopoly, monopoly and monopsony. The
chapter examines both the claims made by pro-market voices
for the virtues of competition as well as the arguments of its
critics as to why monopoly is the resting place of a 'competitive'
capitalism, such as in Joseph Schumpeter's notion of 'creative
destruction'. Finally, it locates these debates in relation to the
dangers of concentrated media ownership and the emergence of
a powerful 'tech-industrial complex' that dominates its markets
and largely shrugs off the ability of antitrust regulation that seeks
to curb monopoly power in the interests of a more full-blooded
notion of capitalist competition.

## Competition: the 'inner nature of capital'

According to the market intelligence platform Tracxn, there are,
at the time of writing, 131,000 media and entertainment companies, 85,000 AI companies, 37,000 telecommunications companies,
27,000 'internet of things' companies, 10,100 music tech companies
and 9,200 streaming video companies.[1] This would suggest the existence of an extremely dynamic situation in which multiple actors
battle it out for market share and in which satiated consumers are
super-served by the wide range of choices available. What drives this
seemingly bustling marketplace is competition, a form of economic
rivalry that is said by its advocates to be the inspiration for capitalist
development and innovation – it is the fuel that powers the system

forward and, much like sharks at night, prevents units of capital from ever switching off or being complacent in case they are eaten up by the morning. Just as individual companies need a 'competitive edge' to prosper, so the wider system fosters a never-ending race open to all participants which pits competitors against each other to serve both corporate and consumer interests. As the pro-market economist Friedrich Hayek puts it, capitalism is above all a 'competitive system based on free disposal over private property' (1944: 52).

In reality – and especially in relation to media and technology sectors – we have a race where the odds are heavily stacked in favour of powerful incumbents and where most participants, if they are even able to afford the entry fee in the first place, drop (or are pushed) out in the early stages, leaving the field clear to just a handful of runners. This is a capitalist landscape marked not by healthy competition and a plurality of producers but by monopolies and oligopolies that dominate their spheres, control the terms of trade and seek to make it as hard as possible for rivals to muscle their way into their business. It is a situation where competition fails to live up to its promise and instead delivers victory to a very narrow set of players.

There are four main arguments put by its supporters about competition: that it is natural, efficient, benevolent and limited. First, pro-competition arguments often rest on the notion that humans are instinctively competitive and that there is, therefore, no reason why economic structures should be protected from its logic. Whether drawing on Hobbes's notion that competition is 'in the nature of man' (1991 [1651]: 88) or Freud's argument that individuals are driven by unconscious psychic urges to compete, a whole range of social institutions are predicated on competitive access to scarce resources, from professional sports to elite universities and from social housing to internships in the financial sector. Yet, even if competition speaks to underlying desires and values, economic competition is seen to be quite different to personal rivalry in that, as Milton Friedman argues (2002 [1962]: 119), 'the essence of a competitive market is its impersonal character. No one participant can determine the terms on which other participants shall have access to goods or jobs.' Economic competition reflects a systemic, not an individualistic, impulse, even if it preys on supposedly natural instincts.

This leads to the second claim: that competition is fundamentally the most efficient way of organizing producers in a market in part because it draws not on petty jealousies, individual psychologies or state machinations but on the incentives that it generates. Competition is essential to capitalism because it forces producers never to rest on their laurels but constantly to develop new products, new production methods, new markets and new tastes in order to stay one step ahead of their rivals. Competition both disciplines and inspires capitalists to seek ever more effective ways of innovating production and stimulating consumption, but it does so in a way that is allegedly more transparent and objective than, for example, planned economies which impose coordination, rather than seeing market exchange as something organic. This is especially the case for large-scale industrial society: 'it is the very complexity of the division of labour under modern conditions which makes competition the only method by which such co-ordination can be adequately brought about' (Hayek 1944: 36). This was an approach adopted with particular vigour by the free-market Chicago School in the 1970s whose leading voice, Robert Bork, was preoccupied by what he saw as the 'efficiency-creating potentials' (Bork 1978: 67) of competition and its potential to deliver the much-vaunted objective of 'consumer welfare', an approach to competition regulation that became dominant under neoliberalism.

Third, precisely because of its familiarity and efficiency, competition is conceived as a value that is best placed to deliver wider consumer benefits. As the International Monetary Fund's explainer on capitalism puts it: 'competition, through firms' freedom to enter and exit markets, maximizes social welfare, that is, the joint welfare of both producers and consumers' (Jahan and Mahmud 2015: 44). Such comforting words may hide the difficulty for many organizations of 'entering' a market and indeed the pain and the consequences of 'exiting' one,[2] but such a conception takes us right back to Adam Smith's notion of the 'hidden hand' guiding economic activity in the public interest. Competition is the default position of the commercial society sketched out in *Wealth of Nations* (Smith 2012 [1776]) and is connected to the ability to generate the lowest price for a commodity in the marketplace – 'the price of free competition' (Smith 2012 [1776]: 65) – which benefits the entire community.

Yet not even its most zealous supporters claim that competition, left completely to its own devices, will deliver consumers the benefits that they seek. There will necessarily be market irregularities, economic crises and unpredictable events (such as pandemics and natural disasters) that may require the gentlest of 'corrective' touches. Somewhat counter-intuitively given his status as the intellectual voice behind the heavily pro-competition regimes of Margaret Thatcher in the United Kingdom and Ronald Reagan in the United States, Milton Friedman acknowledges that 'competition is an ideal type' and that 'there is no such thing as "pure" competition' (2002 [1962]: 120), a point made a generation before by Schumpeter who spoke of the 'impossibility' of perfect competition (Schumpeter 2010 [1942]: 92). As a result of this, it is the responsibility of a range of institutions and actors to foster the conditions in which competition can most freely operate, which means providing a degree of infrastructural support without ever unnecessarily subduing or constraining free-market logic. 'The functioning of competition', writes Hayek (1944: 28), 'not only requires adequate organisation of certain institutions like money, markets and channels of information – some of which can never be adequately provided by private enterprise – but it depends above all on the existence of an appropriate legal system'. For competition to prosper, therefore, states – as I explore in chapter 10 – need to provide a range of legislative, regulatory and at times military protections to mitigate disturbances and crises. Competition, described by Hayek as a 'principle of social organisation' (1944: 27), is everything for capitalists – but it is neither sufficient nor unblemished.

Marx recognized the centrality of competition for the emerging capitalist system of the mid-nineteenth century and acknowledged that this new form of *'laissez faire, laissez passer'* (1973 [1857–61]: 649) exchange was an advance from earlier and more protectionist economic arrangements that depended on guilds, tariffs and blockades. However, rather than welcoming this as an unambiguously positive development, Marx instead noted that only under the unprecedented conditions of an emerging capitalism could the full force of competition be effectively unleashed. As he argues in a famous passage from the *Grundrisse*:

> *competition* is nothing other than the inner *nature of capital*, its essential character, appearing in and realized as the reciprocal interaction of many capitals with one another, the inner tendency as external necessity. (Capital exists and can only exist as many capitals, and its self-determination therefore appears as their reciprocal interaction with one another.) (Marx 1973 [1857–61]: 414)

Competition, for Marx, is part of the very DNA of capitalism because capitalist firms are forced to behave not (despite what they claim) as free agents but as units of capital engaged in battle for control of specific markets: BP versus Shell, Visa versus Mastercard, OpenAI versus Anthropic. 'The influence of individual capitals on one another', he writes (1973 [1857–61]: 657), 'has the effect precisely that they must conduct themselves as *capital*' in these fierce interactions, meaning that they are forced to ramp up exploitation, lower labour costs and seek ever greater sources of profit.

The main consequence of competition is therefore not, as Adam Smith and later free-market voices would argue, that individual welfare could now be served through low prices, transparent trading arrangements and packed supermarket shelves full of different brands but instead that capitalism itself, as a fundamentally unequal system, would be the big winner. 'It is not individuals who are set free by free competition,' writes Marx; 'it is, rather, capital which is set free' (1973 [1857–61]: 650). Far from competition delivering either freedom or endless choice, Marx describes the fetish of competition as 'insipid' and asserts that, ultimately, competition really means nothing other than the 'rule of capital' (1973 [1857–61]: 652). This leads to a situation in which competition is then further legitimized as a 'natural' and efficient incentive for productive activity, even though there are many serious arguments for suggesting that quite the opposite is true: that collaboration and cooperation provide a model for the social as well as the natural world (Raihani 2021), that competition is 'a form of organization, in which actors are formally equal at the outset, and contingently unequal at the conclusion' (Davies 2014: 33), and that competition itself is fundamentally counter-productive. Olin Wright talks of the 'destructive competition' at the heart of the system that demotivates individuals, classifies many as failures and offers a very limited vision of human capacity. Competition, he argues (Wright 2010: 32–3), 'underwrites a culture of accomplishment which evaluates people only in terms of their *relative* standing compared to others. Achievement is defined not as the realization of one's potential but as winning, as being better than other people.' Yet it is not just the limitations of the concept of competition but its very practical failures – specifically its degeneration into monopoly – that have absorbed economists, regulators, politicians and publics over the last 150 years.

## Monopoly: the 'attraction of capital by capital'

For all the references in traditional economics textbooks to 'competitive capitalism' and the virtues of a robust system of economic rivalry, monopoly, the domination of a particular sector by one large firm, never seems to be far away. Milton Friedman blames the media for this – 'monopoly is more newsworthy and leads to more attention than competition' (2002 [1962]: 122) – and despairs that we focus our attention on the blockages to, and not the free flows of, goods and services. Yet, in a situation in which competition is so often held up to be the definitive value of a free market, the blockage *is* the story, either because it highlights the occasional interruption of a normally free-flowing service (like when train services are interrupted by the discovery of a long-dormant, unexploded bomb near the tracks) or because it reveals something more fundamental about the flaws of a market system.

Marx advocated the latter position well before he could even see the giant conglomerates that dominate economies today. He drew attention to the tension between the existence of multiple capitals in competition with one another and what he describes as the 'centralization' of capital, the growth of huge concentrations of wealth and power that result, as he puts it, from the 'attraction of capital by capital' (1977 [1867]: 777). This 'expropriation of many capitalists by a few' (1977 [1867]: 929) tends to lead to a 'constant decrease in the number of capitalist magnates, who usurp and monopolize all the advances of this process of [industrial] transformation' (1977 [1867]: 929). In turn, this generates bankruptcies and inefficiencies for capitalists themselves and also means higher levels of poverty and insecurity for the working people most affected by the shedding of jobs and the communities in which the jobs were previously based. For Marx, this was an irrational and anarchic process and a sign of capitalism's long-term vulnerability: 'The monopoly of capital becomes a fetter upon the mode of production which has flourished alongside and under it. The centralization of the means of production and the socialization of labour reach a point at which they become incompatible with their capitalist integument' (1977 [1867]: 929). This is just one of the contradictions, explored further in chapter 14, that expose capitalism's underlying vulnerability.

Not surprisingly, however, pro-capitalist voices are more likely to argue the opposite. Monopoly, argues Hayek, is not something rooted in the very character of capitalism, caused by greater efficiencies of large firms over smaller ones; nor is it the logical result of an asymmetrical landscape that rewards incumbents over start-ups. Instead, it is all the fault of the socialist planners who pretend that they can manipulate the workings of an innately decentralized system and who 'confer' monopoly status to firms in particular sectors in order to restrict competition (1944: 37). Monopoly, therefore, is the result of the failure to allow the price system to do its job and naturally to 'regulate' the movement of commodities; it is the consequence of an external imposition rather than an organic breakdown. Friedman, in turn, argues that the threat of monopoly has been exaggerated – he speaks of its 'relative unimportance from the point of view of the economy as a whole' (2002 [1962]: 121) – and, in relation to the United States, points to both the absolute number of firms in existence and the healthy turnover of operating enterprises. Monopoly, according to this perspective, stems from the behaviour of regimes who have given up on free trade and who opt for regulation over *laissez-faire* rather than being a specific property of capitalism itself.

One major dissenting voice among pro-market economists is Joseph Schumpeter who, as discussed in chapter 2, was far more preoccupied with innovation than with price-based competition in his analysis of capitalism. He describes monopoly as 'imperfect competition' (2010 [1942]: 21) which, given his statement above about the impossibility of 'perfect competition', suggests that monopoly is in fact endemic, not marginal, to capitalism. This is because capitalism finds itself in a bind: it depends, according to Schumpeter, on constant innovation and intensive technological development, which ultimately rewards the most dynamic players and, in turn, reduces the competition, which is what makes capitalism innovative and dynamic in the first place. Schumpeter believed that monopolies themselves were not the main problem, not least because under a vigorous capitalism they would only be temporary: 'The grocer in a village on the Ohio [river] may be a true monopolist for hours or even days during an inundation. Every successful corner may spell monopoly for a moment' (2010 [1942]: 88) but none of them will last as they are replaced, in a regular cycle, by newer, fresher monopolists.

This is the consequence of Schumpeter's famous notion of 'creative destruction', an organic and continuous form of 'industrial mutation . . . that incessantly revolutionizes the economic structure *from within*, incessantly destroying the old one, incessantly creating a new one. This process of Creative Destruction is the essential fact about capitalism' (2010 [1942]: 73). Schumpeter argues that capitalism is based not so much on meaningful intra-firm competition but on the rivalry between incumbent monopolists and new and more nimble challengers which leads him to declare that the 'first thing to go is the traditional conception of the modus operandi of competition' (2010 [1942]: 74). The problem is that the next thing to go is the energy of innovation itself given that it becomes routinized and rationalized, gradually stifling capitalism's prospects for renewal and eventually leading (regretfully for Schumpeter) to its demise: 'its very success undermines the social institutions which protect it, and "inevitably" creates conditions in which it will not be able to live' (2010 [1942]: 53–4). Monopolies, he suggests, will eventually bring the whole system crashing down. Not surprisingly, given that capitalism has not yet collapsed, Schumpeter is celebrated today – in particular by tech moguls and market fundamentalists – more for his writing on innovation and the role of the entrepreneur than for his economic forecasts.[3]

The Marxist economists Paul Baran and Paul Sweezy soon rubbished Schumpeter's deterministic notion of capitalism – that it is 'inevitably' replenished at regular intervals by the most enlightened and vigorous entrepreneurs who gobble up less competitive rivals – by pointing out that, already by the 1960s when they were writing, it was clear that smaller businesses were quite happy to be bought out by bigger ones and that 'Schumpeter's perennial gale of creative destruction has subsided into an occasional mild breeze' (1968: 82). Baran and Sweezy's study focuses on the rise of the modern corporation in what they describe as 'monopoly capitalism', a quite different set of conditions from the more competitive arrangements of the nineteenth century and one in which the key player is not the entrepreneur or the tycoon but the manager – the archetypal and bureaucratic 'organization man' (1968: 41) of the major corporation. Far from there being a bustling marketplace of small traders, large corporations were now the norm and were able to control prices, set targets and command entire sectors, thus distorting both business and democratic political arrangements. Indeed, given a monopoly capitalism dominated by the largest economic interests, '"free enterprise"', conclude Baran and Sweezy (1968: 327), 'has turned into a shibboleth devoid of all descriptive or explanatory validity'.

Baran and Sweezy were right to highlight the increasingly monopolistic character of twentieth-century capitalism and prescient in pointing out that big companies are just as likely to buy up their rivals than to squash them in open contest – witness the more than 1,100 acquisitions made by the five biggest tech companies (Google owner Alphabet, Amazon, Apple, Microsoft and Meta), and the nearly 1,500 acquisitions by the five biggest media houses (Comcast, Paramount, Sony, Disney and Warner Bros Discovery) in recent years which have helped them to dominate their respective sectors (deWaard 2024: 47–8). They also made a powerful point in connecting capitalism's underlying irrationality to growing experiences of alienation, disorientation and despair in their devastating chapter on 'the quality of monopoly capitalist society'. Yet while monopolization and concentration remain ever-present today, the entrepreneur and the tycoon have not disappeared but resurfaced as key figures in contemporary capitalist landscapes, whether in the shape of French businessman Bernard Arnault, Indian industrialist Mukesh Ambani, Swedish streaming giant Daniel Ek, or the US 'tech bros' that include Jeff Bezos, Larry Ellison, Mark Zuckerberg and of course Elon Musk.

Precisely because monopoly confers extensive power both to companies and individuals unaccountably to shape the contours of specific markets, to determine price levels and to make it more difficult for new actors to enter the market, a range of tools have been deployed by governments to mitigate its most pernicious consequences. This is particularly the case for public utilities – from railroads, postal services and the telegraph in the nineteenth century to digital infrastructures today – where antitrust rules have long been implemented by pro-competition governments in order to address the tendency of market structures to privilege a 'winner takes all' logic. This has involved measures from simply monitoring potentially anti-competitive behaviour to blocking mergers to, in rare cases, the break-up of entire companies, the most famous examples of which were the dissolution of Standard Oil in 1911 following the passage of the Sherman Antitrust Act in 1890, the separation of Hollywood studios from their exhibition arms in 1948, and the requirement in 1982 for telecoms giant AT&T to sell off the vast majority of its assets (Stoller 2020).

Antitrust is now an established part of the regulatory toolkit of capitalist governments, although it has had a rocky journey over the last century. Back in 1940, the pro-market economist Horace Gray was already arguing that the public utility concept underpinning antitrust at the time was effectively 'obsolete' in the face of increased corporate power. He suggested that competition laws were unable to disturb 'in the slightest degree the underlying structure of special [corporate] privilege; they merely reared upon it a superstructure of restraint' (Gray 1940: 8–9). Gray insisted that the concept fostered a delusion that public regulation would ever be sufficiently robust to ward off concentrated private power. Faced with antitrust challenges, '[m]onopoly capitalism, secure in its privileges, shook off the petty irritations of regulation and continued its aggressions against the public welfare' (1940: 9). The odd hiccup in monopoly consolidation was little as compared to the rise of giant corporations. By the 1970s, antitrust had changed in character from a more citizen-based approach designed to challenge undue concentrations of power to a measure, as described earlier in this chapter by the economist Robert Bork, that was predicated on the pursuit of a wholly neoliberal conception of 'consumer welfare'. In practice this involved a return to neoclassical economics and, as Will Davies argues (2014: 90), a new consensus that 'the sole goal of an antitrust intervention should be to increase efficiency'.

Yet antitrust still retains a populist and, at times, anti-corporate edge that reflects wider public anxieties about corporate excess and industry concentration.[4] Responding to the monopolistic power of the biggest tech companies, Lina Khan, the chair of the US Federal Trade Commission under former president Joe Biden, summarized the objectives of antitrust very clearly in a speech in 2024: 'History shows that firms that capture control over key inputs or distribution channels can use their power to exploit those bottlenecks, extort customers, and maintain their monopolies. The role of antitrust is to guard against bottlenecks achieved through illegal tactics and ensure dominant firms aren't unlawfully abusing their monopoly power to block innovation and competition' (Khan 2024).

To what extent, however, can capitalism be relied on to temper its own monopolistic tendencies? Can notions of the 'public interest' and 'public utility' ever be deployed consistently by regulators to challenge anti-competitive behaviour if the ultimate aim is simply to enhance, and not to replace, capitalism? And in what ways have the media and technology sectors either intensified or ameliorated the problems of monopoly?

## Media monopolies and concentrated ownership

Free-market voices insist that commercial media landscapes are exemplars of competition in that they are required to be highly responsive to different political, social and cultural demographics. A plethora of channels, titles, studios, platforms and podcasts cater to diverse audience preferences while the neoliberal conception of consumer welfare suggests that those who fail to do so will disappear, presumably as victims of 'creative destruction'. Robert McChesney neatly summarizes how competition is *supposed* to work inside the media:

> if people desire a particular media content, competition will force media corporations . . . to provide such content. Media firms will be forced to give people what they demand or go out of business. If none of the existing firms has a sufficient grasp of public sentiment, new firms will enter the fray, capture the business, and force the existing firms to get with the program or face ruin. (McChesney 2004: 176)

Except, according to McChesney, this is not at all how media markets work. Instead, they are 'textbook examples' (2004: 177) of oligopolies – markets dominated by a handful of firms – that restrict market entry, diminish competition and raise prices as soon as they are able to do so. Either through strategies of horizontal integration (through acquisitions or growth in order to dominate a particular industry) or through vertical integration (where one firm controls both the production and distribution of content), media concentration is hard-wired into communications landscapes more generally.

According to the legal scholar Ed Baker (2007), the media share some specific properties that make them particularly vulnerable to monopolization. First, while there are very high start-up and production costs (whether in relation to making a high-quality movie, television programme or podcast), it is very cheap to reach additional audience members once the first copy is made. Baker argues that this marginal cost is 'a feature of natural monopoly products' (2007: 31) as is the case, for example, with postal services, energy grids and telecoms systems. Second, Baker describes individual pieces of media content and their associated brands as legal monopolies, enforced by copyright and trademark rules. 'Each product is a monopoly that often can be most profitably priced above not only its marginal cost (often close to zero) but also its average cost, thereby producing monopoly-level profits' (2007: 32), as we have seen not only throughout the history of newspapers and commercial broadcasting but more recently with streaming services and platforms.

This level of systemic 'market failure' is especially significant for media properties given that they are, in theory, supposed to play a decisive democratic role in airing a multiplicity of opinions, representing diverse communities and holding power to account. Private media monopolies, responding to the whims of their proprietors or the desires of their shareholders, are far less likely to pursue the public interest and more likely to align with the commercial and strategic objectives of their owners. Furthermore, occupying a dominant position in their respective markets has allowed a range of proprietors to accrue sufficient power and influence to shape not just media but political landscapes – from William Randolph Hearst, who used his control of US newspapers to push for war with Spain in 1898, to Silvio Berlusconi, whose domination of the Italian media from the 1990s provided the base for his hugely successful political career, to the more recent decision by Jeff Bezos, owner of the *Washington Post*, unilaterally to suspend the newspaper's likely endorsement of the Democratic candidate in the 2024 US presidential election. Little wonder that the journalist and scholar Ben Bagdikian had previously commented that 'media power is political power' (2004: 25).

That comment was from the first edition in 1983 of his influential analysis of US media ownership, *The Media Monopoly*, which links a highly concentrated media system to a series of democratic failures and distortions. Bagdikian notes that a handful of companies control the American media landscape – it was fifty in the first edition and only five by the 2004 edition – revealing a fatal flaw in its claim to be the most competitive media market in the world:

> Corporate life and capitalist philosophy are almost synonymous, and at the heart of capitalism is competition, or the contemporary incantation, 'the free market'. If the dominant media corporations behaved in accordance with classical capitalist dogma, each would experiment to create its own unique product . . . It would mean offering differing kinds of programs that reflect the widely different tastes, backgrounds and activities of the American population. (Bagdikian 2004: 6)

What is actually on display, he argues, are thousands of outlets carrying very similar content, often integrated into a cartel of massive conglomerate entities that show little appetite for risk-taking and diversity. For Bagdikian, concentrated ownership is an effective mechanism for managing the exclusion of marginal voices from political power – a means of massaging news agendas and public priorities in the interests of the most powerful corporations. In his 1962 book, *Communications*, Raymond Williams had already highlighted the emergence of a new form of concentrated media ownership and the resulting commercialization of both content and audience taste. According to Williams, 'the methods and attitudes of capitalist business have established themselves near the centre of communications' (1968 [1962]: 31) – even in a media landscape like the United Kingdom with a significant not-for-profit, public service orientation.

Media markets that have long been associated with critical democratic responsibilities have, therefore, instead been dominated by a range of highly partisan moguls, incorporated into wider conglomerate structures and concentrated into pallid reflections of full-throated competition. In an age of diminishing trust in mainstream outlets and the fragmentation and polarization of many audiences, today's 'global media giants'[5] still command enormous influence over their respective media and political environments – for example, Globo in Brazil, Rupert Murdoch's News Corporation in the United Kingdom, United States and Australia, Clarin in Latin America, Naspers in South Africa, Prisa in Spain, Bertelsmann in Germany, Schibsted in the Nordic countries and Tencent across Asia (and beyond in terms of gaming). The acquisition of media assets in recent years by a range of billionaire entrepreneurs, venture capitalists, hedge-fund managers and private equity firms has swung the pendulum even further towards pursuing financial considerations over public interest ones. As Andrew deWaard (2024) argues in his book on *Derivative Media*, 'financialization is transforming cultural production into a highly consolidated industry with rising inequality, further decreasing the diversity and heterogeneity it could provide the public sphere' (2024: 5). The music, film and television industries in particular are consolidating rapidly, 'supercharged by financial capital' (2024: 47). Similarly, Margot Susca reveals how private equity and hedge-fund capital has increasingly intervened in the US newspaper market, securing high profits and 'treating newspapers and their staff like any other disposable product in a capitalist society' (Susca 2024: 8).

Of course, this kind of consolidation was not supposed to happen, given that the internet – the driving force of the contemporary media landscape – was originally framed by its libertarian early adopters as undermining the very basis of media concentration and centralization, with Nicholas Negroponte, for example, predicting the emergence of an entirely new business model based not on traditional media monopolies but 'a likely cottage industry of information and entertainment providers' (1996: 18). Rupert Murdoch, the archetypal media mogul (and inspiration for the television programme *Succession* [2018–23]), tweeted about the end of concentrated media power in 2012: 'Haven't you heard of the Internet? No one controls the media or will ever again' (quoted in Freedman 2014: 89). Chris Anderson, editor of the Silicon Valley bible *Wired* magazine, spoke of 'the economics of abundance – what happens when the bottlenecks that stand between supply and demand in our culture start to disappear' (2009: 11). Yet none of this has come to pass because the chokepoints, gatekeepers and behemoths that are part of the DNA of capitalism have not been weakened but significantly strengthened by digital developments.

## The 'tech-industrial complex'

The internet has not killed off the blockbuster and platforms have not generated decentralized information and entertainment markets. Digital innovations have simply increased the pressure for consolidation and concentration because of systemic trends close to the ones identified by Baker above in relation to legacy media. Barwise and Watkins (2018) explain that, in addition to high fixed development costs and low marginal costs related to distribution, technology products are 'experience goods' that depend on brand recognition and the maximization of user numbers in order to improve the quality of the experience. These 'network effects' are supplemented by personalization features based on continuous data collection that makes it difficult – or at least provides a disincentive – to switch to rival providers. 'The result', argue Barwise and Watkins (2018: 25), 'is a recursive relationship between adoption and usage, product/service quality, and further adoption and usage, further reinforcing the winner-takes-all dynamic.' This is a logic that AI – based on large-scale machine learning of existing datasets – will only intensify.

The scale of digital dominance is such that, at the end of 2024, the biggest tech companies – the 'magnificent seven' of Alphabet, Amazon, Apple, Meta, Microsoft, Nvidia and Tesla – accounted for just under one third of the *total* value of the entire S&P 500 stock market index (Welsh and Randewich 2024). Nvidia accounts for between 70% and 95% of the global market share of AI chips (Wheeler 2024), while Microsoft commands more than 70% of global desktop operating systems (Sherif 2024). According to Jennifer Holt:

> Google currently has a 90 percent share of the global search market and two-thirds of the world conducts its browsing on Google Chrome, allowing the company to dominate digital information access and the vast online advertising market that goes with it. In the US, the Amazon webstore takes in one of every two dollars spent online, and the company regularly uses data from its third-party sellers to unfairly undercut competition and benefit its own private-label and retail businesses. Apple now has over 50 percent of the global smartphone market and runs the world's largest mobile app store, with an 80 percent market share, taking a 30 percent cut of all transactions. (Holt 2024: 123–4)

The idea, as the British writer Charles Leadbeater claimed back in 2009, that we would have a 'new organizational landscape' in which the mass media 'boulders' that dominated the analogue age would be replaced by a 'rising tide of pebbles' (2009: xix) now seems almost quaint. In fact, quite the opposite is the case: 'With network effects', argues Srnicek (2016: 56), 'a tendency towards monopolisation is built into the DNA of platforms.'

Monopoly and oligopoly control over specific technology sectors has been accentuated by a further problem: that digital markets are distorted not only by the iron grip of a small number of sellers but also by the domination of a handful of buyers. This refers to *monop-*

*sony* power marked by the 'capacity of a buyer-firm to capture more value from suppliers and labour through downward pressure on supplier margins and/or the greater exploitation of labour' (Kumar 2024: 12). This is the lucrative business model for a range of dominant consumer platforms (like Uber and Airbnb) as well as for Amazon in the publishing market, Spotify in music streaming and Apple for apps. In all these domains, the 'buyer', through their gatekeeping capacity, is able to dictate the terms of trade – which in Spotify's case means the payment to the artist of a few hundredths of a cent for a single play (Giblin and Doctorow 2022: 67) – and to demand 'efficiencies' that only increase the exploitation of labour (discussed earlier in chapter 4).

Giblin and Doctorow's book is filled with examples across the cultural industries of what they call 'chokepoint capitalism' and the emergence of 'hourglass-shaped markets, with customers paying money at one end, suppliers and workers creating value at the other, and a small number of predatory rentiers controlling access in the middle' (2022: 15). While monopsony is far from new (farmers have long had to deal with the monopsony power of supermarket buyers) and while it is certainly not confined only to the cultural sector,[6] there is a particular risk posed by the corporate capture of culture that is attached to the ability to control the access points between individual producers and their audiences. Creativity is subjugated to profit making when, for example, 'Google's monopsonies over search, ads, and video translate into dominance over numerous cultural domains, most directly affecting artists, record labels, songwriters, music publishers, journalists and news publishers' (Giblin and Doctorow 2022: 10). The internet's early promise of 'disintermediation' has now evolved into a powerful new form of 'intermediation' that is stifling competition, choice and diversity.

Concerns about monopoly motivated the outgoing US president Joe Biden to speak about the dangers of a 'tech industrial complex' in his farewell address in January 2025. In a nod to former president Dwight Eisenhower's invocation of a 'military-industrial complex' in his own farewell address in 1952, Biden claimed that 'an oligarchy is taking shape in America of extreme wealth, power and influence that really threatens our entire democracy, our basic rights and freedom and a fair shot for everyone to get ahead' (quoted in Holland and Singh 2025). This warning followed a series of antitrust suits launched by the Justice Department and the Federal Trade Commission (FTC) against some of the biggest tech companies during his administration. This included challenges to Apple's control of the smartphone market, Meta's acquisitions of WhatsApp, Instagram and VR company Within, Microsoft's purchase of the gaming company Activision Blizzard, Google's control of search and Amazon's domination of e-commerce. According to FTC chair Lina Khan, Amazon is 'exploiting its monopoly power to enrich itself while raising prices and degrading service for the tens of millions of American families who shop on its platform and the hundreds of thousands of businesses that rely on Amazon to reach them' (FTC 2023). These suits – along with a slew of successful antitrust cases brought by the European Union against tech companies (Chan 2024) – reflect a far more robust conception of antitrust than the neoliberal 'consumer welfare' approach that dominated from the 1980s and suggest that 'antitrust is finally back on the agenda – in a *big* way' (Giblin and Doctorow 2022: 11) to punish corporate excesses and abuses in the tech sector.

Yet there are also many reasons to be cautious, not least because US regulators failed in the vast majority of their competition battles with the tech sector during the Biden administration and because 'Big Tech' profits and market shares have actually grown at a time when antitrust – if only in Europe and the United States – is supposedly being retooled for the digital age. For example, the share of the S&P 500 stock market accounted for by the 'magnificent seven' *increased* during Joe Biden's administration from 24 per cent at the start to 32 per cent by the time Donald Trump took office.[7] Meanwhile, despite the huge fines imposed by the European Union against both companies, Apple's European revenue grew from US$68.6 billion in 2020 to US$101.3 billion in 2024, and Meta's European revenue more than doubled in size from US$29.1 billion to US$62.3 billion in the same period.[8] Antitrust presents a necessary but certainly not a sufficient challenge to monopoly tech power.

This is because antitrust itself – whether of the citizen-based or consumer welfare variety – remains wedded to a conception that monopolies and oligopolies, if adequately regulated, can be brought to heel and forced to act in the public interest. It assumes that, despite structural tendencies within capitalism – and particularly within the media and technology sectors – that favour a 'winner-takes-all' logic, market-based competition is still a desirable and achievable objective. Consider the FTC's 2023 complaint against Amazon for undermining the online retail marketplace, which argues that 'Amazon violates the law not because it is big, but because it engages in a course of exclusionary conduct that prevents current competitors from growing and new competitors from emerging' (FTC 2023). The problem, according to the FTC, is merely bad behaviour and not size, even though the two are inextricably linked as part of capitalism's enduring history of centralization and consolidation. Jennifer Holt is surely right to note that if regulators continue to 'primarily evaluate competition through the lens of neoliberal efficiencies' (2024: 30), then antitrust is unlikely to be able to confront the kind of concentrated corporate power evident in clouds, platforms and networks.

Welcoming a rare antitrust victory in the United States – where a judge ruled in August 2024 that Google had indeed violated competition law by maintaining a monopoly of search – Yeo and Schiller (2024) argue that, while there are some grounds for optimism in the appearance of a more sustained opposition to concentrated power, the very foundations of antitrust are problematic: 'A stronger rationale for mounting a political attack against the titans of the internet would be anchored not in neoclassical economics but, rather, in a sweeping critique of corporate power.' The key question, they suggest, is not how to make companies like Google behave properly: 'Rather, it should be about what strategies we need to employ to pull search and other vital technologies out of the market altogether – and how we should govern them as common resources. The aim must be to limit not only individual corporate power but the market system that grants them that power' (Yeo and Schiller 2024).

Their concerns were entirely borne out by the court decision in August 2025 not to break up a company that had been deemed to be an illegal monopolist but simply to order Google to share its data and not enter into any more exclusive contracts. Little wonder that shares in Google's parent company Alphabet immediately rose by nearly 7 per cent (Palma, Acton and Morris 2025).

## Conclusion

Competition has an almost sacred status within capitalism and yet, far from generating and sustaining vibrant and egalitarian modes of exchange, robust competition is more of a rhetorical than an empirical reality. This is especially relevant to media and tech industries that are particularly susceptible to market failures and network effects that make them vulnerable to monopolization and conglomeration. Initial hopes that the internet would usher in a decentralized and dynamic era of 'perfect competition' have evaporated with the emergence of the chokepoints and oligarchies that characterize today's digital landscapes. Instead of reproducing long-held shibboleths concerning the virtues of competition and the dangers of monopoly, the focus needs to be on the development of a non-market alternative to a system in which the impossible pursuit of 'perfect competition' hides an underlying and irrepressible tendency to generate concentrated markets, media titans and tech oligarchs.

# 7

# Accumulation and Profit

***Overview*** 'Accumulate, accumulate! That is Moses and the prophets!' wrote Karl Marx about capitalism's relentless need to expand the basis of its operations. This involves not simply seeking technological innovation and productivity gains but spreading its footprint, including by the violent imposition of capitalist relations through colonial domination, explored further in chapter 11, to increase value and profits. This chapter explores the genealogy of accumulation and the profit motive and challenges the idea that profit has been superseded by rent seeking and that we are witnessing the emergence of a 'new mode of accumulation' in the shape of Zuboff's 'surveillance capitalism'. The chapter identifies a range of highly traditional accumulation strategies pursued by streaming companies such as Netflix and Spotify, including debt-based content deals, job cuts and price rises.

## Accumulation: 'Moses and the prophets'

Capitalism has an insatiable appetite for growth, a process that demands the systematic accumulation of everything that is potentially valuable, whether that is land, commodities, assets, influence, technology, data or power. At its core, however, capitalism is addicted to the expansion of capital itself and, in particular, to the surplus that is generated by the exploitation of labour. This is not so much a commitment on the part of individual capitalists to engage in the conspicuous consumption that is beautifully illustrated by the ads for private jets, diamond watches and haute couture on offer in specialist publications for the wealthy.[1] Instead, accumulation refers to an economic imperative that reflects the need of individual capitals repeatedly to invigorate themselves in relation to their rivals by engaging in a constant and cyclical process of surplus generation and investment. 'The heart and core of the capitalist function', argue Baran and Sweezy (1968: 55), 'is accumulation: accumulation has always been the prime mover of the system, the locus of its conflicts, the source of both its triumphs and its disasters.'

This relentless commitment to accumulation distinguishes capitalism from its predecessors. Unlike earlier societies, where there was no economic reason to store up goods or capital (unless to stave off hunger ahead of a bad winter or to pay off possible invading forces), capitalism – based on a more advanced division of labour – requires the perennial expansion of tools, materials and resources in order to sustain itself. For Adam Smith, who devotes Book Two of *Wealth of Nations* to accumulation, this is a profitable process for everyone involved in the emerging commercial society: 'As the accumulation of stock is previously necessary for carrying on this great improvement in the productive powers of labour, so that accumulation naturally leads to this improvement' (Smith 2012 [1776]: 268). Accumulation feeds productivity and vice versa; the more surplus you invest, the more efficient your enterprise becomes which, in turn, generates further profits, which allow you to become even more efficient.

In a direct rebuke to landowners eating their way through their profits (and to future capitalists blowing their fortunes on luxury goods), Smith calls for discipline on the part of the emerging business class and urges them to focus on investing their surplus: 'Capitals are increased by parsimony, and diminished by prodigality and misconduct' (2012 [1776]: 332). The strategic decision to invest capital – and not simply to fritter it away on fancy watches – results in both the expansion of productive labour and an increase in the general wealth of the whole society as more jobs and more products circulate in a market which is itself expanding. It is a virtuous circle of moral responsibility, opportunity and wealth creation that continues to populate the free-market corner of economics textbooks.

Smith's emphasis on frugality and parsimony as a driver of accumulation prefigures Max Weber's famous argument about the 'spirit of capitalism', developed more than a century later. Weber suggests that the producer's commitment to accumulation is best expressed by the ascetic, self-denying practices of one branch of Protestantism, the Puritans, during the Reformation in the sixteenth century. The Puritans followed God's work by renouncing personal gain and material consumption and instead pursuing economic activity as a sign of their devotion. The problem for Weber (2001 [1930]: 123) is that while the 'Puritan wanted to work in a calling, we are forced to do so'; in contemporary capitalist circumstances, 'material goods have gained an increasing and finally an inexorable power over the lives of men as at no previous period in history' (2001 [1930]: 124). The religious conviction of the earlier Puritans has been replaced by a far more mundane preoccupation with 'the making of money' (2001 [1930]: 18) in highly rationalized and bureaucratized circumstances. The Puritans' transcendental focus on intensive production has now been brushed aside by the dull compulsion to accumulate in the service of an accountancy, not a religious, logic.

For Marx, however, it is not the ascetic behaviour of religious devotees that epitomizes capitalism but the wealth created by the exploitation of labour which then generates the surplus value used to invest in the new tools that will increase profitability. Marx identifies two main features of accumulation: first, that it is a necessary part of the capitalist DNA and, second, that it is a historical process drowned in blood and sweat. As he puts it in *Capital*, 'Accumulate, accumulate! That is Moses and the prophets! . . . Therefore save, save, i.e., reconvert the greatest possible portion of surplus value or surplus product into capital! Accumulation for the sake of accumulation, production for the sake of production: this was the formula in which classical economics expressed the historical mission of the bourgeoisie' (Marx 1977 [1867]: 742).

Marx writes of the 'juggernaut of capital' that produces profits and possibilities for those who own and control the means of production but agony for those who do not. 'Accumulation of wealth at one pole is, therefore, at the same time accumulation of misery, the torment of labour, slavery, ignorance, brutalization and moral degradation at the opposite pole, i.e., on the side of the class that produces its own product as capital' (1977 [1867]: 799). While Adam Smith sees accumulation as essentially contributing to public welfare by enriching society, Marx sees it as the opposite: the basis for the further impoverishment of working people.

As discussed in chapter 3, Marx argues that capitalism emerges historically out of the 'primitive accumulation' that saw the agricultural population swept off their land and the violent imposition of private property – 'capital comes dripping from head to toe, from every pore, with blood and dirt' (1977 [1867]: 926). Marx saw this as necessary for the consolidation of capital, particularly in its earliest days, but other writers see a more enduring role for this kind of violence. The feminist historian Silvia Federici (2004: 12–13), for example, argues that a 'return of the most violent aspects of primitive accumulation has accompanied every phase of capitalist globalization, including the present one, demonstrating that the continuous expulsion of farmers from the land, war and plunder on a world scale, and the degradation of women are necessary conditions for the existence of capitalism in all times'. It is true that Marx focuses in *Capital* on primitive accumulation as, above all, the 'point of departure' of capitalism (1977 [1867]: 873), yet he also argues that it refers both to 'the pre-history of capital, and of the mode of production corresponding to capital' (1977 [1867]: 875). It refers, therefore, not simply to the expropriation of the peasantry but also to factors including the rise of government debt, the use of coercive legislative instruments and practices of colonization (on which *Capital* ends). Dispossession, expropriation and violence mark all periods of capitalism, not simply its founding, and are core to its reproduction.

This is essentially the argument advanced by Rosa Luxemburg in her account of *The Accumulation of Capital* (Luxemburg 2003 [1913]), in which she writes that capitalism continues to use the tools of primitive accumulation, given that 'capital in power performs the same task even today, and on an even more important scale – by modern colonial policy. It is an illusion to hope that capitalism will ever be content [simply] with the means of production which it can acquire by way of commodity exchange' (2003 [1913]: 350). Like Marx, she sees accumulation as a 'coercive law, an economic condition of existence for the individual capitalist' (2003 [1913]: 12), who is obliged to invest a surplus that would otherwise be 'of no use to the capitalist if it remains hidden in the commodity form of the product' (2003 [1913]: 10). However, Luxemburg was also keen to accentuate the fact that there are two parts to accumulation: both the core economic processes of exploitation and commodity exchange and the 'extra-economic' dimensions of imperialism and colonialism (discussed further in chapter 11). 'The historical career of capitalism can only be appreciated by taking them together. "Sweating blood and filth with every pore from head to toe"', she concludes, quoting Marx, 'characterises not only the birth of capital but also its progress in the world at every step' (2003 [1913]: 433).

Accumulation has remained an imperative for capitalism throughout its different iterations – from the 'free market' spirit that character-ized its birth to the more monopolistic features of the present era and from liberal democratic regimes to more authoritarian forms of rule. This also remains the case whether cotton, oil, knowledge or data provide its underpinning commodity status, even though specific accumulation strategies are context-dependent, for example whether investing in technology, controlling the supply of labour, stimulating consumption, acquiring rival companies or going to war is a priority at any particular time. Yet one objective is inescapable: the pursuit of profit is at the heart of all forms of accumulation. 'If they have no profit,' insists the Keynesian economist Joan Robinson (who wrote the introduction to the first English translation of Rosa Luxemburg's book and whose own book shares the same name), 'the entrepreneurs cannot accumulate, and if they do not accumulate, they have no profit' (Robinson 2013 [1956]: 76). Accumulation and profit are forever intertwined.

## 'Forever renewed profit'

A firm's profits do not just express its economic performance, nor are they simply an accounting mechanism. They are also an indicator of conduct, culture and orientation in that the pursuit of profit normally disciplines firms to take those measures that, *above all*, will stimulate growth and engineer a financial surplus. While it certainly doesn't mean that a 'not-for-profit' company will necessarily act as a model employer, nor that it will *not* look for efficiencies to lower its operating costs or increase its revenue, for-profit organizations are primarily structured around this one main goal. As Kumar notes (2024: 10), the desire to maximize profits involves securing 'the highest revenue for the lowest cost. To achieve this, firms employ pricing strategies, marketing, R&D, and so on, to give them advantages over competitors.' This is apt to make some forms of behaviour more likely – for example a determination to hold down wages, to scrimp on raw materials, to cut corners on health and safety or to minimize ethical considerations.

This was dramatized in a particularly succinct way by James Murdoch, the former CEO of News Corporation and 21st Century Fox and son of media mogul Rupert Murdoch, in a comment in a 2025 interview. Reflecting on the implications of his father's ownership of Fox News and the company's continuing support for Donald Trump, Murdoch told the *Atlantic* that 'I underestimated the ability of a profit motive to make people do terrible things – to make companies do terrible things' (quoted in Coppins 2025). Fox, according to James Murdoch, perpetuates a poisonous and divisive media culture, but it is also a business model predicated on securing ratings, winning influence and making money, no matter the eventual political consequences. James Murdoch himself is in a perfect position to know about the impact of a sensationalist and ratings-driven media, given that he was at the heart of the United Kingdom's phone-hacking scandal that broke out in 2011. As the then chairman of News International, the publisher of the tabloid newspapers the *Sun* and the *News of the World* that were accused of hacking the phones of countless celebrities and ordinary people, including the murdered schoolgirl Milly Dowler, Murdoch was the public face of a profit-driven tabloid culture. According to Nick Davies, the journalist who originally broke the story, these criminal practices emerged directly out of a neoliberal corporate culture marked by 'the casual arrogance of a group of people who take it for granted that they have every right to run the country and, in doing so, to manipulate information, to conceal embarrassing truth, to try to fool all of the people all of the time' (Davies 2014: xiv). As was revealed in subsequent court cases, the profit motive certainly incentivized people and companies to do 'terrible things'.

Of course, there are far more positive views of the profit motive, not least those held by neoclassical economists who see profit as a form of public good. For Adam Smith, profit is the incentive that fuels the self-interested productive activity of commercial entrepreneurs and that then puts food on the table for the benefit of all. 'The consideration of his own private profit is the sole motive which determines the owner of any capital to employ it either in agriculture, in manufactures, or in some particular branch of the wholesale or retail trade' (Smith 2012 [1776]: 369) – a 'consideration' which remains just as relevant today as it did in the eighteenth century. Milton Friedman takes this one step further in suggesting that 'there is one and only one social responsibility of business – to use its resources and engage in activities designed to increase its profits so long as it stays within the rules of the game, which is to say, engages in open and free competition, without deception or fraud' (Friedman 2002 [1962]: 133). Capitalism may, at times, disappoint some of its most enthusiastic proponents because of its 'lapses' into monopoly and corruption, but these are then seen as failures of regulation or blamed on 'bad apples',[2] rather than as systemic or logical outcomes of capitalism itself.

Weber appears to take a predictably pragmatic approach in that, despite its negative consequences for society, he sees the profit motive as a fundamental human trait that precedes capitalism: 'This impulse exists and has existed among waiters, physicians, coachmen, artists, prostitutes, dishonest officials, soldiers, nobles, crusaders, gamblers, and beggars' (Weber 2001 [1930]: xxxi). What is new under a capitalist mode of production, however, is that what used to be discretionary forms of behaviour in previous societies have now become the norm and are, in fact, necessary for its very survival: 'capitalism is identical with the pursuit of profit, and forever renewed profit, by means of continuous, rational, capitalistic enterprise. For it must be so: in a wholly capitalistic order of society, an individual capitalistic enterprise which did not take advantage of its opportunities for profit-making would be doomed to extinction' (2001 [1930]: xxxii). Capitalism, according to Weber, is defined by its commitment to pursue profit in highly rationalized and systematized circumstances, even if this results in higher levels of 'disenchantment' and alienation.

The traditional Marxist account of profit refutes all notions that it is related to public welfare or human nature. Just as with competition, capitalism seeks to naturalize profit seeking and to obscure the fact that a not-for-profit economic system – and ownership models not specifically organized around the pursuit of profit – may be a viable option.[3] For Marx, profit seeking therefore has a very specific genealogy, located firmly in relation to the exploitation of labour under capitalism that was highlighted in chapter 4. Marx himself describes profit as the surplus value created by labour that generates an 'increment or excess' on the original capital (1977 [1867]: 251). He argues that it is not the profit on any single transaction but its contribution to the longer-term accumulation of capital that is decisive. The aim of the capitalist is therefore 'the unceasing movement of profit making. This boundless drive for enrichment, this passionate chase after value, is common to the capitalist and the miser; but while the miser is merely a capitalist gone mad, the capitalist is a rational miser' (1977 [1867]: 254). This may seem an odd conception of a system in which its main protagonists travel around in private jets and holiday on multimillion dollar yachts, but Marx's point is that the most 'astute' capitalist is precisely the one who is committed to 'throwing his money again and again into circulation' (1977 [1867]: 255) in order to accumulate further value. Profit seeking is not a hobby but a compulsion which tends to reward gamblers over misers, even if both profligacy and parsimony are core features of capitalist enterprise.

In recent years, however, some theorists have started to raise doubts about the significance, if not the presence, of profits. Following the turmoil of the 2008 global financial crisis and the emergence of platforms as drivers of a new economic model, the socialist and former Greek finance minister Yanis Varoufakis has argued that the domination of markets and profits has been superseded with that of rent in a new system of what he describes as 'technofeudalism'. 'Markets, the medium of capitalism, have been replaced by digital trading platforms which look like, but are not, markets, and are better understood as fiefdoms. And profit, the engine of capitalism, has been replaced with its feudal predecessor: rent' (Varoufakis 2023: xiii). For Varoufakis, the Apple Store's domination of apps and Amazon's one-way relationship with sellers – both of which, he argues, depend more on the extraction of rent than on the exploitation of labour and generation of profit – express the feudal imperatives of 'cloud capitalism'. This is a situation in which tech overlords benefit from their monopoly control of specific domains of economic activity (as discussed in chapter 6) and in which their subjects (for which the modern term is 'customer') are forced to abide by their terms of service. Rent is especially pernicious as an economic incentive, according to Varoufakis, as it is less vulnerable to competition than profit seeking, given that it 'flows from privileged access to things in fixed supply, like fertile soil or land containing fossil fuels' (2023: 121). This means that the normal cut and thrust of capitalism, no matter how damaging that may have been, has now been replaced by something even more parasitical and less productive.

The wealth, power and lack of oversight of cloud capitalists is such that it is, perhaps, understandable to evaluate 'cloud capitalism' in relation to the emperors and barons (as well as the serfs and vassals) of pre-capitalist societies. But, as with Habermas's notion of the re-feudalization of the public sphere under conditions of publicity as opposed to critical debate in the twentieth century (Habermas 1989 [1962]), it is more metaphor than empirical reality. There has always been a 'feudal' element to capitalism in terms of wasteful, authoritarian, irrational and unaccountable behaviour. Moreover, Varoufakis's argument that Amazon, for example, does not function as a market because it is organized 'by an algorithm that works for Jeff's [Bezos] bottom line and dances exclusively to his tune' (2023: 86) conveniently ignores the failed markets, giant monopolies and proprietorial misdemeanours – from Standard Oil, AT&T and the Hearst Corporation to the *chaebols* of South Korea and *zaibatsu* of Japan – that have consistently featured throughout capitalism's history.

Crucially, rent seeking is not a strategy that is counterposed to profit making but is actually intimately and historically tied to it. Ursula Huws (2013: 87) notes that there are 'three main ways that enterprises generate profit under capitalism . . . rent, trade and the generation of surplus value through commodity production.' The increasing significance of rent is not at all at odds with the pursuit of profit, given that the latter remains the ultimate objective of capitalist enterprise (whether cloud-based or not) and that rent is such a highly valuable source of profit – accounting, for example, for some 86 per cent of the total profits of the oil and gas industries (estimated at approximately US$1 *trillion* a year between 1970 and 2020), according to World Bank data (Carrington 2022). Brett Christophers makes a similar point in his study of *Rentier Capitalism*: that profits remain central to capitalism even if that system is increasingly based on 'income derived from the ownership, possession or control of scarce assets under conditions of limited or no competition' (Christophers 2020: xxiv). Indeed, cloud rent itself is far from an abstract or merely parasitical source of revenue. It relies, as has been highlighted in earlier chapters, on an enormous infrastructure that is based on very traditional forms of exploited labour, including the extraction of precious metals, the production of chips and the building of server farms. Where would Uber be without its drivers, Instagram without its moderators, Amazon without its delivery vans and Meta without its engineers? The extraction of rent, the exploitation of labour and, crucially, the pursuit of profit remain absolutely central imperatives for contemporary capitalism.

## A new mode of accumulation?

The claim that rent has replaced profit and that markets have been superseded by fiefdoms is simply one of the more recent assertions about the end of capitalism 'as we know it' in the light of the 'digital revolution'. The internet has been accompanied at every stage of its development by both academic and 'popular' accounts of the paradigm shift in economic logic that is alleged to have taken place since the birth of the Web in the mid-1990s (Freedman 2016). This has involved eulogies to the 'death of the blockbuster economy' (Negroponte 1996) as well as celebrations of the diversity of the 'long tail' (Anderson 2009) and the emergence of a 'post-scarcity economy' in which, despite the trends presented in the previous chapter, the 'Liliputians have triumphed' over the behemoths (Jarvis 2009: 55). For Tapscott and Williams, the very existence of what they described as 'wikinomics' – an economic model based on collaboration and peer-to-peer networks rather than traditional corporate hierarchies – suggests that a 'new mode of production is in the making' (Tapscott and Williams 2008: ix).

Some twenty years later – and in the context of major innovations in machine learning and cloud computing – this new mode of production has, at least according to some theorists, been firmly established in the shape, for example, of vectoralism (Wark 2019), technofeudalism (Varoufakis 2023) and, in perhaps the most influential and powerful formulation of digital transformation, surveillance capitalism (Zuboff 2019). For Zuboff, Google's highly targeted search-based advertising model signals an entirely 'new mode of accumulation' (2019: 81) that is based on the systematic mining of user data for commercial purposes. She refers to an 'extraction imperative' (2019: 88), hard-wired into Google's operating system, which is necessary to generate a highly lucrative 'behavioural surplus' – the data assets that are beyond those required for core activities, such as service improvements and essential analytics, and which are then funnelled into the predictive algorithms that drive the company's advertising-based profits. Zuboff endows Google with dangerous levels of power as it strips individuals not simply of their data but of their control over their own behaviour and knowledge and does so with minimal levels of accountability and user agreement; it is a 'one-way mirror [that] embodies the specific social relations of surveillance based on asymmetries of knowledge and power' (2019: 81).

Yet instead of seeing the pursuit of behavioural surplus as the epitome of an entrenched capitalist business logic, Zuboff states that 'I could see that this new form [of accumulation] had broken away from the norms and practices that define the history of capitalism and in that process something startling and unprecedented had emerged' (2019: 13). Google – and the behavioural model on which it rests – constitutes a kind of 'rogue capitalism' for Zuboff (2019: 112), even though its commitment to relentless accumulation, monopoly profits and digital dispossession is the hallmark of the capitalist imperatives highlighted throughout this book. Far from establishing a brand-new dynamic to accumulation, surveillance capitalism simply illustrates the system's underlying ability to meet its historical appetite for growth and profitability in the context of changing technological and cultural possibilities. As Muldoon, Graham and Cant argue in their analysis of digital labour, 'the "surveillance aspect" of Zuboff's theory was always just a business model rather than a new modality of capitalism' (Muldoon, Graham and Cant 2024: 13–14).

The technology writer Evgeny Morozov (2022) provides a particularly astute reaction to Zuboff's claim that surveillance capitalism constitutes a meaningful break from traditional capitalist imperatives. He accuses Zuboff of fetishizing data extraction and digital dispossession as uniquely pernicious forms of behaviour (as opposed to more pleasant types of exploitation) and criticizes her for focusing only on Google's lucrative use of its behavioural surplus for advertising purposes, thereby neglecting other platforms which rely on different revenue models. For example, Morozov discusses Spotify's business model which is based not simply on free access to its services and extraction of the data generated but, more significantly, on subscription fees to access content. According to Morozov, both are commodity producers; while Spotify is deeply embedded 'in the capitalist business of producing something' (2022: 110) – which he describes as a 'music-cum-branded-experience commodity' (2022: 111) – Google also produces a valuable commodity in its classification of human knowledge, except that, at least in relation to search, it does not pay for the data on which its service is based. Moreover, rather than acting as 'lazy rentiers' monopolizing fictitious capital, platform companies spend huge amounts of money on research and development, precisely in order to develop more effective accumulation strategies. 'If one accepts that Google is in the business of producing search-result commodities – a process that does require massive capital investment – there is no great difficulty in treating it as a regular capitalist firm, engaged in normal capitalist production' (Morozov 2022: 120).

Zuboff's analysis of surveillance capitalism is certainly comprehensive, but Google's operating system shouldn't be seen as the only exemplar of the contemporary extraction and exploitation of data and knowledge. Indeed, far from encapsulating some ideal type of digital accumulation, Google's business model is contingent both on sustaining a favourable regulatory environment and on advertising continuing to generate the desired surplus. Yet neither can be taken for granted. First, Google's parent company Alphabet's annual filing to the US authorities makes it clear that it is likely to face a range of legal challenges, for example from the Digital Markets Act in the European Union as well as separate investigations in countries including the United Kingdom,[4] India and Japan: 'We are and may continue to be subject to claims, lawsuits, regulatory and government inquiries and investigations, enforcement actions, consent orders, and other forms of regulatory scrutiny and legal liability, including competition matters, that could harm our business, reputation, financial condition, and operating results' (Alphabet 2025: 20). This remains a concern even if the direct threat of breaking up the company appears to be remote, given the actual behaviour of antitrust-influenced regulators (see chapter 6).

Second, it is not at all clear that surveillance-based advertising is a stable revenue model for the future. As Alphabet (along with other tech companies) extends its reach into AI, this is a sector that is not primarily focused on securing 'behavioural surplus' and advertising revenue; rather AI depends, as discussed in chapter 4, on hoovering up entire databases so that emerging AI 'agents' can then generate product sales and stimulate corporate 'efficiencies'. It is the chipmakers and not the online advertising companies that are licking their lips at the prospect of AI. Far from supplanting a capitalist logic of accumulation, it is far more likely that capitalist logics themselves will shape the future of Google and other tech platforms. Ultimately, whatever the technological base of the enterprise, both the need to accumulate and the search for profits will continue to underpin corporate strategy. 'Capitalism is moving in the same direction it always has been,' concludes Morozov (2022: 126), 'leveraging whatever resources it can mobilize – the cheaper, the better.' Data extractivism is just as much a part of the capitalist playbook as the old-fashioned commodity production some thought it would supersede.

## Streaming profits

One possible objection to the claim that traditional profit seeking is central to today's tech companies, notably streamers, is that many of them failed to generate any profits for substantial periods of time. Indeed, profit – and paying back the huge investments in tech start-ups made by venture capital firms – seemed to be a luxury that didn't apply to this particular sector (as exemplified by the dotcom crash discussed in chapter 14). Spotify was launched in 2006 and only declared its full year of profits in 2024, suffering losses of more than €1.2 billion in 2017; Netflix started as a mail-order DVD business in 1997 and took six years to become profitable; Amazon, launched in 1994, had to wait until 2003 before seeing significant amounts of investment eventually transformed into profit. According to its founder Jeff Bezos, losing money was always part of the plan: 'we are a famously unprofitable company', Bezos told the BBC in 2000 after the company declared a US$720 million loss the previous year. 'And that is a conscious strategy and investment decision' (quoted in Agustin 2024). Eschewing short-term profitability and focusing instead on growing capacity and locking in customers with low prices to begin with, successful tech companies were able to ride out apocalyptic headlines (such as *Wired*'s 'Spotify is Screwed' in 2023) and astonishing levels of debt (including Netflix's US$15 billion in long-term debt accrued in 2020) before finally realizing the value of their investments. 'How could we so blindly trust a company that was burning through money?' asked one tech journalist. 'But these are long-term bets and the bets eventually paid off' (Chandonnet 2025). In the cases of Netflix, Amazon and Spotify at least, profligacy seems to have triumphed over parsimony.

In achieving profitability, these companies were not refuting or superseding capitalist principles of accumulation but firmly embracing them by using well-established strategies, initially to dominate a market (or in Amazon's case, a series of markets) and squeeze out the competition before then adopting 'efficiencies' in order to increase profits. If we take the leading streaming companies as an example, three main accumulation strategies are evident: debt-based content and licensing deals, cutbacks in jobs and the restructure of services, and price rises.

The first objective of the streamers was to spend enormous amounts of money to nail down first-mover advantage by adding subscribers to their user-friendly and data-rich services: for Spotify, this meant agreeing licensing deals with record companies and subsequently with 'talent', for example its US$100 million agreement with podcaster Joe Rogan in 2020; for Amazon, it involved expanding its interests from selling books to being a one-stop shop for the widest possible range of goods where streaming (on Prime) eventually functioned simply as a funnel to bring in additional audiences; for Netflix, it meant shifting from DVD rental to licensing other people's content before, in 2013, moving into original production itself. 'Netflix's concern', writes Will Tavlin (2025), 'was scale, rather than the cinema it was scaling. Movies . . . were merely a means to an end: acquiring subscribers who paid for access to Netflix's entire library of content every month.' An article in the *New Yorker* magazine described this as the 'Walmart-ization of Netflix as the platform increasingly prioritized voracious acquisition over curatorial discernment' (Syme 2023). Exploiting their gatekeeping power as both vendor and seller – and extracting highly favourable terms for themselves in their relationships with producers as documented by Giblin and Doctorow (2022) – the streamers' priority was always to accumulate *more* content, *more* users, *more* data and therefore *more* control over their markets in order to reap the dividends that would eventually come with this level of domination. Marx must have been anticipating Netflix when he wrote in *Capital* that the capitalist's 'motivating force is not the acquisition and enjoyment of use-values, but the acquisition and augmentation of exchange-values' (1977 [1867]: 739).

This creates a curious logic in which it is not the quality or distinctiveness of the cultural product that is valued but simply its ability to be stored in a digital warehouse that is sufficiently well stocked to disincentivize users from shopping elsewhere. At one level, this is evidence of the well-established risk-mitigation strategy of developing a repertoire of films, programmes or songs in the hope that one of them may be a hit that will more than compensate for the costs of the 'misses' (Garnham 1990: 161). Netflix, however, built its original content catalogue not in the expectation that any one of its videos would be a blockbuster success but that there would simply be enough of them to entice in, and maintain the loyalty of, users. According to Tavlin (2025), 'Netflix, uniquely, seemed to relish making its films vanish as soon as they were released, dumping them onto its platform and doing as little as possible to distinguish one from the next.' The products of what one agent later described as 'drunken sailor spending' (Shaw 2022) therefore functioned more as shelf-fillers than as cultural goods in their own right, leading Tavlin (2025) to conclude that 'for Netflix, a movie is an accounting trick', a commodity designed to placate investors rather than to entertain and stimulate audiences.

This strategy proved to be highly effective for those streamers who eventually built significant subscription bases on the back of extravagant spending, even if this was based on large amounts of debt and sustained losses. However, in 2022 and in the light of economic uncertainty caused by the Covid-19 pandemic, many streamers saw a major slowdown in new subscribers, forcing them to shift focus 'from subscriber growth to streaming profitability' as the media consultants Enders Analysis put it (Watson, Dalrymple and Harrington 2024). This involved streamlining both their workforces and their services and cutting back on marketing in order to reduce operating costs. Following pressure from investors, Spotify sacked 2,000 staff in 2023, approximately 25 per cent of its entire workforce, leading its chief executive, Daniel Ek, to claim that 'we are being relentlessly resourceful in all of our costs' (quoted in Nicolaou 2024a). This followed a round of layoffs in the previous year, with Elon Musk sacking around 3,700 Twitter employees after his US$44 billion purchase of the platform,[5] Meta cutting 11,000 jobs due to declining advertising revenue, and even the financially robust Netflix laying off 450 people in the light of its first subscriber loss in a decade (Blum 2022).

This retrenchment was not confined only to savings made from redundancies, however. Spotify embarked on a 'demonetizing' strategy in which it said it would stop paying royalties on those songs with fewer than a thousand streams a year (Nicolaou 2024b),[6] while Hollywood streamers such as Disney+, Max and Paramount+ cut their expenditure on original content and prioritized more predictable genres, such as 'reality TV' and true-crime documentaries. Even Netflix changed its emphasis away from an overarching commitment to scale – its 'Walmart-ization' tendency – to commissioning what its chief content officer called 'gourmet cheeseburgers', programmes with both 'premium and commercial' appeal. This was accompanied by a return to 'bundling' services that had previously been 'unbundled' with, for example, mobile phone companies and online supermarkets now offering streaming services as part of a supposedly more cost-effective package. The benefits of bundling, according to Enders Analysis, are 'increased reach, the ad monetisation opportunity, reduced churn and lower subscriber acquisition costs' (Watson, Dalrymple and Harrington 2024), all of which served to assuage investors and bring streamers ever nearer to profitability.

The third response by streamers reflects the classic approach of the emerging oligopolist: once you have locked your audience in (to the extent that this is ever possible in the light of unpredictable tastes and economic uncertainty), you raise prices. After freezing its subscription for over a decade, Spotify increased prices in both 2024 and 2025, contributing significantly to its turnover and eventual profitability. Streaming video companies, confronted with fierce competition and stagnating levels of new subscriptions, also embraced price rises. Seven top US streaming services increased their prices by an average of 23 per cent in October 2023, soon followed by Netflix which has regularly hiked costs in its more 'mature' markets (in the United States, it increased the cost of its premium package eight times between 2013 and 2025 while it has lowered prices in India). Enders describes the situation as one of 'streamflation' (Watson, Dalrymple and Harrington 2024), which risks customers either choosing cheaper ad-supported packages or quitting the service entirely.

The fierce embrace of traditional accumulation strategies has delivered tremendous results for the streaming companies. Netflix earned nearly US$9 billion in profits in 2024 with a profit margin of 22 per cent (Chandonnet 2025), while Spotify made profits of €1.1 billion in the same year with an astonishing 30 per cent profit margin. This level of success allowed senior Spotify executives – including its HR director and head of public relations – to cash out some US$1.25 billion worth of stock in 2024 that included US$900 million in payouts for its two co-founders alone. According to the *Financial Times*, 'the co-founders' transactions have vaulted their stock earnings into the upper echelon of corporate leadership' (Nicolaou and Temple-West 2024), joining other doyens of the corporate world, including Netflix's Ted Sarandos who also sold US$6 million of his own Spotify stock in 2024.

## Conclusion

For all the disruptive behaviour of digital start-ups on legacy markets and for all the new ways in which data are being incorporated into the engine of economic activity across the globe, capitalist cycles involving debt, accumulation, profit and loss are not being eclipsed but intensified. The fact that the leading artificial intelligence company, OpenAI, saw a loss of US$5 billion in 2024 and quickly announced significant price rises – leading the *New York Times* to run a story headlined 'OpenAI is Growing Fast and Burning through Piles of Money' (Isaac and Griffith 2024) – suggests that this is not a process that is likely to end anytime soon. Theories of 'cloud capitalism' and 'surveillance capitalism' that propose that rent has replaced profit or that rates of 'digital dispossession' are hallmarks of a 'new mode of accumulation' ignore the fact that rent seeking, exploitation and dispossession have been intertwined with capitalism for a very long time. Far from breaking with its fetish for accumulation, streamers and AI companies are dependent on some very old tricks of the capitalist trade.

# 8

# Ideology and Hegemony

***Overview*** Capitalism depends for its reproduction on 'bundles' of ideas and supportive institutions that seek to establish a particular 'common sense' about market-dominated societies. This chapter evaluates a materialist conception of ideology – that it is intimately connected to the prevailing mode of production – and highlights the role of hegemony as a means of securing acceptance of dominant ideas. The chapter then focuses on the media's definitional power in relation to its ability to manufacture consent and to shape content around elite frames and agendas. It concludes with a case study of mainstream news coverage of Israel's war on Gaza that illustrates how all too often journalism performs a hegemonic role in reproducing the ideology of powerful groups.

## The realm of ideas

Ideology has a very chequered history, sometimes seen in fairly neutral terms simply as the expression of a particular set of ideas or, in a more pejorative sense, where it is seen as a form of speech that is politically motivated and thus disreputable. As the British cultural theorist Terry Eagleton puts it (1991: 2), 'Ideology, like halitosis, is in this sense what the other person has.' Seeking to rescue ideology from such negative connotations, the French socialist economist Thomas Piketty followed up his bestselling account of capitalism and inequality, *Capital in the Twenty-First Century* (Piketty 2014), with a lengthy study of how specific ideas serve to justify and underpin 'inequality regimes' (Piketty 2020) in different historical and political circumstances. During the course of the more than one thousand pages of *Capital and Ideology*, Piketty argues that inequality isn't simply the result of economic maldistribution or political corruption but is, instead, a deeply ideological phenomenon driven by multiple ideas about how societies should be structured. For Piketty, ideology refers to 'a set of a priori plausible ideas and discourses' (2020: 3) – used by both elite actors and marginalized social groups in negotiating and potentially transforming the world around them. Indeed, he attributes constitutive power to ideology, claiming that 'the realm of ideas, the political-ideological sphere, is truly autonomous' (2020: 7) and concludes that '[t]he history of all hitherto existing societies is the history of the struggle of ideologies and the quest for justice' (2020: 1035).

Piketty's view of ideology is of course a direct challenge to the argument made by Marx and Engels in the *Communist Manifesto* about the primacy of class struggle. But it is also a provocation aimed at the Marxist tradition about the status of ideas and their relationship to the material reproduction of social relations. When Piketty talks of the autonomy of ideology, this is quite different to the traditional Marxist account that ideas are ultimately subordinate to economic factors; and when Piketty claims that it is a mistake to view 'ideological and political constructs as mere veils intended only to conceal the perpetual domination of ruling elites' (2020: 42), this also runs counter to the Marxist assumption that the objective of capitalist ideology – a process in which the media play such a key role – is to mystify the 'real' relations of society and, at least in some accounts, to generate a kind of 'false consciousness'. So while there is a consensus that ideas certainly do matter, there are some significant differences about the relationship between ideological and other spheres of society in relation to two overlapping arguments: where ideas emerge from, and whether ideology can ever provide an independent account of the world.

Marx's great contribution to this debate is, first, to insist that ideas have a material origin and that we do not just pluck ideas out of the sky irrespective of the world around us. Just as misogyny, for example, is neither a spontaneous nor a natural prejudice but one that is intimately linked to the place and role of women in society and the structure of the family (as I explore in chapter 12), ideas about racism are also connected to the material structures that perpetuate racial difference. 'It is not the consciousness of men that determines their existence', argues Marx (1970 [1859]: 21), 'but their social existence that determines their consciousness.' This refers to what

Marx describes as the relationship between base and superstructure: that there is an economic foundation from which emerges an ideological superstructure, a set of beliefs, customs and institutions that correspond to economic variables. In the preface to *A Contribution to the Critique of Political Economy*, he insists that 'it is always necessary to distinguish between the material transformation of the economic conditions of production ... and the legal, political, religious, aesthetic or philosophical – in short ideological – forms in which men become conscious of the conflict and fight it out' (1970 [1859]: 21).

This base/superstructure model has been widely criticized (not least in Piketty's account of ideology) for being crude and mechanical, essentially reducing whole areas of human life to matters of 'the economy'. Yet the model is not designed to evacuate complexity and unpredictability but rather to cement the relationship between economic and non-economic domains and, in particular, to establish economic factors as constitutive forces that cast a shadow over the whole of society. The relationship is indeed a difficult one: it is neither that of a mirror, where the two domains simply reflect each other, nor that of a conveyor belt where economic pressures are automatically translated into their legal, political and cultural avatars. We need, according to Garnham (1990: 23), to avoid both 'the twin traps of economic reductionism and of the idealist autonomization of the ideological level'[1] that Piketty insists on – a position that Jakubowski (1976: 104) pointedly describes as 'the most important form of ideology'.

Engels conceives of the model in terms of a reflexive relationship between individuals and material structures where the former are not passive objects of irrepressible historical forces but nevertheless confront conditions that are not of their own making:

> The economic situation is the basis, but the various elements of the superstructure – political forms of the class struggle and its results, to wit: constitutions established by the victorious class after a successful battle, etc., juridical forms, and even the reflexes of all these actual struggles in the brains of the participants, political, juristic, philosophical theories, religious views and their further development into systems of dogmas – also exercise their influence upon the course of the historical struggles and in many cases preponderate in determining their *form*. (Engels 1972 [1890]: 294)

Ideological forces are, therefore, central to determining the shape of everyday battles but they are not independent of an economic domain which, in any case, is far from static; as Raymond Williams notes (1980: 34), 'when we talk of "the base", we are talking of a process and not a state' that is itself subject to constant renewal and transformation.

Second, Marx develops a theory of ideology based on this material conception of consciousness which itself changes during the course of his life. In one of his earliest pieces of writing, *The German Ideology* (Marx and Engels 2022 [1846]), Marx relates ideology to a *camera obscura*, the nineteenth-century device which projects an image of the world upside down. In suggesting that ideology functions as an illusion that inverts real experiences, Marx asserts the role of ideas in sustaining a gap between what things *appear* to be and their true dynamics, thus mystifying the real relations of society.[2] This is because, for Marx, ideology is not neutral but instead reflects the balance of power at any one time: 'The ideas of the ruling class are in every epoch the ruling ideas: i.e. the class which is the ruling material force of society, is at the same time its ruling intellectual force . . . The ruling ideas are nothing more than the ideal expression of the dominant material relationships' (Marx and Engels 2022 [1846]: 35). This is deliberately fostered by a specific social group of 'active, conceptive ideologists, who make the perfecting of the illusion of the class about itself their chief source of livelihood' (Marx and Engels 2022 [1846]: 35) – a group that, for Marx and Engels, includes most philosophers, historians, religious figures and journalists. So ideology is embedded in a series of practices that generate norms that occlude, mystify and mislead individuals about the true dynamics of the societies in which they live.

Yet Marx refines this understanding of ideology in his later work, especially in *Capital* – away from a sense of 'false consciousness' on the part of the public and instead towards a notion that commodity fetishism has distorted reality itself. 'Ideology', as Terry Eagleton argues in relation to Marx (Eagleton 1991: 85), 'is now less a matter of reality becoming inverted in the mind, than of the mind reflecting a real inversion'. In other words, ideology is not so much about perception and more about the expression of sets of ideas which, in the case of the capitalist class according to Marx, relate to its fetishization of commodity exchange and competition as joyful and liberating. For Eagleton, 'whereas in *The German Ideology*, ideology was a matter of not seeing things as they really were, it is a question in *Capital* of reality itself being duplicitous and deceitful' (1991: 87).

This tension between ideology referring to a means of concealing social relations as well as to systems of ideas that express underlying economic and political dynamics is prevalent in Marx's writing and in that of the Marxist tradition more generally. Raymond Williams notes that Marx uses ideology in two different ways: both in relation to an illusion and as 'the set of ideas which arise from a given set of material interests or, more broadly, from a definite class or group' (Williams 1983: 156). Lukács, for example, also speaks of ideology as a 'veil' and a 'more or less conscious attempt at forgery' (1971 [1923]: 66–7), and yet he simultaneously claims that ideology is far from a simple illusion. 'Ideological factors do not merely "mask" economic interests, they are not merely the banners and slogans: they are the parts, the components of which the real struggle is made' (1971 [1923]: 58). Interestingly, Lukács repeatedly refers to '"false" consciousness' (1971 [1923]: 72) in relation to ideology with 'false' always placed in inverted commas as he seeks to distinguish between the emergent consciousness of workers as they struggle against exploitation and reification and the more profound failure of capitalists to grasp historic realities.

Whether ideology (and ideologists) either distort reality or express the logic of an already distorted reality, the fact remains that ideological articulations are necessary elements of social reproduction and that they contain within them the very tensions and imperatives that characterize capitalist societies. This also means that ideology is most effectively presented not simply as a lie; for ideology to be absorbed, it has to connect with the experiences – as fragmented and alienating as they may be – of ordinary people as they negotiate capitalist society. For example, that is why Marx writes that religion is the 'heart of a heartless world' and not just the 'opium of the masses' (Marx 1844), why 'family values' provide solace for some and violence for others, and why it is usually more common for liberal media to 'frame' reality according to their interests, rather than simply to dissimulate (though of course they do both). As Eagleton puts it (1991: 15), 'ideologies must be more than imposed illusions, and for all their inconsistencies must communicate to their subjects a version of social reality which is real and recognizable enough not to be simply rejected out of hand.' Ideology is best understood, therefore, neither in relation to the existence of an autonomous sphere of thought, nor to the promotion of impeccably neutral sets of ideas, nor simply to purposeful acts of deception but instead to the expression of material interests designed to advantage a specific social group. Under capitalism and in conditions where power is held asymmetrically, this involves 'the ways in which symbolic forms serve, in particular circumstances, to establish and sustain relations of domination' (Thompson 1995: 213).

## Consent and domination

Ideology plays a key role in attempts to normalize capitalist imperatives and values – from competition and profit seeking to private
ownership and patriotism – so as to secure the reproduction of existing social relations. Whether embedded in news bulletins, educational
curricula, religious texts, parliamentary legislation, party manifestos
or national anthems, ideological expressions assist powerful actors
to legitimize their control and, in turn, to delegitimize perspectives
that run counter to their interests. Yet ideology is less able to account
for the broad range of institutions and practices that seek to win
the consent of publics to the priorities of the societies in which they
live and to explain the basis of domination.[3] Instead, a distinct but
related term, *hegemony*, has been used to describe the ways both in
which powerful groups exercise their leadership and in which publics
provide their consent to this domination. As opposed to the threat of
coercion and physical force that is usually monopolized by the state
(see chapter 10), hegemony refers to the 'range of practical strategies
by which a dominant power elicits consent to its rule from those it
subjugates' (Eagleton 1991: 115–16). For Eagleton, hegemony is a
much more expansive category than ideology, helping to add flesh
to ideology's more abstract qualities and providing the latter with
'a material body and political cutting edge' (1991: 115). Raymond
Williams sees hegemony as the pursuit and operation of 'predominance': 'an integral form of class rule which exists not only in political
and economic institutions and relationships but also in active forms
of experience and consciousness' (1983: 145). Hegemony refers
to a process of consent-seeking that is embedded in everyday lived
experience rather than achieved through the top-down imposition of
ideological frameworks.

Hegemony emerges most famously in the work of the Italian revolutionary Antonio Gramsci, who sought to grasp the different ways
in which capitalism maintains its rule and to reflect on strategies
of resistance. He was by no means the first writer in the Marxist
tradition to focus on hegemony, given that Lukács, for example, had
already addressed the issue in his *History and Class Consciousness*:
'For a class to be ripe for hegemony means that its interests and
consciousness enable it to organise the whole of society in accordance with those interests' (1971 [1923]: 52). Gramsci, however,
writing from his prison cell after being jailed for his activism in 1926,
contrasts the coercive power of the state with the '"spontaneous"
consent given by the great masses of the population to the general

direction imposed on social life by the dominant fundamental group' (Gramsci 1971: 12). Both are forms of domination: while the former is more direct and centralized, the latter is the outcome of activities concentrated in a rapidly expanding 'civil society', a sphere that is, at least formally speaking, an intermediate space between the state and private individuals. Yet, because the barriers between state and civil society are so permeable, these activities serve in reality to propagate the overall interests of the capitalist class. Gramsci notes that while the state is quite prepared to use force to defend its interests, it is far more desirable (and productive) to rely on the willingness of its citizens to accept its rules, a relationship that Gramsci describes as 'hegemony protected by the armour of coercion' (1971: 263). This means that, as with ideology, a successful hegemony will have to engage in part with the aspirations and experiences of those they seek to dominate. Hegemony, argue Artz and Murphy (2000: 3), 'does not arise primarily as a result of a dominant group performing some sleight of hand to deceive the "masses" nor by a dominant group conducting a clever propaganda campaign to mislead subordinate groups'. Hegemony involves at least a partial recognition (and rebuttal) of working-class interests.

Gramsci's great contribution was to highlight the importance for the maintenance of capitalist rule of those non-coercive instruments and institutions based in the superstructure and to challenge what he saw as an 'economism' – a depoliticized left-wing version of laissez-faire liberalism – that marginalized this sphere of activity. At the same time, however, Gramsci insists that we cannot lose sight of the determining factors of the economic relations of production: 'for though hegemony is ethical-political, it must also be economic, must necessarily be based on the decisive function exercised by the leading group in the decisive nucleus of economic activity' (1971: 161). Indeed, the 'prestige' and 'confidence' enjoyed by the powerful that allows them to seek and to secure consent exists precisely because of their dominant 'position and function in the world of production' (1971: 12).[4]

Gramsci's other major insight into the operation of hegemony is that it is a process that can never be stable or fixed but is instead attached to the dynamics of political struggles (including the one that landed him in jail). The possibility of change is hard-wired into this conception of hegemony: what at one moment may be seen as a durable kind of 'common sense', arising out of a bourgeois conception of the world and fostered through its leading intellectuals and institutions, can be transformed into the 'more unitary and coherent' form of 'good sense' (1971: 328) as a result of praxis, the interaction between thought and political agency. What is viewed at any one time as 'accepted wisdom' – on issues such as gay marriage, climate change or the 'benefits' of colonialism – can be shifted not through mere argument but only through struggle. Indeed, we may also expect regular *crises* of hegemony when established explanatory frameworks start to break down under the pressure of changing conditions and mobilizations, for example the one famously assessed by Stuart Hall and colleagues (1978) in their analysis of media constructions of mugging in the 1970s, *Policing the Crisis*.

One of the key points made by Hall and his colleagues is that, because the objective of any hegemonic regime is to make its interests seem legitimate and indeed organic to that society, this requires hard work. 'Hegemony was no automatic condition: its very *absence* from Italian political life was what focused Gramsci's attention on it. But it was the condition to which liberal-bourgeois society "aspired"' (1978: 203). There is a sound reason why the 'spontaneous' nature of the consent referred to by Gramsci earlier as the epitome of hegemony is placed in inverted commas in the original quote: precisely because hegemony has to be carefully nurtured and customized in order to make it seem as if consent has been provided willingly and not at all self-consciously. So just as the effective propagation of ideology depends on the labour of 'ideologists', referred to earlier in this chapter, any successful form of hegemony requires the development of institutions and narratives that are relevant and convincing to ordinary people and that enshrine capitalist principles within their operating systems. Not surprisingly, given high levels of instability and regular opposition to specific features of market rule, this is an ongoing and highly delicate process. 'We have to emphasise', argues Raymond Williams (1980: 38), 'that hegemony is not singular; indeed that its own internal structures are highly complex, and have continually to be renewed, recreated and defended; and by the same token, that they can be continually challenged and in certain respects modified'. While hegemony relates to a wide range of cultural, educational, legal and political interventions that seek to cement capitalist domination, that domination is often fragile, contestable and contingent.

## The media and definitional power:
## manufacturing consent, indexing and framing

The traditional liberal democratic conception of the media's role is that, by representing the world to itself and providing a check on power, they help to generate a consensus that can smooth over conflict and, as James Curran summarizes it (2002a: 136), 'assist the collective self-realization, co-ordination, democratic management, social integration and adaptation of society'. In reality, however, the media are key instruments of hegemony; they foster a capitalist 'common sense' that aims to reproduce dominant perspectives about matters of public interest and through the promotion of ideological expressions that recreate the world in the image of the powerful. An early account of media power by Murdock and Golding challenges both liberal functionalism and the abstract economism critiqued by Gramsci: 'In addition to producing and distributing commodities, however, the mass media also disseminate ideas about economic and political structures. It is this second and ideological dimension of mass media production which gives it its importance and centrality and which requires an approach in terms not only of economics but also of politics' (Murdock and Golding 1973: 206–7). In relation to news media, for example, this means that the media have a number of roles: to exercise the 'power to typify, transmit, and define what is "normal"' (Glasgow University Media Group 1976: 348), to 'orchestrate' public opinion given their status as 'primary definers of topics' (Hall et al. 1978: 58), and to secure the reproduction of elite consensus (Bourdieu 1991).

Perhaps the most influential radical account of the media's hegemonic role is Herman and Chomsky's propaganda model (PM) that argues that corporate media are a crucial tool for legitimizing the ideas of the most powerful social actors and, borrowing from the US writer Walter Lippmann, for 'manufacturing consent' for their actions in both domestic and foreign contexts (Herman and Chomsky 1988). They identify five 'filters' working on the media that ensure a systematic bias in favour of capitalist interests. First, the leading media organizations are large corporations with an orientation on profit and, as such, are 'closely interlocked, and have important common interests, with other major corporations, banks, and governments' (1988: 14). Second, these media corporations often depend on advertising as a key source of revenue – a pressure that tends to skew their coverage towards the interests of more 'desirable' (i.e., privileged) audiences and to militate against 'controversial' content that may alienate the most powerful advertisers. Third, news organizations are dependent on elite sources, both because they are seen as 'reliable' purveyors of information but also because they lower the costs of newsgathering. Coverage is dominated, therefore, not simply by established politicians and business leaders but by unaccountable 'experts' and well-resourced think tanks, all of which help to subsidize the cost of newsgathering. The fourth filter is what Herman and Chomsky call 'flak', the systematic rebuttal of material that challenges elite sources and which helps to discipline those journalists who may wish to highlight more critical agendas. The fifth and final filter consists of the construction of an 'enemy' around which populations (and media agendas) can unite. While communism initially fulfilled this role for Herman and Chomsky writing towards the end of the Cold War in the 1980s, the enemy today is more likely to be that of fundamentalist Islam or anti-democratic demagogues (such as Vladimir Putin, Viktor Orbán or Donald Trump). In passing through and interacting with these filters, the mainstream news environment is therefore structured in such a way as to control dissent and to secure public support for the actions of ruling elites. 'They fix the premises of discourse and interpretation and the definition of what is newsworthy in the first place' (Herman and Chomsky 1988: 2).

Through detailed empirical analysis of 'elite media' coverage of US interventions in Central America and South-East Asia, Herman and Chomsky discover a 'conformism' between media agendas and the *broad* aims of US foreign policy and conclude that 'the "societal purpose" of the media is to inculcate and defend the economic, social, and political agenda of privileged groups that dominate the domestic society and the state' (1988: 298). While there is the capacity for limited and tactical disagreement inside the media, coherent oppositional frameworks are largely marginalized, and dissenting viewpoints remain highly bounded. The beauty of the model is that it avoids conspiratorial explanations – in other words, a situation in which editors sit down privately with politicians or generals to plan the contours of media coverage and then instruct their staff to follow suit. In fact, Herman and Chomsky claim quite the opposite: that media performance and complicity is the result of the everyday operation of market forces. The filters are triggered so 'naturally' that journalists are able 'to convince themselves that they choose and interpret the news "objectively" and on the basis of professional news values' (1988: 2). Journalists are, therefore, *formally* free to follow their own hunches and to pursue their own investigations, but they do this within a heavily constrained and hierarchical news system that limits their choices and defines the contours of what is likely to be accepted as news in the first place.

The propaganda model (PM) has been adopted by writers, including Edwards and Cromwell (2006), MacLeod (2019) and Pedro-Carañana and colleagues (2018), whose analyses coalesce around a shared view that mainstream news media ultimately function as 'weapons of mass deception' (Rampton and Stauber 2003) rather than public enlightenment. However, some theorists, for example Sparks (2007) and Freedman (2009), who share the view that the corporate media articulate capitalist interests and do not perform a liberal 'watchdog' role by holding elites to account, are more critical of the model. Although the PM is right to pinpoint the ideological affiliations between states, corporate elites and the media, they argue that the PM underplays the possibility of shifting positions and strategic differences that may be generated by tensions between capitalist elites, and that it underplays the possibility of resistance to mainstream agendas. Others attribute an instrumentalism and functionalism to the PM, claiming that it sees media systems as 'solid, permanent and immovable' (Golding and Murdock 2000: 74) or as 'perfectly unidimensional' (Hallin 1994: 13) and thus unable to account for other roles that they may perform, such as providing a space for elite debate, and for the occasional differences (as opposed to routine similarities) in journalistic output. The PM, therefore, is effective in explaining the ideological orientations of pro-market media but it may be less useful in uncovering exactly how journalistic practices are shaped by news environments, and how the professional values of journalists – including a commitment to 'objectivity' and 'truth-telling' – intersect with their wider surroundings.

Theorists have developed two other ways of explaining the media's broad ideological conformity with capitalist norms: indexing and framing. According to Lance Bennett (1990), journalists' reliance on official sources is conditioned not so much by wider structural forces but by the degree of consensus shared by ruling elites at any one time. To the extent that there is general agreement on the aims and objectives of, for example, foreign policy, journalists are likely to find it difficult to challenge this consensus and to highlight dissenting voices. Bennett develops a theory of press–state relations in which he argues that journalists 'tend to "index" the range of voices and viewpoints in both news and editorials according to the range of views expressed in mainstream government debate about a single topic' (1990: 106). While corporate ownership is certainly a significant factor on their output, 'indexing' explains why journalists

'naturally' orientate themselves on a limited range of 'official' perspectives. It links together economic factors, newsroom cultures and
individual political leanings into an explanation for the narrowness
of the 'journalistic gate' (1990: 107). He also insists that indexing is
not predictable or standard across all types of reporting and that it
is strongest in those areas – like trade and military decisions – which
are 'of great importance not only to corporate economic interests but
to the advancement of state power as well' (1990: 122). Here, the
pressure to take a lead from elite sources and to minimize voices that
challenge these sources will be most intense.

This unacknowledged orientation on a very restricted range of
frameworks and institutions produces a default position that favours
established interests and undermines the ability of journalists directly
to confront these interests and to pursue alternative agendas, even if
they were minded to do so. News, for Bennett, is, therefore, fundamentally 'elite driven' (1994: 24), subject to official sanctions and
government pressure, but also sensitive to the impact of schisms
within these elites which may, at times, provide journalists with
access to '*reportable* opposition voices and viewpoints' (1994: 24;
my emphasis). This doesn't mean that the journalistic gate is thrust
wide open (let alone that it is demolished) but simply that it may be
possible where there is elite disagreement to include a wider diversity
of perspectives than is typically possible, given what is normally considered by risk-averse journalists as 'reportable' or not.

The degree of elite consensus is not sufficient, however, fully to
explain media performance either when there *is* journalistic dissent
(Schlosberg 2013: 205) or, as is more frequent, where there is not.
In order to make sense of the routine distortions and omissions
in mainstream news coverage and the ways in which adherence to
professional values can be undermined without a direct or overt
'command' from editors and proprietors, Todd Gitlin turns to the
US sociologist Erving Goffman's account of frame analysis (Goffman
1974). He argues that frames are crucial ways for journalists to make
sense of and to order public life that are based on 'principles of
selection, emphasis, and presentation composed of little tacit theories
about what exists, what happens, and what matters' (Gitlin 1980: 6).

The latter phrase is particularly crucial: framing is a process that
is an essential part of the journalist's work in helping to assemble
a coherent narrative, but the ability to decide 'what matters' (and,
therefore, what does not) is clearly unequally distributed in a capitalist society. This ability for journalists to discriminate between frames
– whether based on indexing elite consensus or a more profound

ideological sympathy with elite interests – leads, for example, to a persistent favouring of, for example, pro-war voices and the marginalizing of more critical viewpoints. Gitlin (1980) examines the media's long-standing neglect of the anti-Vietnam War movement in the 1960s, while Entman and Page found that, in the lead up to the 1991 Gulf War, out of 118 opinion pieces in the *New York Times*, many of which contained limited criticisms of the administration, not a single one actually argued against US involvement in the war (Entman and Page 1994: 96). Criticism, they argue, was 'procedural' rather than 'substantive', accentuated by a routine dependence on official sources and the 'beat' system that 'encourages the over-representation of administration views' (1994: 96). This is a pattern of coverage that was also evident during the 2003 Iraq War in which, despite substantial public opposition in early 2003, researchers found evidence in allegedly impartial UK broadcast news coverage of a 'subtle but clear bias towards . . . pro-war assumptions' (Lewis et al. 2006: 126).[5]

Entman argues that framing – or what he describes as 'highlighting some facets of events or issues . . . so as to produce a particular interpretation, evaluation, and/or solutions' (Entman 2004: 5) – is the most effective tool with which to explain the elite-dominated nature of media coverage. Reporting of conflict 'does not always fall into the iron grip of hegemonic elite control, nor does it always provide a straightforward index of elite discussion' (Entman 2004: 147), even though the most powerful actors continue to be better equipped to transmit their frameworks and interpretations through the media and on to publics in what he calls a 'cascading activation' model. While this allows for more journalistic autonomy than other 'critical' models, the news process is still dominated by vested interests to produce, particularly in matters of foreign policy, an '"elite" spiral of silence', together with only very limited contestability (Entman 2004: 73).

Framing is certainly a useful way of capturing the dynamics of journalistic practice, but it tends to privilege the internal mechanisms of newsroom culture more than the broader socio-economic contexts within which journalists operate. Entman himself acknowledges that he is 'more concerned with media interventions in the day-to-day contests to control government power *within* the snug ideological confines of American politics' (Entman 2007: 270) than he is to investigate how these ideological parameters condition the frames and routines of journalists themselves. Both framing and indexing provide valuable accounts of the routine pressures brought to bear on journalists, but it is impossible to make sense of the media's general conformity with dominant ideas without highlighting the structural constraints that operate on journalism in a capitalist society. A model of hegemony is needed that accentuates journalism's intimate connection to capitalist power and that simultaneously recognizes the potential impact of elite disagreement and popular resistance.

## Case study: 'impartial' reporting of Gaza

At the time of writing, at least 60,000 Palestinians have been killed by Israeli forces in the Gaza Strip in response to the Hamas attacks of October 2023. Accurate reporting of the war has been made particularly difficult by the Israeli government's refusal to allow foreign journalists into Gaza, together with the Israeli army's targeting of local journalists, more than 200 of whom have been killed in the Strip since 7/10 (International Federation of Journalists 2025). In addition, Gaza presents a particularly difficult challenge for 'impartial' reporting – the obligation placed on UK news broadcasters by regulators (but an aspiration held by mainstream journalists more broadly across the world) not to favour one side over another – because of the perceived political importance of Israel for western hegemony. Seen as a 'strategic asset', western governments have bankrolled and sold arms to Israel for many years, despite both domestic and international opposition to its actions (Chomsky 1999; Stepansky and Kestler-D'Amours 2024). This relationship has been complemented by a long legacy of reporting that diminishes the historical context of Israeli occupation (as discussed in chapter 5), and that tends to privilege Israeli perspectives in a way that reflects the latter's geopolitical and ideological positioning. 'The political status of Israel', write Philo and Berry (2011: 6), 'plus its extensive public relations activity means in practice that its explanations and rationales are much more likely than those of the Palestinians to underpin the thematic structures of the news'.

Studies of the coverage of the war on Gaza by major US and UK news outlets show that this pattern of framing has once again been repeated. Philo and Berry analysed four weeks of BBC coverage immediately after the Hamas attacks and found that references to 'murder' and 'mass murder' were used regularly in relation to Israeli deaths but not to those of Palestinians, thousands of whom had already been killed. 'The Palestinian perspective', they conclude (Philo and Berry 2023), 'is effectively absent from the coverage', overshadowed by the 'status given to the Israeli perspective which stresses that Israel is subject to terrorist attacks motivated by Islamic extremism and antisemitism'. A detailed analysis of elite US news coverage also found that journalists 'disproportionately emphasized Israeli deaths in the conflict; used emotive language to describe the killings of Israelis but not Palestinians; and offered lopsided coverage of antisemitic acts in the US, while largely ignoring anti-Muslim racism in the wake of October 7' (Johnson and Ali 2024).

A comprehensive analysis of broadcast and online UK reporting of Gaza produced by the Centre for Media Monitoring concluded that, all too often, key news outlets amplify official Israeli sources while shutting down pro-Palestinian voices. It found that:

- 76 per cent of online articles described the decimation of Gaza as an 'Israel–Hamas' war, overshadowing other frames;
- broadcast news promoted Israel's right to defend itself, as compared to the right of Palestinians to defend themselves, by a ratio of five to one;
- emotive language about victims was far more likely to be used in relation to Israeli, rather than Palestinian, deaths with more than 70 per cent of all references to 'atrocities', 'slaughter' and 'massacre' attached to Israeli victims;
- television coverage referenced Israeli perspectives three times as much as Palestinian ones which were often 'either dismissed, omitted or minimised';
- journalists failed systematically to challenge unverified claims, for example in relation to allegations of 'beheaded babies', where out of 361 mentions on television news, only 52 actually interrogated these claims. (Hanif 2024)

These findings led the journalist Peter Oborne to argue that 'British journalists and broadcasters have used every trick in the book to paint a false story of the war. They've twisted the facts, promoted falsehoods, collaborated with fabrications, lied by omissions, and far too often failed to correct their mistakes' (quoted in Hanif 2024: 17). Why has a professional commitment to 'due impartiality', or to its related term 'objectivity', failed to provide a fair and even-handed approach to the war on Gaza – let alone one that holds to account a government that has been found to have plausibly engaged in genocide according to the International Court of Justice?[6]

First, a commitment to 'impartiality' cannot overcome the structural inequities and geopolitical realities of imperial and colonial relations of domination (to be explored in chapter 11). Giving equal weight to 'both sides of an argument' in this context means accepting the false premise that one argument, for example Israel's right to defend itself, is a more legitimate starting point than a rival argument, in this case, the right of Palestinians to resist occupation. Even the most pallid version of impartiality should consist of equal treatment of Palestinian and Israeli deaths, eyewitness accounts and lived experiences. Yet the reality is that news agendas all too often dovetail with the ideological views of powerful decision makers and western governments who have both a historic and ongoing investment in maintaining a 'strong' Israeli state. This shapes the framing of both Israeli and Palestinian actors with a degree of agency attached to the former and denied to the latter, as revealed in leaked accounts from CNN journalists that there were 'tight restrictions on quoting Hamas and reporting other Palestinian perspectives while Israeli government statements are taken at face value' (McGreal 2024).

Second, professional values concerning impartiality and objectivity are not innocent and transparent but, in the context of journalism's political economy, may be seen as a 'strategic ritual' (Tuchman 1972) designed to protect journalists against accusations of bias. Given the asymmetrical nature of the war on Gaza, 'objectivity' is a blunt tool that is used to paint a picture of two equal sides battling it out in a 'messy' conflict. Chris Hedges, the former *New York Times* correspondent who reported on the 2008–9 Israeli occupation of Gaza, argues that objectivity serves a highly ideological purpose:

> We retreated, as usual, into the moral void of American journalism, the void of balance and objectivity. The ridiculous notion of being unbiased, outside of the flow of human existence, impervious to grief or pain or anger or injustice, allows reporters to coolly give truth and lies equal space and airtime. Balance and objectivity are the antidote to facing unpleasant truths, a way of avoidance, a way to placate the powerful. We record the fury of a Palestinian who has lost his child in an Israeli airstrike in Gaza but make sure to mention Israel's 'security needs,' include statements by Israeli officials who insist there was firing from the home or the mosque or the school and of course note Israel's right to defend itself. (Hedges 2009)

Due to a range of structural factors that are rooted in contemporary geographies of power – including patterns of corporate ownership, a prevailing consensus on foreign policy objectives and a deep-rooted connection between journalistic and political elites – professional attachments to impartiality and objectivity have repeatedly failed to provide a contextualized, independent and robust account of Israel's long war on Gaza.

This does not mean that there has been no criticism in the mainstream media of Israel's actions in Gaza. The UK broadcaster Channel 4 News has had regular and combative interviews with Israeli spokespeople, while the BBC famously commissioned a moving documentary on the experience of Palestinian children living in a war zone (which was then taken down following complaints that the father of one of the children was an official in the Hamas government); the *Washington Post* produced a forensic investigation into the death of six-year-old Hind Rajab that concluded that Israeli forces were culpable (Kelly et al. 2024), while Al Jazeera, in both its Arab- and English-language versions, has responded to a very different audience demographic by relentlessly attacking Israeli authorities and condemning the genocide.

These limited examples point to the tensions inside many western governments (as well as those in Arab countries) about how to respond to the military objectives of the Israeli government and its destabilizing impact on an already fraught international scene. Yet criticism, where it is made, is confined to specific and dramatic examples of Israeli aggression – such as the killing of aid workers – and not to more 'routine' acts of violence that are somehow justified in the name of self-defence. Just as pro-Palestine protest is sometimes acknowledged but usually derided and misrepresented (Hanif 2024), mainstream media acknowledge the occasional faults of Israeli state violence but fail to base their reporting in the context of a much longer history of Israeli occupation or to challenge the logic of a right to self-defence that involves the denial of that very same right to Palestinians. While this is not a stable or sustainable situation, Israel's genocidal assault on Gaza is nevertheless one in which the media's hegemonic role – and its complicity with power – has been brutally apparent.

## Conclusion

Ideology plays a decisive role in the reproduction of capitalist conceptions about the world, while hegemony involves the ongoing battle to mould specific ideas into a more durable 'common sense' that supports the status quo. Neither, however, is fixed and immutable but is instead intimately linked to the dynamic social relations and ongoing struggles that underpin everyday life. The media are crucial ideological instruments in the contest to secure hegemony – marked both by their associations with private and state power but also sensitive to the need to remain relevant to their audiences. This means that while the mainstream media are wedded to amplifying elite voices and perspectives – not least in relation to critical issues of public interest such as national security and foreign interventions – their role is never settled and secure and therefore needs constant revision and renewal.

# 9
# Freedom and Democracy

***Overview*** Capitalists have long celebrated the idea of 'free markets' and 'free trade' as the basis of individual liberty and liberal democracy. This chapter highlights the restricted meaning of freedom under capitalism – understood in mostly individualistic and negative terms as the absence of constraint – as well as the limitations of a conception of democracy that is confined to a formal and juridical understanding in which questions of economic rights are evacuated. The chapter then explores these arguments in relation to narratives about 'press freedom' and 'democratic media'. Tackling both the abuse of press freedom during the United Kingdom's phone-hacking crisis, as well as the contemporary focus on misinformation and disinformation, the chapter suggests that fundamentally unequal power relations have distorted communications landscapes and diminished the prospects for genuinely free and democratic media.

## A note on the separation between 'economics' and 'politics'

Conventional wisdom tells us that 'politics' and 'economics' are distinct domains of thought and activity; they are taught in separate university departments, reported by separate specialist correspondents, operationalized in separate government offices, and answerable to separate rulebooks. Economics aspires to be a sober and mathematical discipline focused on resource allocation, while politics is ultimately about the play of power based on specific values and beliefs. The difference between the two fields underpins the notion that, for example, central banks should be independent of government and that interest-rate levels should be the preserve of 'expert' economists and not partisan politicians.

But conventional wisdom is wrong: this is an artificial distinction that has been cultivated by capital to hide the highly political character of economic decision-making and is, as such, a highly ideological argument. As Ellen Wood notes (1995: 19), 'there has been a tendency to perpetuate the rigid conceptual separation of the "economic" and the "political" which has served *bourgeois* ideology so well ever since the classical economists discovered the "economy" in the abstract and began emptying capitalism of its social and political content.' This separation both evacuates the politics – the interests, the struggles and the interpretive differences – from the sphere of production and insulates politics from the economic tussles of rival social groups that shape its dynamics.

In reality – and as discussed in chapter 5 in relation to Karl Polanyi's work – politics and economics are mutually reinforcing spheres – incomprehensible without appreciating their interconnections – whose disassociation points to myth making and mystification in the interests of the powerful.[1] This is particularly relevant when it comes to understanding concepts such as freedom and democracy that have been such important motivating forces for popular empowerment and sovereignty throughout the centuries. The distinction seeks to naturalize a sense that these are terms that belong, above all, in a political superstructure with only secondary connections to questions of commodity production and exchange. Yet, far from operating at one remove from the economic base of society, both concepts have been profoundly influenced by core capitalist imperatives and market logic, as both its most engaged advocates and bitter critics make clear.

## Freedom: 'a rare and delicate plant'

This is certainly the case where 'free' economic transactions are seen as the handmaiden of a more general sense of 'natural liberty' and 'perfect freedom' as Adam Smith writes throughout *Wealth of Nations* (Smith 2012 [1776]). 'Commerce', according to the Enlightenment philosopher and writer Voltaire in the eighteenth century (2003 [1733]: 31), 'which has enriched the citizens of England, has contributed to their freedom, and this freedom has in turn stimulated commerce'. The libertarian economist Milton Friedman makes the link particularly explicit in his famous book, *Capitalism and Freedom*, in which he describes capitalism 'as a system of economic freedom and a necessary condition for political freedom' (2002 [1962]: 4). Despite his belief that markets are depoliticized phenomena (as discussed in chapter 5), Friedman insists that 'there is an intimate connection between economics and politics' and that 'economic freedom is also an indispensable means towards the achievement of political freedom' (2002 [1962]: 8). Free markets are not simply a proxy for but the very engine of individual freedom.

I want to highlight just three features of this market-led understanding of freedom that cast a sombre shadow over its emancipatory potential. First, despite the expansive understanding of freedom that has motivated struggles for justice and equality throughout history – the 'sharp invigorating air of freedom' that Mary Wollstonecraft (1995 [1792]: 107) argued should be applied to women and not just men – capital itself has fostered a far more restricted definition of freedom. To the extent that it is based on the benefits of 'free trade' and 'free markets', it operates on a conception that because most people are *formally* free to sell their labour, it is therefore appropriate to focus above all on the juridical relations that allow this. It marginalizes the experiences of ill health, unemployment, precarity, stress, discrimination, low pay, exploitation and alienation that are common features of working lives in favour of a specious form of freedom where, as Marx puts it, the worker is free in only two senses: that 'as a free individual he can dispose of his labour-power as his own commodity, and that, on the other hand, he has no other commodity for sale, i.e. he is rid of them, he is free of all the objects needed for the realization of his labour-power' (1977 [1867]: 272–3).

Wendy Brown, in her foreword to a new translation of Marx's *Capital*, argues that it is precisely this limited and misleading account of freedom that made it hard for workers in Marx's time fully to understand the destructive aspects of an emerging capitalism: 'This was especially so because it took place under the sign of freedom – free markets, free humans, and the free circulation of labor, capital, and commodities' (Brown 2024: xvi). If we are to challenge capitalist logic today, then we will continue to need to grasp 'how its freedoms obscure the drives and effects that make it the greatest system of domination ever made or inhabited by humans' (2024: xvii). Capital's interpretation of freedom is an anaemic one that is confined to the possession of formal property rights rather than to the material conditions that will allow people to exercise these rights. As such, we are, in theory, perfectly free under capitalism to be rich or poor, landlords or tenants, buyers or sellers, satiated or starving – a situation that led Eric Hobsbawm (1989: 24) to note that dominant legalistic conceptions of freedom and equality are 'far from incompatible with real inequality'.

Second, the classic understanding of freedom in relation to 'free' flow of market forces is a negative one in the sense that it privileges the removal of barriers rather than the realization of human potential. Adam Smith's notion of a fully functioning commercial society is predicated on the 'hidden hand' of the market being able to operate without the overreach of an interventionist state that might stifle its creativity and distort the symmetry and reciprocity of a system of free trade. The greatest threat to freedom for capitalism's staunchest advocates is, therefore, any collective voice that claims to know better than an open market about how best to secure the individual welfare of the public. 'Freedom', writes Friedman (2002 [1962]: 2), 'is a rare and delicate plant. Our minds tell us, and history confirms, that the great threat to freedom is concentration of power. Government is necessary to preserve our freedom; yet by concentrating power in political hands, it is also a threat to freedom'. The enemy of freedom is not necessarily the despotic ruler or corporate oligarch but any organization or culture that threatens individual autonomy, whether that is a trade union, the 'red tape' of things like health and safety regulations or social protections – all of which are seen to inhibit the free market's innate and emancipatory dynamism. Friedman laments the fact that, while liberal capitalism initially 'emphasized freedom as the ultimate goal and the individual as the ultimate in society' (2002 [1962]: 5), it came to be associated in the twentieth century with the power of the state as demonstrated by discourses of 'welfare' and 'equality' rather than of individual freedom. Peter Thiel, the venture capitalist founder of PayPal and high-profile supporter of Donald Trump, captures this world view perfectly with his statement that 'authentic human freedom as a precondition for the highest good' is best pursued by an opposition to 'confiscatory taxes' and 'politics in all its forms' – as well as by the promotion and exploitation of 'new technologies that may create a new space for freedom' (Thiel 2009), understood in purely individualistic terms.

Third, even this restricted conception of freedom does not apply equally to everyone but is closely connected to power and status. This reflects the internal contradictions of Enlightenment thinking that accommodated the celebration of individual autonomy with a defence of slavery and that combined appeals to progress and universalism (values that inspired both the French Revolution and a whole series of slave revolts, including most famously in Haiti at the end of the eighteenth century) with emerging class-based hierarchies. J. S. Mill, the British post-Enlightenment philosopher most closely associated with a liberal theory of freedom, argues in *On Liberty* that the right to individual sovereignty is not something that can be uniformly exercised. Articulating the colonial thinking that was dominant at the time among British elites, he distinguishes between those mature enough to be trusted with freedom and those, such as children and the citizens of 'backward states of society', who are 'still in a state to require being taken care of by others [and] must be protected against their own actions as well as against external injury' (Mill 2016 [1859]: 13). Given the 'humanitarian interventions' by western governments in both Iraq and Afghanistan at the start of this century, this is a paternalistic logic that is embedded in the history of liberal accounts of freedom. 'The love of freedom and liberty that is central to the idea of liberalism', writes Gholam Khiabany (2020: 100), 'is indeed one that, in its realisation, has all too often been easily sacrificed on the altar of the interests of capital and (imperial) states'.

Freedom, as understood by key advocates of capital, is therefore ritualistic, negative and selective – the magical outcome of unencumbered systems of free trade. This is the antithesis of a socialist conception of freedom that is rooted in providing the material foundations for human flourishing based on the securing of both economic well-being and political rights. Indeed, Friedman and his former teacher at the University of Chicago, Friedrich Hayek, honed their definitions of freedom specifically in opposition to this vision, with the latter fully appreciating (and condemning) the threat to a free-market system of a commitment to liberty that is based on economic equality and not just the provision of juridical rights. This 'new freedom', as Hayek dubs the socialist perspective, was not simply about freedom from coercion and arbitrary power but 'freedom from necessity'; in order to be truly free, Hayek concludes, 'the "despotism of physical want" had to be broken, the "restraints of the economic system" relaxed' (1944: 19). This involves nothing other than 'the old demand for an equal distribution of wealth' (1944: 19) which, of course, for Hayek as a full-blooded market zealot, constitutes the very opposite of freedom. Yet, in spite of his intentions, his words provide a powerful reminder of the argument that without meaningful levels of economic redistribution, freedom is bound to remain only a formal and incomplete property of contemporary capitalist life.

## The 'thin gruel' of liberal democracy

According to the business newspaper the *Financial Times*, the year 2024 'was heralded as the year of democracy. With more than one and a half billion ballots cast in elections across 73 countries, 2024 offered a rare opportunity to take the social and political temperature of almost half the world's population' (Burn-Murdoch 2024). The article was one of many preoccupied with the same theme: that this was democracy's biggest year to date, given the billions of people eligible to take part in electoral contests in the United States, India, the United Kingdom, Mexico, Indonesia, Japan, South Africa, South Korea, Senegal and many more. The fact that votes took place in countries with varying degrees of freedom of expression and that incumbents performed particularly badly across the board suggested to commentators that this was democracy at its finest: an example of popular frustrations being voiced within the rule of law. The rather significant finding that, as the *Financial Times* noted, 'the year of democracy produced a cry that democracy is no longer working' (Burn-Murdoch 2024) was left to one side, with the increasing number of electoral contests seen as a marker of the system's political maturity. Despite clear frustrations with the actual experience of democratic life, it seems that 'democracy' has been reified into a checklist of indicators, for example, whether there are fair elections, a 'free press', an independent judiciary and an accountable parliament, rather than evaluated in relation to the depth of the fairness, freedom, independence and accountability on offer.

Of course, this is by no means the only way to understand a concept that has long galvanized far broader and more expansive practices related to the term's origins in relation to direct rule by citizens. Just as there is a tension between formal and substantive understandings of freedom, Raymond Williams (1983: 96) notes two competing modern definitions of democracy. There is, first, the more radical account of popular power, seen as 'a state in which the interests of the majority of the people were paramount and in which these interests were practically exercised and controlled by the majority'; then there is also the more 'liberal tradition' that is focused on the 'open election of representatives'. According to Williams, these 'two conceptions, in their extreme forms, now confront each other as enemies' (1983: 96). While capitalism has been forced at times, mostly through popular struggle, to respond to pressure for the 'direct democracy' described by sociologist C. Wright Mills (1970: 130) as 'collective self-control over the structural mechanics of history itself', the more limited, constitutional conception of 'representative democracy' is capitalism's more familiar home.[2]

Following the bourgeois revolutions of the nineteenth century that cemented capitalist hegemony in some areas of the world (Hobsbawm 1964), a specific form of democratic sovereignty emerged that was based on a series of formal rights, including the right to vote, to own property, to freedom of expression and to protest. According to Ellen Wood (1995: 227), however, the new capitalist class purposefully sought 'to shift the focus of "democracy" away from the active exercise of popular power to the passive enjoyment of constitutional and procedural safeguards and rights, and away from the collective power of subordinate classes to the privacy and isolation of the individual citizen. More and more, the concept of "democracy" came to be identified with *liberalism*.'

Yet capitalist democracy followed the precedent of ancient Greek city-states, where participation in public life was reserved only for adult male citizens, and initially denied voting rights to the propertyless, to women, to people of colour and to colonial subjects and only yielded them after significant social struggles. Colonialism and imperialism, as I argue in chapter 11, were not conceived by elites as antithetical to but as engines of a particular kind of democracy, leading Domenico Losurdo in his history of liberalism to speak of a 'master race democracy' which presided over large parts of the world by the end of the nineteenth century. He concludes that 'it should not be forgotten that not only did the classics of the liberal tradition refer to democracy with coldness, hostility and sometimes frank contempt, but regarded its advent as an unlawful, intolerable rupture of the social contract' (Losurdo 2011: 341).

Even though Natalie Fenton is right to state that 'liberal democracy has become the dominant model of democracy precisely because it has proven to be so compatible with capitalism' (2025: 8), the perennial tension between its expansive and limited definitions – in other words, between the active pursuit and exercise of popular control and an occasional trip to the polling station – helps to explain the ambivalence towards democracy that has regularly featured in its analysis by leading advocates of liberal capitalism. Hayek (1944: 52), for example, warns against 'making a fetish of democracy' on the basis that it is effectively only a 'utilitarian device for safeguarding internal peace and individual freedom' – by which he means the unimpeded flow of market forces. Similarly, Schumpeter, in *Capitalism, Socialism and Democracy*, insists that democracy is simply 'a certain type of institutional arrangement for arriving at political – legislative and administrative – decisions and hence incapable of being an end in itself' (2010 [1942]: 217). Democracy, according to Schumpeter, 'means only that the people have the opportunity of accepting or refusing the men who are to rule them' (2010 [1942]: 253) as opposed to a means of actually empowering wider groups of citizens. That both Hayek and Schumpeter were writing during the Second World War – a conflict that was fought, in popular mythology, solely to defend 'democracy' from totalitarianism and fascism – suggests that the relationship between capitalism and democracy resembles more a marriage of convenience than one of pure, unadulterated love.

So, despite claims that capitalism is the 'natural' home for democracy, this relationship is necessarily fragile and contingent. Stuart Hall and colleagues note (1978: 209) that 'a great variety of political regimes have been compatible with the capitalist mode of production' – including liberal democratic, authoritarian, statist and outright fascist regimes, all of which have pursued key capitalist imperatives within very different modes of political organization.[3] This resonates with recent developments in both traditionally liberal democratic and authoritarian states where illiberal and undemocratic practices – including attacks on the judiciary, the media, universities and social welfare programmes (Levitsky and Ziblatt 2024) – coincide with a full-throated embrace of capitalist accumulation. According to Hall and his co-writers (1978: 209), 'it must now be acknowledged that capitalism is also compatible with – and may be required to be "rescued" by – certain quite *exceptional* forms of the state (e.g., the fascist state), in which many of its normal modes are suspended.' Capitalism, therefore, might be economically risk averse (at least in relation to realizing its core imperatives around commodification and accumulation), but it is far more promiscuous when it comes to the political character of the regimes which can accommodate it, even if this accommodation simultaneously undermines some of its key constitutional components.

There are two implications arising from this. First, that democratic rights which are often won after periods of social struggle may be tolerated by capitalism in more stable periods but are increasingly threatened in periods of political and economic uncertainty. According to the British journalist Paul Foot in his history of the battle for universal suffrage, there should be no room for complacency when it comes to the battle for democratic reforms: 'Whatever its chronic weaknesses and paralyses, the parliamentary system and the thin gruel of democracy it offers us are indispensable to any agitation for progress' (Foot 2024: 437). Indeed, both the defence and expansion of democratic rights remains a pressing political challenge. Neoliberalism hollowed out an already anaemic liberal democracy with its concerted attacks on civic and collective rights and its reliance on unaccountable private interests to control key services and industries (Brown 2015; Mair 2013). It is no surprise therefore that these attacks have been met with widespread resistance across the globe both to austerity and to the assaults on democracy and sovereignty carried out in the name of market 'reforms' (Bevins 2023). Second, capitalism is fundamentally an unreliable guarantor of democratic rights because it will sanction and protect these rights only to the extent that their exercise does not damage its core productive activity. Furthermore, while capital is willing to grant limited rights at the political level, it is unwilling to provide them at the economic level, which operates according to a very different, and even more unequal, logic. As Raymond Williams notes (1982: 19), capitalism is based on 'the coexistence of political representation and participation with an economic system which admits no such rights, procedures or claims.' This generates a highly skewed and partial form of democracy.

## Myths of 'press freedom' and 'democratic media'

'King says free press is "cornerstone of democracy"' was the headline in the *Daily Telegraph* on 26 March 2025, accompanied by a photograph of a beaming King Charles shaking hands with media workers at a reception in Buckingham Palace. That the words of an unelected monarch commenting on the crucial role of independent journalism could feature in a newspaper that at the time was the subject of a bidding war between a group of billionaire hedge-fund tycoons, media moguls, sporting oligarchs and Emirati royalty tells you a lot about the mythical status occupied by a 'free press' in the exercise of democracy. Indeed, a 'free press' – together with wider opportunities for freedom of expression – is seen as a marker of a functioning democratic society and as a key mechanism through which liberal democracy is both sustained and invigorated. Similarly, the phrase 'democratic media' is often invoked to describe a system composed of institutions that are independent of both the state and vested interests, whether those based in corporate boardrooms or government departments. Press freedom and democratic media are central components of Friedman's 'competitive capitalism' because they are said simultaneously to nourish the informational needs of free trade, fuel consumption through advertising and branding and limit the risk of concentrated power by scrutinizing those people and organizations in positions of authority.

This conception of a vigorous and critical 'free media' has a specific genealogy, emerging from the press's historic battles against censorship and government control in the early days of capitalism. The media historian James Curran (2002a: 8) argues that this liberal narrative of press history sees the media's evolution 'as a story of progress in which the media became free, switched their allegiance from government to the people, and served democracy'. A newly emboldened press played an important role in cementing capitalism by facilitating information about public affairs, challenging the enemies of 'progress' and acting as a bridge between different social groups in the battle against *anciens régimes*. This was a crucial development that was predicated on two central beliefs: that the state was the main enemy of press freedom and that free enterprise and the free flow of ideas were natural bedfellows. As John Thompson summarizes the liberal perspective (1995: 239), 'The free expression of thoughts and opinions could be practically achieved ... only in so far as the institutions of the press were independent of the state and situated in the private domain where they could carry out their activities with a minimum of constraint.' This was famously described by Siebert, Peterson and Schramm (1956) as the 'libertarian' theory of the press, an account of press freedom that had been dominant for some 200 years in Western Europe and the United States in which 'the press is not an instrument of government but rather a device for presenting evidence and arguments on the basis of which the people can check on government and make up their minds as to policy' (1956: 3). It is an approach which still retains its currency but which, as with other liberal accounts of freedom, comes up well short.

First, it is based on a very narrow and negative framing of freedom which conceptualizes the state as the overarching threat to speech rights and the main barrier to the unrestricted circulation of ideas. Siebert, Peterson and Schramm (1956: 94) acknowledge that the libertarian theory of the press emerged out of 'a concept of negative liberty, which we can define loosely as "freedom from" and more precisely as "freedom from external restraint"', as if the state is the *only* force that can exercise this restraint and curtail press freedom. Damian Tambini in his book on *Media Freedom* (Tambini 2021) rightly notes that, especially given the fresh challenges of digital media, we need urgently to expand our understanding of freedom from the 'negative conception of *freedom from* state-led censorship' (2021: 10) towards a more positive vision of supporting media initiatives that empower audiences and that mobilize more representative sets of voices. This is not meant to minimize the significant threats to press freedom that are posed by authoritarian governments across the globe today but simply to suggest that a robust understanding of the concept also involves rights, responsibilities and opportunities that are broader than defensive strategies, no matter how necessary those may still be. An approach that is focused exclusively on challenging 'negative freedoms' and resisting curbs on individuals (whether private individuals or giant media corporations) will be 'incapable of confronting concentrations of economic power based upon private property and the political and communicative power which results' (Garnham 1990: 18).

Second, the liberal account of press freedom is focused above all on securing the conditions for *commercial* transactions that are unimpeded by state control; it is not primarily focused on providing the conditions in which all citizens are equally equipped to exercise their rights to media freedom. Marx, for example, was a working journalist who was a fierce advocate of press freedom and a staunch opponent of government censorship. But he was also sensitive to the increasing commercialization of the press in Germany and argued that 'the first freedom of the press is not to be a business' (quoted in Hardt 2000: 92). Marx saw press freedom as a collective right that was designed to protect journalists from their own publishers, to equip them with the autonomy to scrutinize the world and to act as the 'ever-present, vigilant eye of the people's spirit' (quoted in Hardt 2000: 91). This is very similar to James Curran's argument that the abolition of press taxes in Britain in the mid-nineteenth century was not, as is commonly seen, an important victory for freedom and democracy that helped give rise to the modern press system. Instead, he suggests, its real objective was to weaken the impact of the radical press of the time, to create the conditions for a commercial newspaper market and to provide a hegemonic pole of attraction for an emerging capitalist class: 'the struggle against press censorship was not imposed solely by a love of liberty. This is to project contemporary sensibilities on to people with different mind-sets from our own. In fact, many leading parliamentary campaigners against press taxes in the nineteenth century were more preoccupied with indoctrinating the masses than with planting the tree of freedom' (Curran and Seaton 2018: 4).

Far from the liberal understanding of press freedom empowering audiences to take control of their destinies, its operationalization has, in reality, led to a rather different outcome, leading to A. J. Liebling's famous quote that 'freedom of the press is guaranteed only to those who own one' (Liebling 1960).

The third criticism of the liberal account of press freedom is simply that it is increasingly out of date. It was developed at a very different stage of capitalist development and was responding to very different configurations of the state (although, as I argue in the next chapter, the state remains a potent source of power). As Curran notes, 'the classic liberal theory for a free press on which we still rely was refined and elaborated in the nineteenth century as part of a political campaign for press deregulation' (2002a: 217). Media landscapes two hundred years ago generally involved small-scale political publications chasing scarce readers in the shadow of the state; today, we have communications landscapes that are characterized by giant transnational corporations, oligopolistic markets, fierce competition for audiences as well as (in many places) the shadow of the state. In such a situation, appeals to the sanctity of individual rights to self-expression and the equation of these rights with those of a fearless and independent media or tech sector is extremely problematic. 'According unrestricted freedom of expression not only to individuals but also to powerful institutions, the media among them, is not *necessary for* but *damaging to* democracy' (O'Neill 2004: 8).

This is borne out by the UK phone-hacking crisis (first discussed in chapter 7) where the criminal activities of some newspaper companies led to demands for more effective forms of regulation and oversight than were already in place. The response of the press was to cry out that this – and not the hacking, blagging and surveillance at the heart of the scandal – constituted a wholesale assault on press freedom, a right that had been won 200 years previously but was now once again under attack. Such was the fury of their response and such is the ongoing impact of their influence on political culture that press regulation in the United Kingdom still remains in the gift of the publishers, who continue 'to mark their own homework'. At one level, this is evidence of the depth of a form of media power (Freedman 2014) that still sets the terms of debate not only in relation to broader political agendas but also to oversight of its own activities. Yet it also points to the vulnerability of a liberal account of freedom which is poorly equipped to confront corporate power. For Natalie Fenton, freedom – at least as deployed by powerful media moguls during the hacking crisis – 'became a narrative device to sidestep the deeper, systemic problems of the newspaper industry of which these ethical misdemeanours were but one symptom' (Fenton 2025: 86). As long as the same concept of freedom is used both in relation to a single individual and to a giant media company, its protections as well as its possibilities will be unequally distributed. 'Concepts of freedom', reflects Fenton (2025: 95), 'must not be abstracted and idealized as indisputable forms of democratic good. They are always interrelated with power and its mediations and hence with issues of inequality and so remain hotly contested'.[4]

This reluctance to acknowledge the asymmetrical power between individuals and giant corporations is just as evident when we consider references to 'democratic media'. This is a label that refers both to the absence of formal restrictions on the independence of media outlets and to the normative role that they play as a 'fourth estate' that mediates between citizens and authority. They are the 'thin red line' holding back the forces of misinformation and disinformation; they are a bulwark both against illiberal 'bad actors' from nefarious parts of the world and against social media companies who have an ambivalent attitude towards providing the checks and balances at the heart of democratic theory; they are what stands between order and chaos, between democratic dreams and authoritarian nightmares. For Fenton, however, the idea that 'media are (in their current forms) one of democracy's vital organs and, without them, democracies (in their current form) will cease to function' is an example of delusional thinking, even if it continues to be 'peddled by the vast majority of media across the world' (Fenton 2025: 5) precisely because it is based on such a pallid conception of democracy.

Robert McChesney is also far from convinced about the democratic credentials of 'democratic media'. He notes that they have three main duties (2004: 57): 'to act as a rigorous watchdog of the powerful and those who wish to be powerful; to ferret out truth from lies; and to present a wide range of informed positions on key issues.' He concludes that contemporary journalism 'fails in all three of its duties' (2004: 57). Far from scrutinizing the powerful, the largest media companies are far more likely to be intimately connected to and supportive of concentrations of power; far from systematically sorting truth from fiction, mainstream news media are tied to a business model that ultimately privileges ratings, attention and clicks over veracity; far from amplifying a diverse range of opinions, journalists are more likely to rely on a small sample of dominant sources and hegemonic values that reflect the consensus opinion relevant to the demographic they are pursuing. Fenton and Freedman have previously described this as the 'illusion of democratic communications' that refers to:

a media where editors and top politicians dine at the same tables, are educated at the same institutions, and share many of the same corporate values and ideological agendas; a media that is disaggregated in theory but centralized in practice; a media where the tools may be open source but where the most powerful networks remain closed. This is a media marked by commerce, complicity and caution rather than critique, creativity and a journalism of conscience. (Fenton and Freedman 2018: 133)

The concern is not so much about the sudden predominance of 'fake news' but the circulation of 'fake democracy' – the veneer of democratic participation without the possibilities of substantive political impact and accountability.

While it is true that largely unregulated social media platforms have entrenched (an already existing) polarization, spread conspiracy theories and amplified voices that lie outside of previously carefully cultivated consensual positions, the fact is that X didn't invent silos and Facebook didn't invent disinformation. They are the latest products of highly unequal information environments that lack accountability and oversight and that cynically exploit the frustrations of their users that were partly exacerbated in the first place by the failure of the established media adequately to represent their experiences and to voice their concerns. According to Farkas and Schou (2024: 7), the idea that we now live in 'post-truth' environments characterized by declining trust and rampant infodemics 'fails to acknowledge that democracy, as a political system, has never only been about truth in the first place. In doing so, it neglects that contemporary democracies were by no means in a stable condition before the supposed villains of post-truth suddenly knocked them off course.' 'Bad' information, far from being an outrider in the history of 'democratic media', should instead be seen as an innate property of a system that never adequately integrated democratic criteria into its own operations. It is a curious irony, therefore, that while liberal democracy has long extolled the value of a 'free' and 'democratic' media, the nature of that freedom and the meaning of that democracy have rarely been investigated in relation to the internal workings of the media themselves.

Embedding democratic principles into the structure and behaviour of the media and tech industries would demand levels of accountability that are overwhelmingly absent from today's communication environments. Initiatives might include, for example, the requirement for algorithms to be made transparent and changeable according to the public interest; the provision of audiences with opportunities for selecting content through public commissioning procedures (Hind 2010); the setting up of member-led news outlets, such as the *Bristol Cable* in the United Kingdom or *De Correspondent* in the Netherlands, where members are able to influence editorial agendas; elections to the boardrooms and senior editorial positions of media organizations; or the redistribution of revenue via levies on the largest companies to allow the widest possible diversity of voices to self-manage their own media outlets, including community radio stations, local newspapers or hyperlocal platforms where market failure is particularly stark (see Fenton 2025: 210–11 for an outline of the 'conditions of possibility for a transformative media commons'). The objective would be to expand the footprints of freedom and democracy away from their current limited and juridical definitions. As the campaigning journalist Paul Foot argued back in 1982 when discussions of 'alternative' economic programmes and worker participation were more common:

> We want economic and industrial democracy as well as parliamentary democracy. We want to see not just those who make the laws elected, but those who enforce them elected too – the judges, the police, the armed forces. We want to see those in authority in the factories and workplaces subject to election too, and those who control the media. (Foot 1982)

Today, such a conception would be interpreted by the most powerful voices in media and tech as an attack on corporate freedom and as an overreach of representative democracy. Yet without such a bold programme of democratic renewal, 'press freedom' and 'democratic media' are going to remain mythical and unfulfilled concepts – the products of capital's ideological grip on society – rather than the vital and fearless institutions that their audiences and users need more than ever.

## Conclusion

The record of liberal democracy and capitalist notions of freedom is a contradictory one. They have facilitated political opportunities for sovereignty and justice while restricting their scope for those who need them most; they have celebrated equality but confined it to a constitutional rather than an economic right; they have embraced discourses of transparency and accountability while simultaneously purging them from the domain of production; and they have fetishized electoral contests while transforming them into performative spectacles dominated by marketing consultants and PR gurus. Capitalism, according to Ellen Wood, has fostered not the overall expansion but the 'contraction' of democracy as it 'leaves untouched vast areas of our daily lives – in the workplace, in the distribution of labour and resources – which are not subject to democratic accountability but are governed by the powers of property and the "laws" of the market, the imperatives of profit maximization' (1995: 234). There can be no substantive democracy or freedom – in the media landscape and beyond – without meaningful political *and* economic equality.

# 10
## Capitalism and the State

*Overview*  Despite the pervasive influence of the market, the state continues to be a central actor in structuring media and communications systems, as well as in coordinating social relations more generally. This chapter[1] considers a range of debates on the changing status and power of the state and acknowledges the contribution of both Marxist and Weberian approaches. It then outlines six roles performed by the state in relation to the media: as propagandist, bully, data controller, rulemaker, entrepreneur and sponsor, addressing issues from policymaking and public service media to surveillance and suppression.

## A 'helping hand' or the 'monopoly of the legitimate use of force'?

More than 50 years ago, Ralph Miliband opened his influential book on *The State in Capitalist Society* by insisting that we live increasingly 'in the shadow of the state . . . It is possible not to be interested in what the state does; but it is not possible to be unaffected by it' (1969: 3). For Miliband, the state – as both institutional arrangement and instrument of power – was perhaps *the* critical actor in the political, economic and ideological battles that mould contemporary society. Fast forward to today and, despite the degree of state surveillance of and penetration into everyday life – including our communication systems – many theorists insist that the state is not the powerful force it once was and that our lives are shaped more by private interests than by either the disparate units or hollowed out framework of a modern state. According to Susan Strange, for example, the state is on the retreat and global markets are now 'more powerful than the states to whom ultimate political authority over society and economy is supposed to belong' (1996: 4). Clearly, the state has not entirely disappeared as its officials still issue passports and wedding licences, stop migrants from crossing borders and directly administer (admittedly declining levels of) social security benefits, but its overall coordinating power is seen to have been significantly diminished.

Such a conception, however, underestimates both the scale of economic activity still managed by the state as well as its continuing ability to set broader terms of reference for a range of private actors. While authoritarian countries are necessarily predicated on the existence of a highly visible and deep-rooted state machinery, liberal democratic nations are not free from the influence of a central administrative force that presides over key areas of public life including education, health, defence, welfare, trade and investment. As Streeck (2024: 26) puts it, even the dramatic rise of the private sector 'does not preclude a powerful state presence in the hyperglobalised world of neoliberalism, for example when they impose economic sanctions on other states, demand that "the markets" take account of the requirements of "national security", deny the firms and governments of other countries access to superior technology, or use military means "to secure their trade routes".'

The ramping up of European defence spending to meet what is described as an imminent Russian threat, the tariffs and part nationalizations implemented by Donald Trump's second administration designed, in particular, to respond to China's growing economic power and the huge investment in infrastructure by the Indian state – including the emergence of a National Infrastructure Pipeline – are examples of the active capacity of the state to pursue economic benefits and geopolitical advantage. Yet, while the capitalist state retains a profound influence on everyday life, there is a stark debate about whether it plays a necessary and ultimately benevolent role or whether it is committed fundamentally to protect the interests of a small minority.

Even the fiercest advocates of the free market agree that some sort of coordinating mechanism is required to facilitate market exchange and to ensure that rules are followed. In *Wealth of Nations*, Adam Smith accepts that 'public institutions and public works [are] necessary for the defence of the society, and for the administrative justice' (2012 [1776]: 721) and argues that the restrictions imposed by this overarching authority might impinge, at times, on the freedom of specific capitalists. Just as he was also in favour of banking regulation, he notes that the 'obligation of building party walls, in order to prevent the communication of fire, is a violation of natural liberty' (2012 [1776]: 319), yet one that is necessary. Sensitive and proportionate 'administration' is required, he insists, to ensure that the fruits of competition are experienced by all.[2] 'The functioning of competition', notes the free-market economist Friedrich Hayek (1944: 28) nearly 200 years later, 'not only requires adequate organisation of certain institutions like money, markets and channels of information – some of which can never be adequately provided by private enterprise – but it depends above all on the existence of an appropriate legal system'. Even Milton Friedman, widely associated with the philosophy of neoliberalism, insists that some sort of coordinating body is required to mediate differences between capitals and 'to enforce compliance with the rules on the part of those few who would otherwise not play the game' (2002 [1962]: 25). The state is conceived here as an unobtrusive participant that aims to ensure fair play in free trade and to resolve conflicts as they emerge.

Marxist accounts argue something quite different: that the capitalist state emerges not as an umpire adjudicating between different interests but as a means of cohering and articulating ruling-class interests. This was necessary in the early days of capitalism to assist the transformation of property relations (explored in chapter 3) and has remained necessary ever since to protect capital against challenges to its authority. For Engels, 'the modern state . . . is essentially a capitalist machine, the state of the capitalists, the ideal personification of the total national capital' (Engels 1947 [1878]: 338). Far from representing a 'universal' or 'public' interest as Adam Smith argued, the state promotes and protects the values, protocols and property of only one section of society. The state may *claim* that it is equally loyal to all social groups, and it may, at times, be forced into recognizing competing demands but, above all, it seeks to secure hegemony for the '1 per cent' and to neutralize its opponents through the use of coercive *and* non-coercive means. As such, the state is able to mobilize both repressive forces, for example the security services, the police and the army, as well as 'administrative' institutions, such as the civil service, education, welfare *and* media, in order to maintain the necessary infrastructures for social and economic reproduction. In this way, the state is linked, but not reducible, to concepts like 'government', 'public sector' and 'nation', all of which lack the particular emphasis on an underlying 'apparatus' and set of relationships around which capitalist interests can coalesce. Governments, for example, are necessarily more fragile and impermanent than the more durable structure of the state which is 'staffed by "professional" people who owe their position not to any election, popular or otherwise, but to the allegedly rational internal bureaucratic norms of the sector of the state for which they happen to work' (Sparks 1986: 76).

Bob Jessop (2002: 45) outlines some core 'functions' of the capitalist state: that it needs to secure a legal framework for capital accumulation, to assert the rights and capacities of capital over labour, to define the boundaries between what is seen as 'economic' and what is seen as 'political' and, crucially, to address the consequences of capitalist contradictions. The state, according to this logic, presides over large infrastructure projects that private (and more short-termist) interests might not otherwise invest in; it polices trade unions and opposition groups that challenge specific accumulation strategies; it regulates the political and legal circumstances in which capitalism operates; and it supervises the 'social equations' (Hall et al. 1978: 214) that naturalize the values and domination of the status quo. Despite recent developments, for example the increased use of outsourcing and the growth in transnational capital flows, the state remains for Jessop 'the most significant site of struggle among competing global, triadic, supranational, national, regional and local forces' (Jessop 2002: 211). Mitchell and Fazi, confronting the idea that globalization somehow supplanted state power when it was 'largely the product of state-driven processes' (2017: 7), conclude that the state has not declined but is instead in the process of being reconfigured: 'Capital remains as dependent on the state today as it was under "Keynesianism" – to police the working classes, bail out large firms that would otherwise go bankrupt [and] open up markets abroad (including through military intervention)' (2017: 9). The prevalence of wars of occupation, international trade rivalries and the bank bailouts after the 2008 financial crash appear to bear out this conclusion.

Yet for some critics this invocation of the continuing power of the state and its core functions smacks of an instrumentalism that overstates the homogeneity of the state, fails to do justice to the conflicts within elites and ignores the perceived 'autonomy' of state institutions and personnel from capital itself. There have been decades of debate on the left about the extent to which 'politics' and 'economics' are not only distinct categories (as discussed in chapter 9) but are themselves relatively independent of the state (see Poulantzas 1980). Such an interpretation would mean that the state should be seen not simply as the enforcer of capitalist interests but as a potential site of struggle for marginalized groups who might be able to take advantage of tensions between different 'fractions' of capital to secure limited advantages. Far from being a well-oiled machine of class domination, the state is seen here as a sprawling, messy and unreliable agent of capitalist social reproduction.

Raju Das fiercely rebuts this claim and criticizes the 'fetishism of autonomy' (2022: 5) in many contemporary studies of the state. The idea that the state has any meaningful independence from capital mistakes appearance for reality: the capitalist state is designed in such a way as to secure the *overall* interests of capital, even if this means at times distancing itself from more sectional interests. The fact that the state is staffed both by highly ideological figures (such as security agents and generals) as well as by more 'neutral' people (like junior civil servants and teachers) lends it an illusion that it does indeed operate 'at arm's length' from capital. According to Das, however, 'the degree of autonomy is much less than often assumed. Very little autonomy is needed to subjugate the masses and to reproduce capitalist property relations. The separation of the state from capitalist economy is more a matter of the surface reality of capitalism' (2022: 6). So while there is the veneer of independence and separateness from any kind of underlying mission, in reality the state – in all its different guises[3] – continues as the main backstop for capitalist interests understood collectively.

Of course there is an instrumentalist tone to, for example, Marx and Engels' definition of the state in the *Communist Manifesto* as 'a committee for managing the common affairs of the whole bourgeoisie' (Marx and Engels 1973 [1848]: 35) and in Lenin's description in *State and Revolution* of the state as 'an organ of class *rule*, an organ for the *oppression* of one class by another' (Lenin 1977 [1917]: 9; emphases in original). This reflects their origins in conditions in which state power was exercised in brutal and visible ways. But this has not prevented Marxist theorists from further acknowledging that the state is far from homogeneous in its composition, that different sections are constantly struggling for hegemony within state circles and that there is a need for both coercive and ideological methods for reproducing class power. Instrumentalism need not mean predictability or the absence of contradiction; it simply illustrates the determination, on the part of those with power, to act in ways that are designed to secure the reproduction of unequal power relations. As such, the state is engaged every day in what could be seen as 'instrumental' activities to secure the established order, even if it does not operate as a monolithic bloc.

Ralph Miliband (1969: 46), for example, argues that the state is not a simple object, a 'thing', but instead 'a number of particular institutions which, together, constitute its reality'. It is bound to be a 'nebulous entity' (1969: 47) until it is materialized by actual people and structures in very different and unpredictable circumstances. Miliband is particularly interested in the state's participation in what he calls 'political socialisation': '[p]rocesses through which values, cognitions and symbols are learned and internalised, through which operative social norms regarding politics are implanted, political roles institutionalised and political consensus created, either effectively or ineffectively' (Miliband 1969: 164). This is far from a mechanical picture of social reproduction but refers instead to an ongoing process of legitimation. Miliband draws very heavily here on Gramsci's description of the state as 'the entire complex of practical and theoretical activities with which the ruling class not only justifies and maintains its dominance but manages to win the active consent of those over whom it rules' (Gramsci 1971: 244). Here, we have not a blunt instrument or a singular object but a hegemonic *architecture* composed of government, media, civil service, military, police, judiciary, parliament and so on that, ultimately, supports the reproduction of class power. It is the relationship between these institutions that 'shapes the form of the state system' (Miliband 1969: 50), a point developed by Pierre Bourdieu when he conceptualizes the state as a relational force – 'a set of specific resources that authorizes its possessors to say what is good for the social world as a whole' (2014: 33) – and that allows them vigorously to defend this authority.

For Das, however, the state is both a social relation *and* a 'thing'; it is defined both by the dynamic interpenetration between state and non-state actors as well as by a series of spaces and institutions. 'This "thing" aspect of the state', he suggests (2022: 9), 'its formidable material solidity, cannot be obscured by saying that the state is [simply] a relationship. The state is a thing and it is not a thing.' Ultimately, the state is the property of a system that is bound up with conflict and exclusion; far from being autonomous (relatively or otherwise) of the underlying imperatives of capitalism, 'the state is the political form of the content of [a] social relation which is fundamentally antagonistic' (2022: 9). This means that, while there can be a shifting balance of power inside state formations at any one time and while it can *appear* that the state does not operate simply to reproduce class power, it is ultimately inseparable from capitalist interests that dominate precisely through a combination of consent and coercion.

This latter point is closely associated with Max Weber's famous definition that 'the state is a human community that (successfully) claims the *monopoly of the legitimate use of physical force* within a given territory' (2013: 78; emphasis in original). The state is an archetypal bureaucratic structure that is characterized by a 'monopoly' on coercion specifically so that it can settle conflicts in an ordered and productive way (for those who have power). This is only possible so long as its domination is seen as 'legitimate' and its authority validated by the creation of a formal legal system with a codified set of rules. It is seen as a vital response to the increasing complexity of modern societies and a necessary bulwark against the vagaries of individualized forms of exchange. Yet even though Weber shared some of Marx's criticisms of capitalism, he is essentially arguing that the state is a necessary component of a highly rationalized society in which class reproduction is far from the only objective (as discussed in chapter 4). Instead, he argues, 'the state cannot be defined in terms of its ends' (2013: 77) but rather understood through the different forms of domination – including an appeal to traditional authority, the use of charismatic leadership and the 'rule of law' – that secure the consent of its citizens.

While the Weberian and Marxist perspectives may disagree about many things, not least the purpose and beneficiaries of state power, there are at least two aspects on which they do agree: first, that the state refers to a set of relations, institutions and processes that are at the heart of economic and social reproduction and, second, that the state plays a key *organizational* role in this process. As the neo-Weberian theorist Theda Skocpol puts it, the state refers to 'a set of administrative, policing, and military organizations headed, and more or less well coordinated by, an executive authority' (1979: 29). In what ways is this relevant to contemporary media and communications landscapes?

## The state and the media: six roles

Back in 1986, Colin Sparks produced a very useful account of the different roles adopted by the state in its effort to influence media systems and to reinforce the status quo. The state, he argued, could be seen as a 'patron' (in terms of its subsidies to media outlets), a censor, an 'actor' (providing source material), a 'masseur' (involved in public relations to shape coverage), an 'ideologue' and a 'conspirator' (representing shared class interests) (1986: 77–85). Sparks highlights the mutual bond between the unelected personnel of the state and the unaccountable structures of a corporate media: 'The state and the media are two of the weapons that the people who rule us use to ensure their continuation in power' (1986: 84). To what extent can this be argued to fit contemporary realities marked, on the one hand, by fragmentation, polarization and marketization and, on the other, by residual concentrations of power and influence? In what ways have globalization, neoliberalism and digitization reshaped the role of the state in its relationship to communications, and how do these developments affect the usefulness of Sparks's model?

Despite these changes, Sparks's core assumptions remain largely relevant and the state continues to be a powerful, structuring force in the communications field. However, I would like to propose six roles that better reflect the specific activities and typologies of the twenty-first-century state, even if there are significant continuities with Sparks's twentieth-century model. This updated list conceptualizes the state as *propagandist*, *bully*, *data controller*, *rulemaker*, *entrepreneur* and *sponsor*. Of course these roles overlap – for example, the state's interest in sponsoring media is often connected to a propaganda pay-off, while its use of targeted surveillance is predicated on its control of the regulatory landscape – but they refer, nevertheless, to some of the key ways in which the state is able to exercise power over communications.

## *Propagandist*

The state is an energetic and prolific communicator. It exerts a significant amount of time and money in generating its own original content as well as source material for third parties, notably the media. Vast resources are poured into the production of public information campaigns, press releases, social media content and advertising material that seek both to inform and persuade citizens about specific initiatives, whether they relate to public health promotions, electoral contests, benefit entitlements or national security. This is usually discussed in relation to 'government communication', referring to the promotional activities of, for example, the Government Communication Service in the United Kingdom, the Federal Press and Information Service in Germany and the Government Information Service in the Netherlands, and is often seen as an inevitable consequence of a 'public relations democracy' (Davis 2002). Perhaps not surprisingly, therefore, the strategic communication of liberal democracies is sometimes conceived by its supporters as a relatively harmless and consensual form of information exchange in contrast to the 'propaganda' emanating from authoritarian regimes.

Yet, while some government communication may indeed be the routine output of bureaucratic political life, it is nevertheless far from an innocent form of PR that simply reflects the responsibilities of an elected government. The state continues to be a prolific and influential source for highly ideological news content, often operating behind a protective cloak of anonymity, such as when a 'senior serving general' was widely quoted in the UK press promising that the army would take 'direct action' to prevent the election of a government headed by the then left-wing Labour leader Jeremy Corbyn (Kennard 2019). This is just one example of a larger system of 'organized persuasive communication' (OPC) that is 'central to the exercise of power across all social spheres' (Bakir et al. 2019: 2), not least the more permanent interests that circumscribe the actions of specific governments. According to Bakir and colleagues, insufficient attention is paid towards 'manipulative OPC' where 'citizens are routinely incentivised, deceived and coerced by powerful actors' (2019: 15) and to an overemphasis on things like public relations and branding that are seen as relatively benign forms of organized persuasion. So while it is easy to condemn the 'fake news' coming out of Putin's Russia and Xi's China, it is also important to be attentive to the multiple forms of propaganda emanating from inside liberal democratic states that have been used, especially since 9/11, to market the 'war on terror', to install security regimes in which Muslims have been positioned as prime suspects and to foster support for foreign policy initiatives, no matter how disastrous. Media operations, strategic communication, public affairs, public diplomacy, perception management, information warfare, information operations and psychological operations (PSYOPS) are just some of the ways of labelling the means by which both authoritarian and liberal democratic states justify military interventions, legitimize domestic surveillance apparatuses and talk up the need for increased defence spending as a response to threats to 'national security'.

## Bully

The state's 'monopoly of the legitimate use of physical force' means that it is well placed to use coercive tactics both to control information flows and to delegitimize voices with whom it disagrees. Traditionally, this has meant formal and informal systems of censorship that range from pre-publication bans and the seizing of material that contravenes rules on what is argued to be legally publishable to the use of official 'flak machines' (Herman and Chomsky 1988: 28) to undermine opponents and voluntary mechanisms like the United Kingdom's 'D-Notice' that pressures editors to avoid publishing sensitive political content.

In a digital age, the more obvious forms of censorship are difficult to get away with, although censorious authorities – from China and North Korea to Sudan and Eritrea – still persist in policing media outlets and clamping down on any semblance of independent journalism. The annual World Press Freedom Index, curated by Reporters without Borders, demonstrates the extent to which media censorship still remains a hallmark of authoritarian regimes. The most dramatic illustration of the coercive power of the state, of course, is the number of journalists killed while carrying out their professional duties. This includes the high-profile murder of the *Washington Post* journalist, Jamal Khashoggi, allegedly by Saudi officials in their embassy in Istanbul in 2018, as well as the more than 200 journalists and media workers killed by Israeli forces in Gaza between 2023 and 2025. A search of the database of the Committee to Protect Journalists (CPJ) reveals that 932 reporters were killed either by 'government' or 'military' personnel across the world between 1992 and 2025.[4]

In liberal democracies, First Amendment absolutism and liberal conceptions of 'free speech' undergird arguments against the suppression of what have often been seen as fundamental speech rights. Pre-publication censorship is therefore relatively rare even if there still exists a barrage of legislation that can be used against journalists including, for example, official secrecy, anti-terror, libel and bribery laws. This has allowed even the most 'liberal' states to attack investigative journalism, one of the hallmarks of a functioning 'fourth estate' and a vital defence against demagogues and tyrants. In the United States, before 2008, a grand total of five cases had been brought against whistle-blowers and leakers under the terms of the Espionage Act for helping journalists report on classified government programmes. The Obama administration (2008–2016), however, used the Act to launch nine cases, leading the *New York Times* to comment in 2016 that if 'Donald J. Trump decides as president to throw a whistle-blower in jail for trying to talk to a reporter, or gets the F.B.I. to spy on a journalist, he will have one man to thank for bequeathing him such expansive power: Barack Obama' (Risen 2016). Obama's war on journalists was then, perhaps not surprisingly, followed by the further prosecution of six whistle-blowers under the Espionage Act in Trump's first administration.[5] In his second administration, Trump has – according to a detailed report published by the Committee to Protect Journalists (Jacobsen 2025) – instigated a series of targeted attacks against journalists and news organizations that includes suing a range of news outlets and initiating regulatory investigations into the conduct of major broadcasters including National Public Radio and CBS's flagship current affairs programme, *60 Minutes*. The report concludes by stating that the United States 'is now at a critical juncture concerning both the future of freedom of the press and democratic institutions more broadly' (Jacobsen 2025). Censorship and state intimidation remain very pressing concerns for journalists all over the world.

### Data controller

The state's monopoly of coercive power also allows it to gather extensive information about the lives and activities of its citizens. This is nothing new. For years, institutions such as the Stasi in East Germany and the FBI in the United States built up enormous, bureaucratic surveillance operations that generated huge amounts of data concerning personal communications and political affiliations. Digital technologies, however, have allowed the state exponentially to increase the volume of personal data that can be collected and processed and to track the movement of capital, people and communicative interactions with unprecedented detail (Dencik et al. 2022). Of course, the state is by no means the only institution with surveillance power. Private-sector tech companies like Meta, Amazon and Alphabet have accumulated vast repositories of data about consumer preferences and have used this to disrupt and reshape fields from business to politics and from media to medicine. As discussed in chapter 7, this is connected to Zuboff's claims that we live under 'surveillance capitalism', a data-intensive system that 'replaces legitimate contract, the rule of law, politics, and social trust with a new form of sovereignty and its privately administered regime of reinforcements' (2019: 514). Yet, even with 'surveillance capitalism', the state retains a unique capability to link the collection and storage of data to the provision of key services and to enforce sanctions against those it deems to be acting in ways that run counter to the 'national interest', including journalists.

The events of 9/11 and the emergence of a 'homeland security agenda' were used to justify the construction of a datafied security state. This has generated what Frank Pasquale (2015: 216) describes as a 'defense/intelligence/policing complex' that is part of a wider 'Black Box Society' based on opaque algorithms and the fusion of corporate and state interests. This was, of course, most dramatically illustrated both by the revelations in 2013 of the American whistle-blower Edward Snowden about the scale of the surveillance apparatus overseen both by the US National Security Agency and the United Kingdom's GCHQ, as well as the witch-hunts against those who sought to expose this, including Snowden, Chelsea Manning and Julian Assange. Programs like PRISM, that took data straight out of the 'back door' of the largest tech companies (that handed the NSA the keys) and Boundless Informant that processed billions of phone calls and emails in the United States (Lyon 2015), demonstrate the overarching capacity of the state to monitor the communications landscape with hugely significant consequences for both individual privacy and journalist safety. Surveillance systems operated either directly by the state or in partnership with private third-party providers are becoming increasingly ubiquitous.

For example, according to a report by Amnesty International (Rueckert 2021), the phones of more than 180 journalists in 20 countries were hacked using Pegasus spyware developed by the Israeli firm NSO Group at the behest of a range of governments, including Azerbaijan, France, India, Mexico, Rwanda, Spain and the United Kingdom. According to Amnesty's secretary general, Agnes Callamard, the scale of the operation reveals that 'the abuse is widespread, placing journalists' lives, those of their families and associates in danger, undermining freedom of the press and shutting down critical media' (quoted in Rueckert 2021). A 2024 report published by the International Press Institute found evidence of mass surveillance by government and intelligence agencies of investigative journalists in Greece and Hungary. The report concludes that such activities pose 'a fundamental threat to media freedom, the digital safety of journalists, and source protection within the European Union' (Wiseman et al. 2024: 17). The aim of this use of spyware is designed, above all, to pressurize journalists into *not* reporting on matters of public controversy. According to Roman Gressier, a journalist for the El Salvadoran news outlet *El Faro*, whose phone was hacked when he attempted to report on the activities of the country's president, 'Part of the role of this type of spyware is also to intimidate. It's like, we don't only want to get information from you, we also want to let you know that nowhere is safe. And we also want you to feel corralled, and in a corner. We want you to feel like your sources aren't safe' (quoted in Farrow 2022). Surveillance regimes impinge on not only the lives of ordinary citizens but undermine the very possibility of investigative journalism.

*Rulemaker*

Despite predictions of a shift from *government* to *governance* in which outsourced actors like self-regulatory and multi-stakeholder bodies assume some of the responsibilities previously performed by the state, it has not yielded its legislative role. The state continues to provide the legal infrastructure through which rules and regulations affecting the communications environment are developed, implemented and policed. Laws concerning online harms, privacy, media ownership, election advertising, intellectual property, tax breaks and spectrum allocation all shape the character of individual communication landscapes and are subject to oversight and sanctions by regulatory bodies whose authority is vested in the state.

The state, therefore, has certainly not divested itself of the power to set the terms of debate and to devise the rules that structure communicative interactions. Indeed, given the rise of online disinformation and misinformation as a public policy priority in recent years – that 'fake news' is disrupting democratic elections and undermining trust in established sources of authority – we are seeing a raft of new laws being passed that are likely to grant additional powers to the state, even if they are claimed to protect the rights of individuals. France was the first country to pass a law, in 2018, on the 'manipulation of information' that enabled judges to demand the immediate removal of fake content online during an election period. The law hands the regulator, the Higher Audiovisual Council, a series of new administrative and executive powers to police enforcement and even to suspend media outlets who are deemed to be controlled or 'under the influence' of a foreign state. While there were some welcome initiatives concerning the transparency of algorithms and the labelling of digital content, the law was criticized both for strengthening the power of the state and for failing to address the underlying causes of the problem of misinformation. 'The concentration of property in the media sector, the low working conditions of journalists, and the conflicts of interests within the sector are the three main diseases of contemporary journalism', argued the leader of the left-wing La France Insoumise party, Jean-Luc Mélènchon, at the time. 'The law appears to deal with the symptoms, not the causes, of the diseases of the media sector' (quoted in Ricci 2018).

Today, dozens of countries and trade blocs are passing laws on online harms, cybercrime and cyber libel, and data protection. In some cases, such as the European Union's Digital Markets Act and Digital Services Act, they are explicitly framed so as to curb the powers of Big Tech companies and to require at least degrees of financial transparency and behavioural accountability. However, in many countries, legislation is often double-edged: allegedly designed to stamp out the most nefarious examples of disinformation and hate speech but in reality enhancing the state's ability to define these terms according to its own priorities and to punish those they deem to be contravening its interpretation. One of the most celebrated examples was the targeting in 2020 of the award-winning Filipino journalist Maria Ressa under cybercrime charges in the hope of shutting down her investigative journalism outlet Rappler. According to the Centre for News, Technology and Innovation (2024), 'a majority of cybercrime laws include few safeguards to protect against investigatory overreach and incorporate provision with vague or broad wording that can be used to target journalists, thus threatening an independent press and free expression.' This use of 'lawfare' is now a popular tool for states to selectively interpret legislation in order to punish journalists who are investigating corruption and seeking to hold powerful figures to account.

## Entrepreneur

Thus far I have identified largely negative roles where the capitalist state uses its power to reproduce its hegemony, defend its own interests and diminish its opponents. To what extent can the state mobilize its power and resources for the public good and not only for the special interests with which it is intimately associated? This might suggest a *welfarist* role in which the state guarantees a minimal allocation of communication rights, acts as a counterweight to market failure and privileges the public interest in communications. This approach is perhaps best expressed in the public subsidies for non-mainstream content and continuing support for public service media that I consider in the next section. The state, however, also has a *developmental* aspect in which it seeks to build capacity – in terms of infrastructure, skills and technologies – both to accrue economic advantage and to improve opportunities for its citizens. This involves large-scale public investment, partnerships with industry and a focus on the end-user as well as on the bottom line.

In her book, *The Entrepreneurial State* (Mazzucato 2015), the economist Mariana Mazzucato argues against neoliberal advocates of a 'small state' that, far from being a bureaucratic restraint on innovation and creativity, the state – where it is confident and not apologetic – is able to engage in long-term planning that market forces have little appetite for. According to Mazzucato (2015: 4), 'the State has historically served not just as an administrator and regulator of the wealth creation process, but a key actor in it, and often a more daring one, willing to take the risks that businesses won't.' Her book contains a detailed analysis of innovations in the technology, health and energy sectors in which the state has played a leading role and focuses, in particular, on the role of public investment in generating the conditions in which digital transformations became possible. Apple, she notes, 'was able to ride the wave of massive State investments in the "revolutionary" technologies that underpinned the iPhone and iPad: the Internet, GPS, touch-screen displays and communication technologies. Without these publicly funded technologies, there would have been no wave to foolishly surf' (2015: 94). Indeed, in the United Kingdom, crucial developments in colour television, microcomputing and digital broadcasting have all emerged out of the laboratories of the publicly funded BBC (Klontzas 2025).

For all the democratic possibilities of a forward-thinking and risk-taking state that is committed to serving the public interest, it is, however, virtually unthinkable for the capitalist state to shrug off its underlying commitment to existing property relations. Mazzucato is quite right to challenge the myths about a 'sluggish' public sector versus a 'dynamic' private sector, yet even the most entrepreneurial states remain in hock to the logic of capital accumulation and the reproduction of the status quo. Neoliberalism has not eviscerated the entrepreneurial state but has instead attempted (where it is able to do so) to change its immediate priorities away from welfare delivery to the provision of infrastructure, the securing of inward investment and increased spending on defence. There will continue to be large-scale investment by the state in areas like artificial intelligence, transport infrastructure and green technologies, but as long as the state maintains its intimate connections to vested interests, it is unlikely that this investment will be predicated, above all, on the needs of ordinary citizens.

### Sponsor

Where Sparks talked of the state as a 'patron', 'a direct economic benefactor of the media' (1986: 77) through its funding of media outlets and its granting of licences, tax breaks and advertising subsidies, it is probably more appropriate in the twenty-first century to use the commercial language of 'sponsorship' to indicate the different financial relationships that the contemporary state maintains with the communications sector. Broadly speaking, this refers to two types of arrangements: public funding for media that is formally independent of the state and funding that is seen as a direct extension of the state. In current circumstances, the crucial distinction between these two categories is under enormous stress.

There is of course a significant difference between public service media (PSM) and the systems of press subsidies in Sweden, Norway, Finland and Denmark that Syvertsen and colleagues (2014) describe as a crucial pillar of the Nordic 'Media Welfare State' *and* state-funded international news channels that are wholly answerable to their funders and that are generally closer to the propaganda function discussed earlier in this chapter. It is worth noting, however, that while the former systems are under increasing financial and political strain, the latter approach is booming, with a growing number of states more than happy to underwrite their own broadcast itera-tions of 'soft power'. Early adopters like the Voice of America and the BBC's World Service have now been joined in a very crowded marketplace by Al Jazeera, RT, China Global Television Network, France 24, Press TV, Rai Italia, Globo TV International and many more. Each channel has a quite different relationship to its state sponsor, but none can be said to be wholly independent of the sphere of influence and control exerted by its paymaster.

The lack of editorial autonomy may be more obvious when it comes to the output of Chinese, Russian and Iranian international news channels, but Kate Wright and colleagues are right to point out (Wright, Scott and Bunce 2024: 11) that, 'despite the claims made by international PSM [public service media] regarding their editorial independence and impartiality, they are not apolitical organiza-tions.' All these news outlets are engaged in public diplomacy at the behest of their controlling states and all – although in very different circumstances – are affected by trends towards 'government capture' and 'democratic backsliding' that Wright and co-authors analyse in detail in relation to Donald Trump's politicization of the Voice of America in his first term in office.[6] Even the BBC World Service, widely seen as a model of public service journalism, is hardly immune to this kind of strategic power play, given that the introduction of new language services was funded by the UK government's 2015 Strategic Defence and Security Review and that the World Service itself is part-funded by the government's Foreign, Commonwealth and Development Office.

Domestic public media services are equally embroiled in the poli-tics of their 'funding states'. For example, both Hungarian and Polish public service broadcasters have long faced legislative reform and political attacks that have curbed any semblance of independence. In Poland in 2016, the then ruling Law and Justice party introduced the state appointment of broadcast executives and presided over the sacking of 120 journalists (Goclowski 2016) while Hungarian public media remain dominated by government appointees with virtually no editorial autonomy; instead, 'reporters are told by their editors what and how to report, and which terms to use and to avoid, and if they do not like it, that they can pack and leave' (Human Rights Watch 2024). The very concept of public service media – that it should provide a counterweight to the distortions of a commercial media system – is at risk as PSM outlets are increasingly constrained by funding crises, political intervention and forms of media capture (Dragomir 2024).

Yet this is not an unprecedented situation but rather one that reflects the historic ties between capitalist states and PSM institutions. Public service broadcasting may have been designed to avoid some of the problems and exclusions of a wholly market-led model, but it was also a shrewd strategic move on the part of specific states to develop media systems that were nominally independent but, in reality, accountable to dominant interests as part of more widespread exercises in 'nation building' and, in the case of post-Second World War Germany, 'depoliticization'. This is the case where public service outlets have been most clearly captured by the state as well as where they have a reputation for independence, such as in the United Kingdom, but where the fingerprints of elite power are nevertheless visible. PSM, as I found (2024b: 474) reflecting on the BBC's proestablishment framing of key topics such as the economy, defence and Gaza, may have, at certain points, improved the communications landscape, but it has simultaneously acted as 'an accessory to state actors and contaminated media markets that reproduce elite power. What it is not, and has never been, is an effective and consistent antidote to the shortcomings of commercial media and a reliable bulwark against the consequences of private property, concentrated ownership and state control.'

## Conclusion

The state retains a central coordinating force in contemporary capitalism and neither neoliberalism nor protectionism has made the state disappear from our communication landscapes. Indeed, due to the outsourcing and hollowing out that has taken place in the last 30 years, the state has become *more* concentrated, hierarchical and centralized in its articulation and defence of the capitalist interests with which it is intimately connected and which shape the dynamics of contemporary media systems and technological infrastructures. State power is neither a simple conspiracy nor an irresistible instrument of class domination – indeed, it is contradictory, self-denying and opaque – but it remains central to the reproduction of capitalist social relations inside the media and beyond.

# 11
# Imperialism, Colonialism and Globalization

***Overview*** This chapter sets out to clarify the complex relationship between imperialism, colonialism and globalization. It explores the extent to which capitalism spread across borders and continents not because it was intrinsically curious, adventurous, cosmopolitan or philanthropic but because, like so many other dimensions of capitalism explored in this book, there was an imperative to do so in order to foster accumulation and increase profits. The chapter assesses the role of media and communications technologies as both (partial) cause and effect of capital's internationalization and discusses theories of cultural imperialism and media globalization. In identifying the emergence of global communications and platform infrastructures, it reflects on case studies, including Netflix's content strategy, and the phenomenon of data colonialism.

## The internationalization of capitalism

In late 2024, the *Wall Street Journal* carried an opinion piece from Pulitzer Prize-winning journalist Karen Elliott House headlined 'The Middle East Is Up for Grabs'. It focused on the opportunities for the then incoming president, Donald Trump, to exploit global insecurity to the advantage of the United States. Israel's bombing of Gaza and Lebanon, the toppling of the Assad regime in Syria, the destabilization of Iran, China's sabre-rattling in the South China Sea and Russia's invasion of Ukraine all complicated the project 'to make America, and the world, safe again' (House 2024). It was a clear reminder that America's domestic interests are intertwined with its foreign policy and that US hegemony is directly related to the weakness or vulnerability of its rivals in China, Russia and Europe. The headline was resonant of the so-called 'scramble for Africa' at the end of the nineteenth century where European powers, notably Britain, France, Belgium and Germany, competed to carve up the continent of Africa, described at the time by the Belgian king as a 'magnificent cake' (quoted in Carmody 2011: 2), in order to revive their own economic and political fortunes. The strategic objectives of the most powerful states and corporations then and now have been realized through the attempted domination and expropriation of weaker ones across the globe involving a combination of military force, economic pressure and cultural inducements that has long been understood in relation to practices of imperialism, colonialism and globalization.

Marx and Engels were among the first writers to address the expansionist impulse at the heart of capitalism in famous words in the *Communist Manifesto*. 'The *need* of a constantly expanding market for its products chases the bourgeoisie over the whole surface of the globe. It *must* nestle everywhere, settle everywhere, establish connexions everywhere' (1973 [1857–61]: 37; emphases added). This was not a moral choice but an economic requirement related to capitalism's addiction to accumulation – a drive that originated in, but could not be confined to, nation-states. Capitalists moved speedily in the second half of the nineteenth century to internationalize their operations in ways that not only unsettled more traditional and insular producers but undermined the very basis of nation-based autarchy: 'In place of the old wants, satisfied by the production of the country, we find new wants, requiring for their satisfaction the production of distant lands and climes. In place of the old local and national seclusion and self-sufficiency, we have intercourse in every direction, universal inter-dependence of nations. And, as in material, so also in intellectual production' (1973 [1857–61]: 37). This is achieved, they suggest, through a range of measures such as intensive technological innovation (including developments related to communications), urbanization, industrialization and the increased circulation of cheap goods. 'In one word', they conclude (1973 [1857–61]: 38), 'it creates a world after its own image'.

Marx and Engels wrote these prescient words in 1848, well before capitalism had significantly expanded its scope beyond a few European countries. In the last quarter of that century, however, and in the grip of sustained economic crisis, these states were in desperate need for increased access to raw materials and cheaper sources of labour if they were effectively to compete with one another. It was at this stage that European nations stepped up their attempt to 'create a world after their own image' in what the historian Eric Hobsbawm (1989) describes as the 'age of empire'. It is of course not the case that these were the first empires in human history as Hobsbawm himself admits: 'Emperors and empires were old, but imperialism was quite new' (1989: 60).[1] The difference is that while previous empires – from the Roman to the Ottoman and from the Persian to the Mongol – controlled vast swathes of land and populations, they were not predicated on the same competitive economic dynamic and, in particular, on the same fusion of state and private power that was developing in the capitalist era and that underlined the new imperialist drive. As the leader of the Russian Revolution Vladimir Lenin writes in his short book on imperialism, it was the emergence of a new and highly monopolistic form of capitalism at the end of the nineteenth century that accelerated imperialist interventions and territorial division: 'capitalists partition the world, not out of personal malice, but because the degree of concentration which has been reached forces them to adopt this method in order to get profits' (1933 [1917]: 68).

Lenin's book was one of several on imperialism by writers in the Marxist tradition who were motivated by the threat of mass slaughter ahead of the First World War and its characterization as an imperialist conflict, including work by Rosa Luxemburg (2003 [1913]) and Nikolai Bukharin (1929 [1917]). While there are different emphases in their analyses, they share the conception that imperialism is, above all, related to a competitive struggle between leading capitalist states to enhance their economic standing – or, as Bukharin argues, to competition between 'state capitalist trusts' where states act as the 'defender and protector' (1929 [1917]: 124) of capitalist enterprise. For Luxemburg, imperialism is the outcome of capitalism's singular devotion to accumulation and the resulting fact that economic activity could no longer remain locked within national borders. 'Since capitalist production can develop fully only with complete access to all territories and climes, it can no more confine itself to the natural resources and productive forces of the temperate zone [the West] than it can manage with white labour alone' (2003 [1913]: 342–3). Capitalism can sustain itself only through expanding the sphere of exploitation and, in particular, as the great African-American writer W. E. B. Du Bois puts it, 'subjecting the labor of yellow, brown and Black people to the dictation of capitalism organised on a world basis' (2013 [1935]: 563).

Lenin saw imperialism as related to a specific stage of capitalism that is marked by multiple factors: intense economic concentration, the hegemony of finance capital, the increasing significance of the international circulation of capital, the growth of international corporate monopolies and, crucially, the means by which the 'territorial division of the world by the greatest capitalist powers is completed' (1933 (1917): 81) – in other words, the pressures that led to the Great War. What Lenin describes as 'territorial division' is a violent process for two fundamental reasons. First, because it has so often involved military competition between imperial powers as we have seen in two world wars and numerous inter-imperial conflicts and proxy wars; second, because it is frequently based on the forcible conquest and occupation of other people's land (even when carried out by occupiers in the name of 'civilization' and 'democracy' – terms that were used in recent years to justify US interventions in Iraq and Afghanistan). For Luxemburg, violence was not an optional extra in, for example, the British colonization of India or the French settlement of Algeria that she saw as classic examples of imperialist manoeuvring but a core and unconcealed feature of colonial policy. 'Force', she argues (2003 [1913]: 351), 'is the only solution open to capital' in order to secure its expansionism and protect its interests.[2]

This raises the important question about the relationship between imperialism and colonialism. For some theorists, they are virtually interchangeable. Weber, for example, argues that imperialism's main objective was the 'possession of territories from which goods (raw materials) could be imported' (2013: 163). Imperialism, he insists, is based on the direct occupation and subjugation of foreign territory for domestic economic gain: 'Besides women, cattle and slaves, scarce land is one of the original and foremost objects of forceful acquisition' (2013: 165). Edward Said writes in *The Question of Palestine* that, 'Imperialism was the theory, colonialism the practice of changing the unoccupied territories of the world into useful new versions of the European metropolitan society. Everything in those societies that suggested waste, disorder, uncounted resources, was to be converted into productivity, order, taxable, potentially developed wealth' (2024 [1979]: 130).

While Said's acerbic characterization of the 'civilizing' and 'rationalizing' mission of colonialism is painfully accurate, it is not so clear that imperialism simply provides the theoretical impulse for – or the state-centred 'policy' (Young 2016: 17) guiding – the violent practices of colonization. Imperialism is a practice of its own that refers to the struggle between the most powerful capitalist nations to assert hegemony while colonialism refers to the brutal conquest of, and long-term rule over, territories by occupying powers that was often, but not always, at the heart of the imperial project. Imperialism refers to a form of competition between states, usually on behalf of major capitalist enterprises, for influence and power that relies on military superiority; colonization involves the conquest of land, resources and labour and the attempted imposition of an occupier's culture. They are distinct but intimately related phenomena.

For example, Walter Rodney, in his important book, *How Europe Underdeveloped Africa,* notes that imperialism is 'essentially an economic phenomenon and [that] it does not necessarily lead to direct political control or colonization' (1982 [1972]: 137). Racism was pervasive among imperial elites in the nineteenth century but, nevertheless, he argues that 'it was economics that determined that Europe should invest in Africa' while 'it was racism which confirmed the decision that the form of control should be direct colonial rule' (1982 [1972]: 141). This points to an important difference between the overall strategic objectives of the largest imperial powers to extend their influence and the specific mechanisms through which they choose to do this – for example, colonial rule enforced by major European powers in the nineteenth century, proxy wars, occupations and clientelist regimes in the case of US imperialism since the Second World War, and China's 'Belt and Road Initiative' that has, up to this point, relied on massive infrastructural investment across the globe backed up by military power. This is not in any way to suggest that colonialism has been somehow less central to capitalist development but is simply a recognition of the fact that imperialism and colonialism are different, if closely linked, forms of capitalist violence and control.

Of course, colonialism in particular has not always been discussed in these terms. Adam Smith, for example, rejected the idea that colonization was a necessary part of capitalist expansion even if he also welcomed its contribution to economic growth and the 'enjoyments' of the home population. Smith's main concern with colonization was neither moral nor political but economic: that it was largely a monopoly enterprise which was expensive to run and generated only marginal benefits. 'For the sake of that little enhancement of price which this monopoly might afford our producers, the home consumers have been burdened with the whole expence [sic] of maintaining and defending that empire' (2012 [1776]: 659). Two hundred years later and in the light of the terrible violence perpetrated by colonial forces against Indigenous populations – from the Congo to India and from Algeria to Indonesia – Fernand Braudel was nevertheless able to conclude that colonialism, 'like almost all culture-contact between civilizations, had both positive and negative cultural impact' (1995: 133). It is as if innovations related to education, technology, medicine and public administration could not have been developed by the people who lived in those countries had they been free to do so (bearing in mind, of course, that many crucial technological innovations such as paper and printing, as well as alcohol and algebra, originate from outside the West in the first place).

For the colonized themselves, colonial rule was decidedly neither 'evangelism, nor a philanthropic enterprise' as the Martiniquais activist and writer Aimé Cesaire put it in his influential 1950 anti-colonial manifesto, *Discourse on Colonialism* (2000 [1950]: 32). Cesaire clearly identifies capitalist competition as a key motivation for colonial conquests:

> the decisive actors here are the adventurer and the pirate, the wholesale grocer and the ship owner, the gold digger and the merchant, appetite and force, and behind them, the baleful projected shadow of a form of civilization which, at a certain point in its history, finds itself obliged, for internal reasons, to extend to a world scale the competition of its antagonistic economies. (Cesaire 2000 [1950]: 33)

In a hugely powerful account of the savagery and hypocrisy of western 'civilization', he describes colonization as an extreme form of capitalist commodification – a 'thingification' whereby human subjects are objectified in the most brutal ways possible: 'Between colonizer and colonized there is room only for forced labor, intimidation, pressure, police, taxation, theft, rape, compulsory crops, contempt, mistrust, arrogance, self-complacency, swinishness, brainless elites, degraded masses' (2000 [1950]: 42).

Cesaire's fellow Martiniquais, Frantz Fanon, was inspired by the experience of anti-colonial struggle against the French in Algeria in the 1950s and provides a valuable account of both how colonizers view those they seek to dominate as well as their impact on the dominated. According to Fanon, through systematic misrepresentation and brute force, 'it is the settler who has brought the native into existence and who perpetuates his existence' (2004 [1963]: 28). Fanon argues that there are series of powerful binaries in the relationship between the settler and the colonized: the former is seen as ethical, the other as devoid of values; one is generative, the other 'corrosive'; one is civilized, the other 'constitutionally depraved' (2004 [1963]: 33). In reality, the colonized suffer from an extreme form of alienation and live in a world that is 'divided into compartments' (2004 [1963]: 29) beyond which they are not allowed to go – both physically *and* imaginatively. Imagining themselves as active, autonomous individuals who re-occupy the spaces that the colonizers have deprived them of, they are able initially only to dream of liberation: 'the native never stops achieving his freedom from nine in the evening until six in the morning' (2004 [1963]: 40).

The violence of and liberation from colonial rule are part of capitalism's history. They are not, however, obscure debates, confined to Westphalian nation-states in an analogue age but aspirations and processes that remain relevant to contemporary struggles and experiences. The Middle East, for example, remains a crucial hotspot of imperial rivalry and source of energy security that is also dominated by a settler colonial state, Israel, which plays a crucial geopolitical as well as regional role. The experience of Palestinians is directly tied both to imperial power plays as well as to the violence of this settler colonial regime. On the other hand, successful anti-colonial movements in the second half of the twentieth century did indeed see the colonized able to regain control of their territories, if not their economies (Young 2016) and studies of both colonialism and imperialism now have to engage with a fresh set of circumstances: the emergence of postcolonial nations, the changing balance of power between the state and market (that was explored in the previous chapter) and the increasingly global footprint of capitalism itself. None of this means that we should no longer understand imperialism, as Aijaz Ahmad once argued (1994: 41) in response to a new wave of decolonization theorists, 'as a hierarchically structured system of global capitalism but as a relation, of governance and occupation, between richer and poorer countries, West and non-West'. Capitalist imperatives remain the central driving force of contemporary geopolitical relations.

This has not always been universally accepted. Schumpeter long ago criticized Marxist theories of imperialism as overly simplistic and suggested that they exaggerated the notion that governments were under pressure from monopolistic capitalists to smooth the path to capital export. 'As a matter of fact', he argues (2010 [1942]: 47), 'very little influence on foreign policy has been exerted by big business ... The attitudes of capitalist groups toward the policy of their nations are predominantly adaptive rather than causative', more opportunistic than strategic. David Harvey has more recently explored what he describes as the 'dialectical relation between territorial and capitalistic logics of power' (2003: 183) – in other words, the tension between more traditional, state-based conceptions of power and increasingly deregulated flows of capital. For Harvey, 'these two logics intertwine in complex and sometimes contradictory ways . . . sometimes to the point of outright antagonism' (2003: 29). Harvey's argument is that we now have a more unstable and multipolar world marked by the growing influence of capital, as distinct from the state, together with regional sub-imperialisms in, for example, South Asia and South America, that constitute a 'new imperialism' marked by the 'geographical dispersal of capitalistic class power' (2003: 186).

While this exaggerates the extent to which capital is ever able to detach itself from the military, technological and legal infrastructures which remain to this day largely the preserve of nation-states, Harvey's emphasis on emerging sub-imperialisms was understandable. New trade routes and patterns of exchange paved the way for the rapid rise in the late twentieth century of globalization as an explanatory framework that seeks to make sense of this perceived 'geographical dispersal' of power and to replace well-established narratives of imperialism and colonialism in both scholarly and popular debate with a conception of the world that is better suited to the paradigm of neoliberalism.

Globalization theory emerged at a particular conjuncture in the 1990s. It was the perfect perspective to make sense of the confluence of rapid changes in communications (not least the widespread adoption of domestic satellite dishes that facilitated transnational footprints), the increased salience of information as a commodity, intensive marketization, the predicted decline of nation-states and a far more permissive attitude towards cross-border trade. A combination of technological innovations, economic agreements and political shifts helped to produce an 'actually existing' version of Marshall McLuhan's notion of a 'global village' that he first speculated about decades earlier (McLuhan 2001 [1964]). Globalization's more zealous proponents spoke about a frictionless version of capitalism in which the old, fixed relationship between time and space had been reconstituted in a new world marked by mobility and speed. Not just goods and services but people, ideas, taste and culture could be exchanged beyond traditional national borders that would change forever the very texture of our lives. The *New York Times* columnist Thomas Friedman argued in a widely read book, *The Lexus and the Olive Tree*, that globalization referred to:

> the inexorable integration of markets, nation-states and technologies to a degree never witnessed before – in a way that is enabling individuals, corporations and nation-states to reach around the world farther, faster,

deeper and cheaper than ever before, and in a way that is enabling the
world to reach into individuals, corporations and nation-states farther,
faster, deeper, cheaper than ever before. (2000: 9)

To its advocates, globalization was the welcome expression of
the broader reshaping of capitalism in neoliberal circumstances – a
cosmopolitan flowering of free-market forces and triumph of transnational corporations that might even deliver world peace. As Friedman
(1996) famously argued in his 'golden arches theory of conflict pre-
vention', 'No two countries that both have a McDonald's have ever
fought a war against each other.' It may have been a tongue-in-cheek
comment, but it nevertheless struck a chord with those who believed
that what was now described as 'global capitalism' would enrich
populations to the extent that wars would become redundant among
those that signed up for neoliberal capitalism. Sadly for Friedman –
and more significantly for the civilians caught up in conflict – many
countries with McDonald's have indeed gone to war including Israel
and Lebanon, India and Pakistan and, of course, Russia and Ukraine.

The British sociologist, Anthony Giddens, struck a more cautious
note. Globalization was a hugely uneven process best expressed by
a structural interdependence which meant that 'larger and larger
numbers of people live in circumstances in which disembedded
institutions, linking local practices with globalised social relations,
organise major aspects of day-to-day life' (1991: 79). This involved
both a transformation of the economic sphere as the production of
goods and services (and not just the extraction of raw materials) was
outsourced to countries with fresh sources of cheap labour as well
as the 'stretching' of social relations that soon became ever more
elastic with the emergence of digital networks and worldwide connections. According to Giddens, these developments reached deep
into every household: 'Globalisation isn't only about what is "out
there", remote and far away from the individual. It is an "in here"
phenomenon too, influencing intimate and personal aspects of our
lives' (Giddens 1999). Above all, Giddens argues that globalization
is an example of the anarchic nature of capitalism and that, for all its
opportunities, it is also 'fraught with anxieties, as well as scarred by
deep divisions. Many of us feel in the grip of forces over which we
have no control' (Giddens 1999).

To its opponents, however, globalization marked an escalation of
trends that had long been enshrined in capitalism: the pursuit of profit
across the entire globe, the asymmetrical accumulation of wealth and
power not just by corporations but their home states as well, and the

intensification of labour exploitation in order to increase productivity (Klein 2005 [1999]). The world had become not more cosmopolitan or more peaceful but increasingly unequal and divided, just as the US sociologist Immanuel Wallerstein (1974) had predicted in his analysis of the 'capitalist world economy', into different zones: the core, the semi-periphery and the periphery. For all the absolute increases in cross-border trade and population movement, James Fulcher (2015: 101) suggests that the very idea of 'global capitalism' is based on a series of myths: first, that its internationalizing tendencies are new and unprecedented when, as we saw earlier in this chapter, Marx and Engels had already identified capitalism's expansionist imperative some 150 years earlier; second, that 'capital circulates globally, when in reality most of it moves between a small group of rich countries'; third, that nation-states play a marginal role in a global world when, as we saw in the last chapter, transnational companies still rely on the power of their home states; and finally, that the world has become more integrated which obscures the reality that inequalities in wealth have increased, not decreased, in the global era – a development most famously analysed by Piketty (2014). Globalization, therefore, should be understood not simply as an unambiguous fact of global connection but as an ideological correlation to the neoliberalizing tendencies that emerged in the 1970s. That both globalization and neoliberalism are now facing major challenges from growing protectionism and renewed imperialist rivalry should not distract from their role as mobilizing categories for economy, politics and culture in the last 50 years.

## From cultural imperialism to data colonialism (via media globalization)

How have processes of capitalist imperialism, colonialism and globalization shaped communications and what theoretical approaches have been developed to grasp this dynamic? Daniel Headrick (1981) illustrates how innovations in transportation, pharmaceuticals and military hardware – including the vicious 'dum-dum bullet' which 'was considered so cruel that even the "civilized" nations refused to use it against each other' (1981: 103) – acted as crucial 'tools of empire' in facilitating imperial control in the nineteenth century. Media technologies have also long acted both as instruments of internationalization – vehicles that have assisted in the roll-out of supranational relationships and intensified domination – and as forms and systems whose logic has been moulded by capitalism's expansionist logic. Journalism, for example, has been connected to the ambitions and narratives of the biggest European governments from the earliest days of imperialism and the most powerful nation-states of the time were keen to establish international news wire services that would reflect their strategic interests. The earliest news agencies, Havas, Wolff and Reuters, were all closely linked to their home states in France, Germany and the United Kingdom respectively in the second half of that century. 'In Britain', writes the media historian Paul Starr (2004: 180), 'though the state did not directly control Reuters, the foreign news service was so reliably in line with official opinion that it was given exclusive access to internal government information, such as telegrams from India, and gained an aura as the semiofficial imperial news agency'.

In their fascinating account of the creation of nineteenth-century communication infrastructures, Winseck and Pike (2007) nevertheless warn against the danger of exaggerating the impact of imperialism on communications development when globalization and economic interdependency, they suggest, were more decisive drivers of international connections. Yet what they describe as communications cartels that were 'devised to divide and share global markets' (2007: xvi) were hardly immune from the protections and priorities of their home states and the fact that undersea cables reached Alexandria in 1861, Suez in 1863, Bombay in 1865 and Australia in 1871 certainly complements the geography of imperialist expansion (O'Hara 2010: 611). According to Paula Chakravartty (2019: 247), 'colonial and postcolonial infrastructures of empire can be traced from nineteenth-century imperial rivalries and the long twentieth century of US domination', infrastructures based originally on innovations in telegraphy and telecommunications and, more recently, on developments in broadcast, satellite and digital technologies. All are implicated in fostering a 'colonial logic of racialized information infrastructure' (2019: 248) that justifies a continuing focus on imperial power as well as corporate strategy. This relationship remains central to more recent disputes around, for example, disputes between the United States and China over who will dominate AI (Kennedy 2025) and military tensions between NATO and Russia in the Baltic over the safety of undersea cables (Schiller 2025).

In response to this history of western infrastructural and cultural hegemony, theorists and activists sought to account for what they saw as the structural inequalities that are sutured into the media's role in the world. The concept of cultural imperialism first surfaced in the

1960s and was inspired not just by the expansive reach of western corporate power but also by the impact of decolonization movements across the globe. This wave of struggles for self-determination had also generated a new group of voices who sought to highlight the cultural element of anti-colonial resistance including Frantz Fanon, Amilcar Cabral, Ariel Dorman, Phong Hien and Luis Ramiro Beltrán.[3] According to Chakravartty (2019: 257, emphasis in original): 'It was these internationalist intellectuals from socialist, third-world, feminist, civil rights and decolonization movements . . . that ultimately aimed for *liberated infrastructures* to combat colonial propaganda and build transnational circuits of transport and communication (radio and newspapers) in the service of the commons'.

A significant example of the attempt to liberate a communications infrastructure from colonial rule was seen in the Algerian struggle in the 1950s against French occupation. Here, Fanon was particularly absorbed by the emancipatory role played by radio and how it had been transformed from being a tool of the colonizer to being an essential part of anti-colonial resistance. In the early days of the revolt, Algerians refused to buy radio sets as they were seen as enemy objects, as 'civilizing tools'. This changed as a result of the revolts when French domination started to crack and when, as Fanon puts it, 'the occupier's lie becomes a positive aspect of the nation's new truth' (1965 [1959]: 76). In 1956, the insurrectionary radio station, the Voice of Fighting Algeria, was launched and brought a level of self-consciousness and organization to the people of Algeria. Having a radio now meant, as Fanon argues, 'paying taxes to the nation' (1965 [1959]: 84) and indeed it became so popular that people actually *imagined* they had heard broadcasts even when they had not. Jammed by the French and constantly closed down, the Voice of Fighting Algeria nevertheless allowed Algerians to imagine the spreading of resistance: 'behind each modulation, each active crackling, the Algerian would imagine not only words but concrete battles' (1965 [1959]: 88). For Fanon, 'having a radio seriously meant *going to war*' (1965 [1959]: 93; italics in original).

Theories of cultural imperialism that emerged in the west, however, were generally more absorbed with confronting the dynamics of capitalist hegemony than with vocalizing anti-colonial struggles themselves. For many proponents of the cultural imperialism thesis, the ubiquity of, in particular, American representations, images, sounds and narratives constituted a form of domination that was achieved not directly through the barrel of a gun but through the tantalizing appeal of phenomena like Donald Duck, Hollywood movies,

Coca Cola and *Dallas* (the television programme, not the physical place). This was combined with funding and trade arrangements that made it viable for major cultural producers to 'dump' content on smaller and less developed markets. The international circulation of western cultural commodities would come to be known as a form of 'soft power' (Nye 1990) but at the time, it was seen simply as the imposition of western capitalist norms over countries that were less equipped to resist or to counter with their own cultural products.

Herbert Schiller's *Mass Communications and American Empire* (Schiller 1971) was one of the first titles in that period to excoriate US communications policy and its component institutional structures. It speaks of a 'military-industrial communication complex' (1971: 54) that corrupts both domestic and international audiences through its advocacy of a wholly commercial orientation on public life. With chapters that include 'The Global American Electronic Invasion' and 'The Developing World Under Electronic Siege', Schiller saw the overseas activities of giant US communications conglomerates as a key element of a renewed American 'imperial surge' (1971: 16) that was designed to respond to contemporary anti-colonial movements. Schiller later expanded on this approach with a definition of cultural imperialism itself as: 'the sum of the processes by which a society is brought into the modern world system and how its dominating stratum is attracted, pressured, forced and sometimes even bribed into shaping social institutions to correspond to, or even promote, the values and structures of the dominating centre of the system' (Schiller 1976: 9–10). These processes include language, religion, liberal beliefs, political institutions but, above all, media and communications as part of a hegemonic strategy to enforce not mutuality or equality but new conditions of dependence on US power.

Following Schiller, Oliver Boyd-Barrett (1977) developed the slightly narrower concept of media imperialism to describe the way in which the media system of one country is shaped by that of another without the opportunity for reciprocal arrangements. This relationship is marked by three key features: the unidirectional nature of international communication flows, effectively from the West to the East and from the North to the South, the very small number of source countries and the disruption, if not dissolution, of indigenous cultural forms. Media imperialism speaks to a situation in which transnational corporations and media moguls increasingly operate across borders but also where they act as active agents *of* imperialism – 'when they prioritize the voices, justifications and discourses of imperial actors over the voices of victims, dissidents and alternatives, and when they omit or marginalize details and perspectives that would serve to critique imperial power' (Boyd-Barrett 2015: 13).

Resistance to cultural imperialism was especially strong in Latin America where, for example, Ariel Dorfman and Armand Mattelart's *How to Read Donald Duck* (Dorfman and Mattelart 2019 [1971]) was a sharp and popular critique of capitalist propaganda masquerading as a harmless cartoon strip. The Bolivian journalist and researcher Luis Ramiro Beltrán focused on the lack of possibilities for reciprocity in the imposition of dominant cultures over the 'periphery' and suggested that this was a purposeful strategy on behalf of the wealthiest countries. 'Cultural imperialism through communication is not an occasional and fortuitous event. It is a vital process for "imperial" countries to secure and maintain economic domination and political hegemony over others' (1978: 185). Indeed, such was the anger in the Global South that the debate even reached the hallowed halls of the United Nations where, in 1980, UNESCO circulated a call for a 'New World Information and Communications Order' that proved to be a brief rallying point for change before it was 'derailed by the US media and advertising industries and the ideologically hostile Reagan administration of the 1980s that overturned even the weakest calls for reversing any form of US media imperialism' (Chakravartty 2019: 253).

Theories of media and cultural imperialism were welcome and powerful critiques of imperial overreach and testimony to the pressure exerted by anti-colonial and anti-imperialist movements in the 1960s and 1970s. But they also had their own problems, not least that they skirted over the 'sub-imperialisms' that were changing the political and economic geography of the postcolonial era with undemocratic regimes emerging in, for example, Mexico, Brazil, Egypt and India that exerted significant regional power. Mattelart argues that there was a further problem in that theories of cultural imperialism also exaggerated the dependency and vulnerability of indigenous cultures that were, as Jeremy Tunstall put it, 'being battered out of existence by the indiscriminate dumping of large quantities of slick and commercial media products, largely from the United States' (1977: 57). For Mattelart, cultural imperialism all too often ended up as a catch-all phrase that reinforced the unassailable power of the United States and undermined possibilities for resistance. The very notion of a 'monolithic, triumphant imperialism, wiping out all diversity and homogenizing all cultures can provoke a legitimate refusal to recognize the very existence of imperialism' (Mattelart 1979: 61) and, in turn, to make it harder to design an effective anti-imperialist politics. Finally, cultural imperialism was often used not to describe intra-capitalist rivalry but to capture the poisoning of local cultures by the export of foreign goods, a phenomenon that is closer to Said's definition of colonialism – 'the subjugation of the universe or a vast part of it to that [occupying] people's language, customs, ideas and laws' (2024 [1979]: 130) – than it is to imperialism as I have defined it in this chapter.

By the 1990s, however, theories of media and cultural imperialism were far less popular, increasingly challenged by critics influenced by emerging discourses around postmodernism and cultural globalization. 'What replaces "imperialism"', argues John Tomlinson (1991: 175), 'is globalisation . . . a far less coherent or culturally directed process'. Globalization, for Tomlinson, 'suggests interconnection and interdependency of all global areas which happens in a far less purposeful way' (1991: 175) than that of theories of imperialism. Instead of media flows originating in Los Angeles, London or Paris and being foisted on vulnerable populations in the Global South, a new audio-visual landscape was said to be emerging – one that did not conform to the inflexible and one-dimensional model of cultural imperialism. This was a far more fluid and decentralized landscape, characterized not by a lack of reciprocity but by what two Australian scholars called 'a new diversity in program sources' (Cunningham and Jacka 1996: 29) and what Anthony Giddens described as 'reverse colonisation' (Giddens 1999). This involved the creation of new hybrid circuits of media exchange involving, for example, TV Globo's exports of *telenovelas* from Brazil to Portugal, Phoenix's programming from Hong Kong that reached across China and South East Asia, Zee TV's Hindi output that was based in India but had millions of subscribers in Europe and the global popularity of South Korean pop music. Culture no longer moved simply from the North to the South and the West to the East but was wrapped up in more complex distribution patterns that reflected emerging regional centres of power and included 'contra-flows' along with more traditional, colonial trade routes (Thussu 2007).

Globalization theory has had the advantage of not treating audiences like passive victims of foreign interference and has certainly attempted to make sense of the consequences of technological change, the lived experiences of diasporic populations and the rise of a more multipolar world. But it all too often overstates the decline of US cultural hegemony, underestimates continuing 'systematic global inequalities in cultural prestige and economic profit' (Hesmondhalgh 2026: 408) and neglects the crucial fact that globalization was – and remains – a strategy pursued by capitalist interests not because they want audiences to get to know each other better but because economic imperatives have forced them to internationalize their operations. As the largest US media conglomerates have outgrown their domestic market, they are obliged to look abroad for new markets and for cheaper sources of (creative) labour in ways that are far closer to older imperialist logics than to a decentralized or deterritorialized conception of cultural trade.

Consider the case of Netflix which is seen as the epitome of a global streamer given that it has some 300 million subscribers in over 190 countries and that, at the time of writing, four out of ten of its most popular television shows ever are non-English language productions (*Squid Game*, seasons one and two [2021, 2024], *Money Heist*, part four [2020], and *Lupin*, part one [2021]).[4] The fact that a South Korean drama is the most viewed title ever of a California-based TV behemoth is of course significant and much has been made of Netflix's commitment to building up regional production bases. Yet it remains the case that Netflix content is disproportionately North American – 42 per cent of its programming originates in the United States and Canada (Harrington 2025) – and that English-language content is disproportionately popular as compared to the linguistic diversity of its subscriber base. Indeed, given that Netflix's business model depends on scale rather than quality, non-English content has the advantage both of being less expensive to produce and a useful way of locking in global audiences. As media consultants at Enders Analysis noted in their report to subscribers:

> Netflix has been illuminating the global success of cherry-picked non-US/English language shows for some time in order to ease through the perception that expenditure on this content is *not* inefficient – as it is also readily consumed outside of the market where it is made – and as content expenditure outside of the US has grown, this narrative has intensified. *However, while we think that it is clear that locally-produced content is an important driver of local engagement (not to mention usually relatively cheap) we are sceptical in most cases that it travels globally.* (Harrington and Sutcliffe 2024; emphasis added)

Netflix's commitment to 'localization' appears to be focused less on a desire to negotiate with or to promote global difference than a corporate strategy to diversify and de-risk its production base and to deliver regional audiences into the orbit of a US-based transnational. 'Netflix imperialism', as Davis (2021) describes it, is an attempt to secure a global streaming monopoly designed to undermine corporate rivals and exploit user engagement. Indeed, in a speech in 2019, the former president of the Canadian public broadcaster CBC, Catherine Tait, compared Netflix to nineteenth-century colonialists who argued that they were 'educating' the people of Africa and India and 'bringing their resources to the world' as an act of charity. The rise of Netflix, she argued, marked the 'beginning of a new empire' (quoted in CBC 2019).

Similar concerns animate ongoing concerns about 'data colonialism' (Couldry and Mejias 2019) which revolve around the expropriation of data and commodification of users that intensifies the asymmetrical power between a handful of wealthy countries and the rest of the world. This resonates with Shoshana Zuboff's claim that in surveillance capitalism, our very nature 'is scraped, torn, and taken for another century's market project' (2019: 94), but here it is the specifically *colonial* aspects of dispossession and resource theft that best express contemporary 'data relations'. For Couldry and Mejias, this involves an especially high degree of alienation in which 'human beings become not just actors in the production process but raw material that can be transformed into value' (2019: xvii), a transformation particularly associated with colonialism. They suggest that we are seeing the re-emergence of traditional patterns of colonial behaviour in new digital conditions with, for example, data infrastructures that still privilege the Global North and projects like Facebook's Free Basics that reproduce imperialist logics rather than encouraging meaningful sovereignty in countries of the Global South.[5]

Couldry and Mejias locate data-driven developments in relation not only to colonialism and imperialism respectively but also, firmly, to capitalist logics; they do not see these developments as already having ushered in a new mode of production or as superseding capitalism's fetish for accumulation. Yet, just as we saw earlier that Mattelart was worried that theories of cultural imperialism often exaggerated the power of western commodity producers and undermined the prospects for resistance, so too have some critics suggested that colonialism is a problematic framework for making sense of data relations, in particular because of the difficulties in equating the violence that underscored colonization with the expropriation inherent to data-driven capitalism. For example, Couldry and Mejias suggest that data colonialism 'represents both a progression of capitalism and its turn, potentially, to more brutal forms of exploitation' (2019: 85) and while they acknowledge that there is a 'world of difference between slavery's direct and violent ownership of bodies and minds and the more indirect forms of surveillance and dataveillance that characterise contemporary data relations', they nevertheless argue that 'they have something crucial in common' (2019: 160–1). Other writers do not see such a clear correspondence. The concept of data colonialism, argue Segura and Waisbord,

> diminishes the centrality of violence in colonialism. Put it simply, colonialism is unthinkable without violence – the takeover of lands and populations by sheer physical force. Similar to colonialism, data capitalism denies populations their humanity by turning them [into] resources and value-creating subjects. It does not, however, employ force the way colonialism did. Data capitalism uses insidious and duplicitous techniques to extract value, but its tactics are not backed up by standing armies and slavery. (Segura and Waisbord 2019: 416)

To be fair, the same criticism could be made of some advocates of cultural and media imperialism theses who, at times, elided the difference between the violence used in imperialist war and colonial conquest, and the political and economic pressure that was exerted on poorer countries to accept western goods and services.

## Conclusion

Imperialist competition and colonial relations of domination remain ever present in the world today, whether in relation to the ban on TikTok proposed by western governments, the limitations on the use of equipment produced by the Chinese firm Huawei, the Chinese government's 'Belt and Road' initiative or the dramatic increase in defence spending fuelled by sympathetic media coverage. There is, however, a significant difference between 'civilization' enforced with the barrel of a gun and the expropriation of data from social media users, even if both are important weapons in the capitalist armoury. Indeed, capitalism, rather than a specific communications-related form of imperialism, colonialism or globalization, remains a wholly relevant (and probably more useful) explanatory framework with which to engage in the contemporary battles, wherever they take place in the world, to control our digital futures.

# 12
# Oppression

***Overview*** Capitalism depends on unpaid labour to ensure social reproduction as well as on various forms of, in particular, racialized and gendered discrimination to divide communities and weaken opposition. This chapter tackles the intimate relationship between capitalism and oppression by examining critical work on racism, the family and misogyny and explores how capitalism has systematically weaponized differences between social groups. The chapter then discusses ways in which culture and media have both contributed to and been shaped by the lens of discrimination. It highlights Edward Said's work on Orientalism and changing representations of women over time as a means of illustrating the media's central role in reproducing structures of oppression.

## Weaponizing difference

According to its most vociferous supporters, capitalism provides the best defence not only against inequality and poverty but against discrimination and injustice. 'It is a striking historical fact', notes Milton Friedman in *Capitalism and Freedom* (2002 [1962]: 108), 'that the development of capitalism has been accompanied by a major reduction in the extent to which particular religious, racial, or social groups have operated under special handicaps in respect of their economic activities; have, as the saying goes, been discriminated against.' In Friedman's world, the prevalence of discrimination is precisely correlated with the degree of economic competition because things like racism, sexism and religious persecution are, ultimately, bad economic choices that lead to labour inefficiencies and higher prices. The free market is more interested in securing the fruits of labour than it is in treating people differently on the basis of what Friedman describes as 'irrelevant characteristics' (2002 [1962]: 109). Discrimination, therefore, becomes a matter of opinion rather than an exercise of power: 'It is hard to see that discrimination can have any meaning other than a "taste" of others that one does not share' (2002 [1962]: 110).

This faith in the ability of capitalism to operate in such a disinterested way and to treat populations without prejudice would be quaint if it was not for another 'historical fact': that capitalism owes its very existence to the profits accrued from slavery, the violent colonization of whole swathes of the globe, the systematic downgrading of the rights of women and the subjugation of minority groups. Capitalism has, since its inception, effectively mobilized the differences between its citizens – on the basis of faith, geography, ethnicity, sex, sexual orientation and much more – in order to cement its domination and to fragment resistance. It has set 'civilized' against 'barbarian', colonizer against colonized, men against women, white against Black, able-bodied against disabled, Christian against Jew, cis against trans and straight against gay, and it has sought to justify these distinctions through spurious concepts of 'human nature' and 'common sense'. This book views oppression both as the systematic discrimination against different social groups because of specific background characteristics and as an intrinsic component of capitalism's origins and its development. This is very different to Adam Smith's use of the term throughout *Wealth of Nations* as a kind of suffocation or stifling that could be experienced by *any* individual as a result of the overreach of power. Oppression, however, is connected not simply to a series of individual harms and grievances – as real and as deep-rooted as they are – but to the structural dynamics and imperatives of capital and, in particular, to the reproduction of labour power (discussed in chapter 4).

Of course, differences based on, for example, ethnicity, sex and religion long pre-date capitalism but they have been redefined, intensified and reproduced in the specific circumstances of a system predicated on exploitation and the expansion of private property. Oppression offers certain specific advantages to capitalist accumulation: it provided the initial justification for the super-exploitation of slave labour that fuelled the Industrial Revolution; it underscored the subjugation of peoples and nations that assisted the colonial and imperial projects that enriched capitalists; it normalized the conditions in which the care of and responsibility for the next generation of labour was outsourced to women; and it sought to accentuate division between social groups as a means of undermining prospects for a united opposition to capitalism. While it's true that oppression itself has generated the resistance that capitalism has sought to suppress – from slave revolts through to contemporary civil rights and social justice movements – social division remains a critical and powerful tool in the hands of a status quo committed to defending existing property relations.

Nancy Fraser has written extensively about the relationship between exploitation and what she describes as 'the back-story of expropriation' (2022: 8), the confiscation of the raw materials and land of historically marginalized peoples, together with the uncompensated affective work that supports current and future labour and that enables accumulation to take place. Although she acknowledges that 'expropriation and exploitation work hand in hand' (2022: 15), and that without the former, the latter would be unable to continue, she argues that the 'expropriated' have been (and continue to be) denied the status of the 'exploited' both by capitalism itself but also within the classic Marxist tradition which, after all, privileges 'productive' labour as the key site of accumulation and class as the overriding social division. Echoing the work of Federici (2004) on the historic separation of production and reproduction that occurs as a result of capitalism, and of Robinson (1983) in relation to the embedded role of racism in capitalist development that perpetuates a specific type of 'racial capitalism', Fraser suggests that working people are divided into two further structural categories: 'one suitable for "mere" exploitation, the other destined for brute expropriation' (Fraser 2022: 15). This requires a further shift in attention on the part of anti-capitalists from their preoccupation with production to a full engagement with struggles around social reproduction and expropriation.

Fraser's comprehensive analysis of the structural imperatives of capitalism that drive discrimination is a powerful reminder that oppression has a systemic genesis and orientation and is not simply the outcome of a flawed 'human nature' or reactionary individual beliefs. Moreover, her identification of the interconnections between capitalism, climate crisis, misogyny and racism is especially helpful, as is her claim that a renewed interest in critiques of capitalism suggests a growing appetite 'for an analysis that clarifies the relations among the disparate social struggles of our time' (Fraser 2022: 1). However, her notion that Marxism has paid insufficient attention to questions of reproduction overlooks the key point that the site of production is especially significant not because of a moral question around what matters most but because capitalism has consistently redefined the very contours and practices of oppression in order to facilitate accumulation and, additionally, because this is the space in which capitalism – because of the contradictions I discuss in chapter 14 – is most vulnerable.

## Race and racism

Let me try to clarify this point by discussing capitalism's relationship first to racism and then to misogyny as key and enduring examples of oppression. As has already been stated in this chapter, slavery was absolutely central to the consolidation of capital in the eighteenth and nineteenth centuries. As the economists Anievas and Nişancıoğlu point out, the profits generated from slavery were crucial in generating the capital to develop a whole range of industries, effectively 'jump-starting the engine of industrial accumulation' (2015: 165). While wage labour is fundamental to the capitalist project, they suggest that this doesn't preclude the exploitation of 'unfree labour' in conditions where this was economically or politically viable. Slavery, however, didn't start simply because of pre-existing prejudice against people of colour. 'Slavery', as the Trinidadian historian Eric Williams argues in *Capitalism and Slavery* (1964 [1944]: 7), 'was not born of racism; rather racism was the consequence of slavery. Unfree labor in the New World was brown, white, Black and yellow; Catholic, Protestant and pagan.' Servitude, for Williams, was essentially an economic phenomenon: 'The reason [for slavery] was economic, not racial; it had to do not with the color of the labourer, but with the cheapness of the labor' (1964 [1944]: 17).[1] Given that there simply wasn't enough 'free labour' to pick cotton, tobacco and sugar cane, those with capital initially turned to the Indigenous peoples of the Caribbean followed by impoverished white people, including convicts and indentured servants. When these groups didn't furnish sufficient numbers, planters then turned to the mass enslavement of Black Africans which required a 'moral' justification for the extreme brutality of the Middle Passage.

This hinged on the notion that Black Africans were somehow less 'civilized', indeed less human, than their white counterparts and that the ownership and full commodification of the Black body could be sanctioned.[2] This generated an ideology of white supremacy and Black inferiority that was developed and enforced in the most traumatic ways. According to the West Indian historian C. L. R. James:

> the conception of dividing people by race begins with the slave trade. This thing was so shocking, so opposed to all the conceptions of society which religion and philosophers and others had . . . that the only justification by which humanity could face it was to divide people into races and decide that the Africans were an inferior race. It is the beginning of the modern conception of people being divided into different races. It did not exist before. (James 2013: 127)

The Guyanese academic Walter Rodney makes a similar point in his classic text, *How Europe Underdeveloped Africa* (Rodney 1982 [1972]). First, he argues that it would be a mistake to think that European capitalists enslaved and exploited Africans for purely racist, as opposed to economic, reasons. African labour became necessary specifically because of the lack of alternatives, caused in particular by the genocide against Indigenous Americans. Second, he argues that once the basis of slavery had shifted to African labour, Europeans then 'found it necessary to rationalize that exploitation in racist terms as well. Oppression follows logically from exploitation, so as to guarantee the latter' (1982 [1972]: 89).

This 'rationalization' of racial superiority does not in any way mean that racism is simply an ideological construction or a mere accessory in the capitalist toolkit. Racism has real material origins and enduring, everyday consequences, even if the concept of 'race' itself is far more ambivalent. As the sociologists Robert Miles and Malcolm Brown point out (2003: 88–9), 'race' refers not to biological realities but to a 'process of signification whereby certain somatic characteristics are attributed with meaning and are used to organise populations into distinct groups that are defined as "races"'. This is very similar to Stuart Hall's celebrated description of 'race' as a 'floating signifier' and his notion that it is 'more like a language than it is like the way in which we are biologically constituted' (Hall 1997). This means that 'race' needs to be constantly renewed in specific historical circumstances and repeatedly amplified through a series of elite institutions (including the media).

For example, following the abolition of slavery, capitalists modified their justifications for racism in order to continue to benefit from its advantages. This saw the emergence of a 'pseudo-scientific racism' based on what were claimed to be the unequal biological and social characteristics of distinctive social groups (as opposed to the effective denial of any humanity to Black Africans that characterized racism during the slavery era). For Peter Fryer (1984: 165), racism was too 'valuable' a property for capitalist elites to be dispensed with and instead a 'new basis and new purpose for it had emerged. It was to become a principal handmaiden to empire.' The great African-American writer W. E. B. Du Bois was a harsh critic of 'organized capital' and notes that, following the end of the US Civil War, American bosses 'founded and retained' racism in order to ensure the 'subordination of colored labor to white profits the world over' (2013 [1935]: 29).[3] Speaking about what were described as 'race wars' in various American cities at the beginning of the twentieth century, Angela Davis argues that 'racial conflict did not emerge spontaneously but rather was consciously planned by the representatives of the economically ascendant class. They needed to impede working-class unity so as to facilitate their own exploitative designs' (Davis 1983: 73). Throughout history, therefore – from slavery to the identification of a 'new racism' towards the end of the twentieth century, based on cultural difference rather than biological inferiority (Gilroy 1987) – 'race' has been used as a divisive instrument on the part of capital. At the same time, it has had to be constantly resignified in order to maintain its relevance to capital, not least in the light of significant movements against racism itself. As such, it's important to focus on processes of 'racialization' rather than the definition of 'race' – in other words, the investment of meaning into the alleged characteristics of minority groups that is intimately related, if not reducible, to capitalism.

### Misogyny

Of course, there is one social group to whom this process applies that is not in a minority: women. Yet the same principle – of attributing specific characteristics to and establishing the status of a group in changing historical circumstances – can be seen here. Practices of gendering, therefore, have the same relationship to misogyny as racialization has to racism where the latter are the outcome of systematic classification and signification. It may appear as 'common sense' that fundamental differences between men and women account for the different ways in which they have been valued, regulated and represented, and yet these processes have a very specific genealogy.

Engels (1972 [1884]) provides an influential account of the roots of women's oppression by arguing that the formal equality of men and women in what he describes as early 'primitive communist' societies was broken apart by the creation of a surplus that was overseen by men. Women, for the first time, were punished for their role as mothers and relegated to the private domain while men organized and took control of the distribution of the surplus. Engels describes this as the '*world historical defeat of the female sex*. The man took command in the home also; the woman was degraded and reduced to servitude; she became the slave of his lust and a mere instrument for the production of children' (Engels 1972 [1884]: 120; emphasis in original). Women – as Black Africans were to suffer many years later – were turned into commodities, a situation that led to the first comprehensive form of oppression and to a structural antagonism between men and women that had not previously existed.

Capitalism, however, intensified this form of oppression in two main ways. First, given the opportunities for factory work at the start of the Industrial Revolution, it increased the pressure on women to act as both wage labourers and carers. 'Capitalism', argued the Russian revolutionary writer Alexandra Kollontai (1977: 252), 'has placed a crushing burden on woman's shoulders: it has made her a wage-worker without having reduced her cares as housekeeper or mother. Woman staggers beneath the weight of this triple load' (1977: 252) – a weight that has only grown heavier with the expanded numbers of women entering the workforce. As the feminist writer Sheila Rowbotham notes (1973: 56), there was by the middle of the nineteenth century 'a new demand for female labour in the factory, but somehow children had to be cared for, and families fed. Women were not able to turn this contradiction to their advantage. Instead, they were forced to labour both at home and at work.'

Second, it radically transformed the nature of the 'traditional' family unit by disconnecting social reproduction from the sphere of production. Where the two had previously been intimately connected – in the fields or in craft labour that took place in the home – capitalism instituted a sharp distinction between paid and unpaid work, privileging the former and devaluing the latter. According to Nancy Fraser, this involved the downgrading of women's status and the need to tell a new story about the role of the family: 'liberal-colonial capitalism elaborated a new gender imaginary of separate spheres. Figuring woman as "the angel in the home," its proponents sought to create stabilizing ballast for the volatility of the economy. The cutthroat world of production was to be flanked by a "haven in the heartless world"' (2022: 34). While this separation between paid labour and family life was experienced very differently by the poor and by racialized minorities as opposed to more privileged women, the implications of this break between production and reproduction has preoccupied both Marxist and feminist theorists.

For Federici, this break was the consequence of a new sexual division of labour that she argues was even more significant than the new industrial division of labour. It consigned women to second-class status – a situation that remains the case today – and effectively hides a major part of their contribution from public view. She writes that 'the economic importance of the reproduction of labor-power carried out in the home, and its function in the accumulation of capital, became invisible, being mystified as a natural vocation and labelled as "women's labor"' (Federici 2004: 75). Angela Davis, too, talks of a 'fundamental *structural* separation between the domestic home economy and the profit-oriented economy of capitalism' (1983: 131; emphasis in original). However, this was always a highly unstable and ideological process – not least because of women's increasing role in paid labour and the fact that this separation requires constant justification and normalization. Davis, for example, writes about the construction through 'popular propaganda' of the housewife in the nineteenth century in a situation in which 'sexism emerged as a source of outrageous super-profits for the capitalists' (1983: 131). For the feminist sociologist Lise Vogel, the structural separation of production and social reproduction is a vital weapon employed by capital to divide men and women, but one that is sustained through ideological work, even if this ideology 'takes a particularly stubborn institutional form' (Vogel 2013: 161).

Rather than seeing the sphere of social reproduction as materially separate from and counterposed to paid labour, I want to emphasize the extent to which it has *purposefully* been detached, devalued and hidden by capital with huge implications for the lives of women. Indeed, if we follow Fraser's argument that expropriation is the 'enabling condition' (2022: 16) of wage labour-based exploitation, then we can identify both the underlying interconnections between the two spheres and the significant ideological work required to rationalize and hide this separation. This reflects the point made in chapter 1 that capitalism actively seeks to obscure the conditions of its own reproduction – to fragment social relations that are, in reality, fundamentally intertwined – and to deploy a range of techniques and institutions to reinforce the logic of divisions that work in its interest. This means that, as Ferguson and McNally put it:

> While the family is fundamental to women's oppression in capitalism, the pivot of this oppression is not women's domestic labour for men or children, however oppressive or alienating this might be. Rather it pivots on the social significance of domestic labour for capital – the fact

that the production and reproduction of labour-power is an essential condition undergirding the dynamic of the capitalist system, making it possible for capitalism to reproduce itself. (Ferguson and McNally 2013: xxv)

This condition provides the material base for the very real misogyny, sexual violence and discrimination that continues to be attached to the diminution of women's roles in a capitalist society.

These two examples – of the oppression of women and people of colour – reveal how capitalism has weaponized differences between social groups in order to serve its own purposes. Yet the great irony is that for all that capitalism relies on and fetishizes division, it simultaneously provides the basis of unity if oppression is understood not just as a discrete form of harm but as a *structural* element of the reproduction of the status quo. Kimberlé Crenshaw, who is credited with developing the concept of intersectionality, has written eloquently about how the Black women she studied in US anti-discrimination cases don't experience racism and misogyny in an atomized fashion but instead are 'multiply-burdened' (Crenshaw 1989: 140). She calls for 'bottom-up approaches' to the law, which 'combine all discriminatees in order to challenge an entire employment system' (1989: 145). The goal of an intersectional approach, she concludes, 'should be to facilitate the inclusion of marginalized groups for whom it can be said: "When they enter, we all enter"' (1989: 167).

All too often, however, this structural approach founders on a desire to focus on one oppression at a time without looking to systemic causes. Crenshaw herself has criticized what she sees as a descriptive approach, where intersectionality is reduced to 'just multiplying identity categories rather than constituting a structural analysis or a political critique' (quoted in Guidroz and Berger 2009: 70). The intersection which all oppressed groups have to navigate is class which can not only act as a source of integration but also points to the system's vulnerability in terms of its ultimate orientation and dependence on exploitation, accumulation and the defence of private property. This is certainly not meant to downplay the very real harms, inequalities and injustices faced by oppressed groups but to identify the mutual interests of those defined by their class position. As Rhian Jones (2014) has argued: 'The problems of the "ordinary" working class are inherently intersectional: material disadvantage amplifies, and is amplified by, racism, sexism, homophobia, and ageism, all experienced as real and immediate issues enforced by existing structures of power.'

Meanwhile, across all forms of oppression, what should be seen as inconsequential distinctions (at least in relation to their status in society, not in relation to the actual experiences of the members of an oppressed group) are instrumentalized and amplified through a series of legal, political and ideological processes presided over by capitalist interests. Oppression, therefore, provides the powerful with a material resource to reproduce unequal social relations and simultaneously requires the constant renewal and modification of this resource to adapt to specific historical circumstances. It is here – in the justification for and resignification of oppression – that media have long played such a central role.

## Reproducing division

Marx noticed this over 150 years ago when writing about tensions between English and Irish workers and their propensity to identify not with each other across class lines but with their own national interests. 'This antagonism is artificially kept alive and intensified by the press, the pulpit, the comic papers, in short, by all the means at the disposal of the ruling classes . . . It is the secret by which the capitalist class maintains its power. And the latter is quite aware of this' (Marx 1870).

This is an explicit recognition of the benefit for the powerful of both fomenting and reproducing division – a practice that requires the circulation of harmful narratives about oppressed groups. From newspapers in the southern states of the United States that reported on lynchings of African Americans as street theatre through to the anti-Semitic propaganda films of the Third Reich that sought to glorify and energize an 'Aryan race'; from portraying women as compliant and domesticated appendages of male breadwinners in 1950s television ads to the virtual invisibility of older people in contemporary commercial film and video; and from the barrage of headlines in UK tabloid newspapers portraying asylum seekers as either criminals or benefit scroungers (or both) to the historic representation of Muslims in the West as bombmakers and religious zealots, stereotyping, vilification, distortion, marginalization and misrepresentation of (mostly) minority social groups are common ways in which primary definers attempt to assert their superiority and cement their control.

Perhaps the most influential account of this process is Edward Said's work on Orientalism, a historical account of western cultural representation mainly of the Arab world or, as he puts it, an analysis of the 'Western style for dominating, restructuring and having authority over the Orient' (Said 1979: 3). This refers to the ways in which entire populations have been *animated* by, for example, western poets, writers, filmmakers, artists and historians, who are able to make the Orient 'speak' but only in their own image. Talking about the French novelist Flaubert's meeting with an Egyptian courtesan, Said notes that 'she never spoke of herself, she never represented her emotions, presence or history. *He* spoke for her and represented her' (1979: 6).

Orientalism works through a form of Gramscian 'common sense' that aims to naturalize particular ways of thinking about 'others' that stems from material divisions and real inequalities of power. Far from being a conspiratorial project devised in palaces and parliaments, it is the routine cultural expression of imperial domination and a powerful means of producing the 'other' as different and inferior. In order to delegitimize, diminish and control its subjects, the latter are portrayed as subservient or dangerous, childish or violent, naive or threatening. Said emphasizes the point that Orientalism reveals relatively little about the identity of this 'other' and much more about the ideological frameworks and political objectives of those who seek to define and dominate them: it has 'less to do with the Orient than it does with "our" world' (Said 1979: 12). Nevertheless, it provides western interests with an intellectual framework that underpins the brutal realities of occupation and domination.

Said deploys this approach in his later book on *Covering Islam* (Said 1997), in which he assesses the flaws and biases in mainstream western journalism on the Middle East.

> It is only a slight overstatement to say that Muslims and Arabs are essentially covered, discussed, apprehended, either as oil suppliers or as potential terrorists. Very little of the detail, the human density, the passion of Arab-Muslim life has entered the awareness of even those people whose profession it is to report the Islamic world. What we have instead is a limited series of crude, essentialized caricatures of the Islamic world presented in such a way as, among other things, to make that world vulnerable to military aggression. (Said 1997: 28)

This chimes with the analysis I proposed in chapter 8 where 'impartial' reporting of the atrocities in Gaza has often assisted in consolidating the strategic assumptions of the Israeli state in relation both to its right to self-defence and to its treatment of Palestinians as a dehumanized minority. It also echoes the findings of a report into UK mainstream media coverage of Muslims produced by the Centre for Media Monitoring (Hanif 2021). The report argues that the media bear a particular responsibility for normalizing Islamophobia and perpetuating the idea that Muslims constitute a separate social group that is hostile to the 'Indigenous' majority. The CfMM examined dozens of online news outlets and found that some 60% of articles mentioning Muslims identified them with negative behaviour, such as terrorism and extremism – a number that dropped to 47% on the more tightly regulated broadcast news media. Of these pieces, 14% were assessed as 'biased' or 'very biased' against and 21% as 'antagonistic' to Muslims (Hanif 2021: 30–1). More than one in five articles specifically associated Muslims with terrorism and extremism, while narratives linking Muslims with anti-Semitism and feudal behaviour were widespread. The report concludes that 'a large section of the media still favours voices that echo colonial era tropes which see Muslims as dangerous fanatics, terrorists and misogynists while giving preference to voices which regurgitate these tropes' (2021: 283). The circulation of these tropes across the media has 'mainstreamed' these ideas, pushed political discourse to the right and emboldened far-right actors who wish to scapegoat Muslims for existing social problems (Mondon and Winter 2020).

This kind of analysis – where media intensify the antagonism towards specific social groups whether they be Muslims, LGBTQ people or other minorities – is especially useful in pointing out the potential links between the 'othering' of such groups and wider discriminatory practices against them, for example higher rates of 'stop and search' against young Black men or the enduring pay gap between women and men. Media in a capitalist society are always likely to reinforce the unequal status of oppressed groups because, as embodiments of capital, they are fully beholden to the imperatives I have attempted to map out throughout this book – their adherence to, for example, private property, commodification and accumulation that foster division and inequality. Yet, as I have also argued, capitalism is a constantly changing and highly volatile system, shaped by technological innovation, its own internal contradictions (as I outline in chapter 14) and resistance to its exploitative and oppressive conditions. Representations of oppressed groups, therefore, are never frozen in time and instead are always historically contingent and regularly contested.

This takes us back to Said's powerful but sweeping condemnation of western domination of the Orient. Aijaz Ahmad, in a sympathetic but also fiercely critical analysis of *Orientalism*, accuses Said of overgeneralizing the Orientalist project and underplaying the tensions within 'the West'; in other words, that he treats the Occident in the same crude way that he accuses the Occident of treating the Orient. 'Said quite justifiably accuses the "Orientalist" of essentializing the Orient, but his own essentializing of "the West" is equally remarkable' (Ahmad 1994: 183). Ahmad argues that Said conceives of the West as 'unified, self-identical, transhistorical, textual' (1994: 183), despite the very different political histories and social struggles that pertain to its constituent elements. Indeed, just as Said makes it clear that Orientalism doesn't correspond to a 'real' Orient,[4] Ahmad questions why he appears to perpetuate the notion that there is a 'real', singular and unchanging Occident – an approach that flattens the very real tensions inside western societies.

The implication of this is that media representations of all oppressed groups – not just those related to Arabs and Muslims with which Said is particularly preoccupied – need to be grasped in relation to their specific historical contexts and to the media's intersections with other social forces. For example, the representation of women in British media has undergone a dramatic shift since the start of the Industrial Revolution when, as James Curran notes, 'a new generation of middle-class women's magazines . . . sought to professionalize home-making by offering a flow of advice about domestic management, followed subsequently by tips about how to be beautiful' (2002b: 139). Changes in the labour market, the prevalence of women's struggles for equality and the needs of the economy at any one time helped to shift representations of women so that by the Second World War, for example, images of female workers liberated from purely domestic roles were increasingly common. In the post-war period, there was a renewed emphasis on the woman as the pillar of the private family unit. Yet the gradual increase in women's participation in the workforce saw a further transformation of their representation, even if there remained some stark continuities related to the underlying commodification of the female body: 'bikini-clad women adorning the bonnets of cars in 1960s press advertisements gave way to poised, confident women behind the wheel in some 1990s television car commercials. These were but some of the ways in which the media responded to the increased economic power and prestige of women' (Curran 2002b: 140).

Catherine Rottenberg provides further evidence of both continuities and discontinuities in the portrayal of women. She analyses a form of feminism in the early twenty-first century that chimes with the disciplines of neoliberal capitalism and explores how 'this new and increasingly popular form of feminism has been curiously and unsettlingly unmoored from those key terms of equality, justice and emancipation that have informed women's movements and feminism since their inception' (Rottenberg 2018: 11). Based on critiques of 'mommy blogs', programmes like *The Good Wife* (2009–16) and bestselling 'feminist' books, such as Ivanka Trump's *Women Who Work* (2017) and Sheryl Sandberg's *Lean In* (2013), she argues that these texts all privilege women's search for 'a felicitous work–family balance based on a cost–benefit calculus' (2018: 55). Mainstream media are key vehicles in promoting this kind of 'neoliberal feminism', which expresses the simultaneous desire for women's autonomy and its seamless incorporation into contemporary capitalist priorities. Similarly, Sarah Banet-Weiser highlights contemporary advertising and marketing campaigns that draw on and reinforce a 'market for feminism' (2018: 13). Her book, *Empowered*, focuses in particular on a depoliticized and entrepreneurial 'popular feminism' that has shifted from a political demand for representation and rights to an 'economy of visibility' in which 'visibility becomes *the end* rather than a means to an end' (2018: 23).

We can see many of the same tensions being explored more recently with a plethora of blogs, TikTok videos and YouTube content produced by women that cultivate the desire for a return to traditional domestic roles while not entirely giving up work. Women like Gwen the Milkmaid and Hannah Neeleman, @Ballerinafarm, who lives on a huge estate and makes money by selling protein powder to her millions of Instagram followers while taking care of her eight children, are two examples of the 'tradwives' who reject their feminist histories and project right-wing positions on reproductive rights and politics more generally. Although not exactly a homogeneous movement, through their promotion of pro-Christian, pro-consumerist, pro-nuclear family and pro-conservative values, tradwives, according to Sykes and Hopner (2024: 480), fit the Trump moment: they 'replicate and contribute to wider societal conversations about the role of the government in economic markets and labor relationships'.

The tradwives phenomenon is a useful reminder that analysis of the media's role in publicizing and attempting to normalize specific gender roles – or indeed the meanings attached to any minoritized group – needs to extend beyond representation and into broader practices of media-making and the dynamics of the media industries more generally. For example, while acknowledging the substantial impact of negative media representations on people of colour, Anamik Saha switches the question 'from how cultural industries *represent* race, to how cultural industries *make* race' (2018: 11). In highlighting the racialization of the cultural commodity, Saha explores the conditions under which traditional racialized stereotypes are often perpetuated by media, but his approach also allows at least some room for messy challenges to these stereotypes. As with many examples of 'othering', this is neither a seamless nor a predictable process but one shaped by relentless capitalist imperatives, historical shifts, political aspirations, popular resistance and the sheer weight of ideological pressure which, for Saha, helps to explain 'the content churn of racialized, Orientalist representations of racial and ethnic groups' (2018: 173).

Returning to the example with which I started the chapter in order further to illustrate the process of racialization, it could be argued that the media's iconography of slaves coincided with the actual role of the press in organizing and facilitating the slave trade itself. In a fascinating and horrifying piece of research, DasSarma and Fisher analysed over a thousand advertisements in eighteenth-century US newspapers related to the capture and sale of enslaved people. They suggest that the press played a key part both in articulating how colonists conceived of the institution of slavery and of slaves themselves and in policing the trade as a whole. They note the 'central role the newspaper industry played in nascent systems of surveillance over people of colour, including enslaved and unfree Indigenous men and women. Newspaper advertisements turned reading (largely white) citizens into self-appointed slave patrollers who felt empowered and financially incentivized to maintain slave hierarchies by identifying and turning in self-emancipated Native and African people' (DasSarma and Fisher 2023: 270–1).

This was an important part of a process of racialization, in which, in response to legal changes, slave owners were forced to change the ways in which they talked about enslaved people and to 're-race' them in order to abide by the law. Newspapers thus both shaped the public understanding of 'race' but also were handsomely rewarded for their role in sustaining the trade itself. The authors conclude by noting 'the newspaper industry's deeply complicit role in sustaining slavery and turning citizens into "slave catchers" – all while pocketing a profit' (2023: 286).

## Conclusion

Instead of representing different social groups to themselves and to others in order to generate mutual recognition and collective rights, mainstream media have all too often reproduced a culture of division. Through their use of stereotyping or simply marginalizing minority groups, the media have been implicated in active processes of, for example, racialization and gendering that connect to and reinforce the dominant economic and ideological consensus at any particular moment in time. This isn't a static or frictionless process, given that struggles for recognition by those groups are bound to shift prevailing norms. However, the examples given in this chapter are a powerful illustration of the broader embedding of culture within capitalist logics of oppression and a reminder of the media's contribution to sustaining a very old and very destructive political strategy: to divide and rule.

# 13
# Nature and Environment

***Overview*** Capitalism involves the domination and exploitation of nature in order to increase productivity and maximize profit. This chapter addresses the costs of these imperatives in the shape of an escalating climate crisis and considers the role of media and communications in exacerbating this crisis in two ways. First, it highlights the superficial and individualistic framing of climate change journalism and second, it notes the rapid increase of 'digital rubbish', as well as the environmental cost of an AI boom fuelled by a huge demand for energy.

## The 'metabolic rift' with the Earth

Where does responsibility for the rapid and unsustainable warming of the planet lie? With individual consumers whose appetite for cars, meat and flying has intensified climate change? With governments whose reticence to rein in consumption and whose refusal to switch to and invest in renewable energy sources with sufficient speed means that we are highly unlikely to meet internationally agreed targets for emissions reductions? With individual corporations (not least technology companies) whose enormous energy requirements mean that they continue to pollute the physical environment in their pursuit of profits and dividends? Or with right-wing politicians who insist, in the face of overwhelming scientific consensus, that climate irregularities are a long-standing feature of the planet's ecological history? There may be a grain of truth in each of the above attributions of blame, but what they lack is a systemic orientation – a narrative thread that locates this self-destructive behaviour in relation to wider social forces. By focusing solely on individual motivations, lifestyle choices and fringe political positions, the role of an overarching and coordinating force – in this case, capitalism – is minimized and deflected.

Capitalism is, indeed, at the heart of the environmental crisis. The Industrial Revolution was fuelled by the coal that continues to spew out $CO_2$ emissions; colonialism expanded the brutal extraction of natural resources without any thought of sustainability; military conflicts between imperialist rivals have long been a major source of greenhouse gas emissions; neoliberalism intensified the drive for profits, whatever the cost to nature, while simultaneously cultivating a climate denial industry of think tanks and astroturf campaigns. Climate change is not simply anthropogenic – the result of specifically human activities – but intimately related to the needs and imperatives of capital. According to Carbon Majors (2024: 13), more than 70% of $CO_2$ emissions (which themselves account for 80% of all emissions) have historically been generated by just 78 industrial producers, including not only private companies like Chevron, ExxonMobil and BP but also state groups like Saudi Aramco, GazProm and the National Iranian Oil Company. And the situation is getting worse: the period between 2016 and 2022 alone generated 12.2% of all global emissions since 1751, but in only 2.6% of the time, while six of the ten highest emissions years on record occurred *after* the Paris Agreement on emissions reductions that was adopted in 2015 (2024: 13). The geographer Matthew Huber argues that, because of the role of the industrial sector in generating the products used by all other sectors, 'industrial emissions are the *foundation* of all other emissions' (2022: 62); for Huber, therefore, capitalist production 'is the core metabolic force causing the climate crisis' (2022: 64).

At the heart of this crisis is the undoing of a sustainable and reciprocal relationship between humans and nature. In its early days, proponents of capitalism – energized by a post-Enlightenment belief in the possibility of science and progress – argued that the Industrial Revolution promised potential liberation from the vagaries and catastrophes of the natural world. As Naomi Klein puts it in *This Changes Everything: Capitalism vs the Climate* (2014: 174), 'The harnessing of fossil fuel power seemed, for a couple of centuries at least, to have freed large parts of humanity from the need to be in constant dialogue with nature, having to adjust its plans, ambitions and schedules to natural fluctuations and topographies.' Humans could, for the first time, use technology to assert control of their destinies and not be passive victims of the idiosyncrasies of weather and climate. The idea of being helpless in the face of tsunamis, hurricanes and drought was to be replaced by human domination of the natural world based, in large part, on the use of fossil fuels to make things, stay warm (or cool) and travel to and from work. Yet, precisely because capitalism fostered neither reciprocity nor sustainability in its relation to the natural world, we are now facing the terrible consequences of climate change: 'the cumulative effect of those centuries of burned carbon is in the process of unleashing the most ferocious natural tempers of all' (Klein 2014: 175).

Marx was one of the first writers to highlight the delicate and dialectical relationship between humans and nature in relation to the act of labour. He describes labour as, above all, 'a process by which man, through his own actions, mediates, regulates and controls the metabolism between himself and nature' (1977 [1867]: 283). This is a kind of double movement in that the worker both 'acts upon external nature and changes it, and in this way he simultaneously changes his own nature' (1977 [1867]: 283). The problem is that capitalism – with its insatiable appetite for accumulation – upsets this balance and separates humans from the natural world. Marx talks about how the 'blind desire for profit' has 'exhausted the soil' (1977 [1867]: 348) and how, as a result of intense and unplanned urbaniza- tion, capitalism upsets 'the metabolic interaction between man and the earth' and 'hinders the operation of the eternal natural condition for the lasting fertility of the soil' (1977 [1867]: 637).[1] It is not only the worker who suffers at the hands of capitalism's determination to exploit everything in its scope but the soil and the land which are robbed of their fertility and their value. That Marx makes this argu- ment in *Capital* should perhaps come as little surprise, given that 20 years earlier one of the key demands of the *Communist Manifesto* was 'the bringing into cultivation of waste lands, and the improvement of the soil generally in accordance with a common plan' (Marx and Engels 1973 [1848]: 60).

Marx's belief that capitalism was responsible for a fundamental separation between labour and nature – resonant of the argument in the previous chapter that capitalism also fostered a decisive break between production and social reproduction – highlights the fact that, in a system dominated by commodity exchange, humans are alienated both from their own labour power *and* from the natural world. Nature becomes an asset to be exploited rather than an envi- ronment to be nurtured, and any former organic connection to nature needs to be nullified – or at least fully mediated by capital. Raymond Williams (1980) suggests that capitalism has instrumentalized nature by mining it for its market value rather than appreciating its intrinsic properties.[2] Using the language of improvement, domination and control, capitalism transformed the very idea of nature and placed it at a distance from human endeavour: 'now nature, increasingly, was "out there", and it was natural to reshape it to a dominant need, without having to consider very deeply what this reshaping might do to men' (1980: 79). For Williams, this transformation of nature was not only dangerous and counter-productive but also effectively 'unnatural', given that humans have long 'mixed our labour with the earth, our forces with its forces too deeply to be able to draw back and separate either out' (1980: 83). Yet such was capitalism's power that it was indeed able to break this bond, to subjugate nature as it was able to exploit labour, and to create, as John Bellamy Foster famously describes it following Marx, 'a metabolic rift between human beings and the soil' (Foster 1999: 383).

Foster provides a staunch defence of Marx's perspective on ecological issues and his promotion of a 'historical–environmental materialism that took into account the coevolution of nature and human society' (1999: 373). By the time Marx started on *Capital*, Foster suggests that he was already deeply concerned about the application of 'modern' techniques – for example, the widespread use of fertilizers – that might stimulate short-term yields but also cause long-term damage to the soil. Technology which *might* have been used to protect the land was instead used further to corrupt it. This was by no means an argument against technology per se but simply about its deployment exclusively for capitalist development: 'Marx had become convinced of the contradictory and unsustainable nature of capitalist agriculture' as a result of the 'depletion of the natural fertility of the soil, which was in no way alleviated, but rather given impetus by the breakthroughs in soil science' (Foster 1999: 376). Foster also notes that Marx wasn't only interested in the exhaustion of the soil but also about the destruction of forests, the squandering of energy reserves and the polluting impact of coal – all of which were the logical properties of an economic system that treated 'society' and 'nature' as wholly distinct realms.

Indeed, coal was a decisive driver of the Industrial Revolution, and while its use was already well established in Britain, the invention by James Watt of the steam engine in 1776 – the same year in which Adam Smith's *Wealth of Nations* was published – transformed its possibilities and generated the opportunity to fuel not just an isolated cottage but an entire economy.[3] This gave rise to what Andreas Malm has called 'fossil capital' – defined as a 'self-expanding value passing through the metamorphosis of fossil fuels into $CO_2$' (Malm 2013: 52)

– that promised both a new relationship between capital, labour and nature as well as a 'revolutionary' industrial and economic process. Malm discusses the reasons why British industry turned from water, which up to that point had been its main source of energy, to steam, with all the environmental problems that were to follow. He makes it clear that this was a class project in which questions of sustainability were secondary: 'Water power was a barrier that had to be knocked down for the fossil economy to emerge' (2013: 19). In place of a technology that was subject to the irregular availability of its core resource, coal-powered steam offered predictability, control and – above all – 'superior power over labour' (2013: 44). While water was, for obvious reasons, closer to natural cycles, the use of steam further separated individual producers from nature and entrenched the command of capitalists over the labour power of workers. Malm argues that this is an important lesson for today: that the world *could* run on renewable energy – the natural resources of wind, sun and water – but this would conflict with the systemic privileging for capital of reliability and productivity over sustainability.

Capitalism, therefore, needs to be placed at the very centre of public discussion and actions in relation to stopping climate change. This is the motivation for Jason Moore's argument that we need to describe the current geological era not as the 'Anthropocene' but the 'Capitalocene', understood as a 'world-ecology of capital, power, and nature' (Moore 2016: xi) if we are fully to grasp capital's destructive impact on the environment. Yet this is also recognized by pro-market voices who both acknowledge that the origins of climate change lie in the development of capitalism and simultaneously assert that capitalism can also furnish the solutions to impending environmental disaster. For example, Newell and Paterson speak of the emergence of a 'climate capitalism' – 'a model which squares capitalism's need for continual economic growth with substantial shifts away from carbon-based industrial development' (2010: 1) – that is increasingly evident in relation to the carbon markets and emissions trading that is flourishing today. Meanwhile, the US environmentalist Bill McKibben argues that while markets may have been the problem, they are also, pragmatically, going to have to be the solution: 'Greed has helped destroy the planet – maybe now it can help save it' (McKibben 2008). McKibben suggests drawing on the same imperatives of accumulation and exchange that made pollution an externality apparently worth bearing – including auctioning off carbon permits and driving up the cost of fossil fuels in order to disincentivize their use.

The *New York Times* columnist Thomas Friedman provides a particularly fulsome account of how capitalism can ride to the rescue with a 'green revolution' in his book, *Hot, Flat and Crowded* (Friedman 2009). According to Friedman, capitalism had no grand plan in its initial approach to the environment; instead, there was the haphazard emergence in the eighteenth century of what he describes as a 'dirty fuels system', characterized by the wasteful use of fossil fuels and the unsustainably intensive exploitation of natural resources. This was a generally efficient way of powering the economy, but its overuse means that a different, cleaner market-led strategy is now required, although one that still draws on capitalism's history of innovation and dynamism. 'Only the market can generate and allocate capital fast enough and efficiently enough to get 10,000 inventors working in 10,000 companies and 10,000 garages and 10,000 laboratories to drive transformation breakthroughs; only the market can then commercialize the best of them and improve on the existing ones at the scope, speed and scale we need' (2009: 244).

Friedman concludes by calling for a wholesale green capitalist transformation of the US economy, even if one with deeply colonial implications: 'We are all Pilgrims again. We are all sailing on the *Mayflower* anew. We have not been to this shore before' (2009: 412). Considering how colonized people were some of the first to suffer from the environmental damage caused by capitalism and that the impact of climate change is very unequally distributed – most severely affecting populations in some of the poorest countries on the planet (Barca 2024) – Friedman's choice of language is particularly revealing about who is likely to pay the price for a market-led green restructuring of the economy.

Pro-market solutions to a climate crisis caused by market fundamentalism are not only implausible but, additionally, seek to place the burden for mitigating the climate crisis away from corporations and systems and onto individuals. For example, the whole premise of carbon footprint accounting is to provide atomized consumers with a quantitative metric of their emissions in order to persuade them to reduce their carbon-producing activities: to drive a smaller car, to eat less meat and to take fewer international holidays (unless they travel by train). The suggestion here is that individual lifestyle choices and not systemic economic imperatives are to blame – or at least that they are easier to shift. This is what Naomi Klein refers to as the ecological strategy of focusing on 'low-hanging fruit', given that 'it's hard and expensive to try to convince politicians to regulate and discipline the most powerful corporations in the world' (Klein

2014: 200). Yet the problem lies not only in the difficulty of targeting corporations but also in individualizing the problem itself. Matthew Huber (2022) points out that while the sphere of social reproduction is often forgotten in broader discussions of where power lies in society, it appears, in popular discourse at least, to be the sphere that matters the most when it comes to addressing carbon footprints and reducing emissions. Huber argues that carbon footprint analysis is deeply shaped by neoclassical economics and attached to a notion of consumer sovereignty rather than producer control. By fetishizing individual consumption, we underestimate the extent to which capitalist investment decisions shape consumption choices and prioritize not what is sustainable but most profitable. The key question, according to Huber (2022: 13), is: 'Who do we believe has real *power* over society's economic resources? Consumer sovereignty theory suggests power is diffuse and scattered among individual consumers. But, in fact, power over the economy is not diffuse, but concentrated in the hands of those who control productive resources.'

Huber proposes a response to climate change that focuses not on individual lifestyle decisions – which, in any case, unhelpfully assumes that all consumers are equally able to change their consumption patterns despite huge economic disparities across populations – but capital's outsized share of emissions. This means an orientation on capitalism's major institutional polluters: the energy companies primarily responsible for the burning of fossil fuels but also those data centres, factories, mines, shopping malls and transport networks whose appetite for fossil-based profits remains undiminished, despite claims to the contrary. It means rejecting the idea that the near exhaustion of the planet's natural resources was an unexpected outcome of centuries of capitalist development and innovation – just an 'externality' that can be mitigated with yet more capitalist development and innovation. Market mechanisms cannot rescue society from a problem for which they are responsible. As Mark Fisher writes: 'The relationship between capitalism and eco-disaster is neither coincidental nor accidental; capitalism's "need of a constantly expanding market", its "growth fetish", mean that capitalism is by its very nature opposed to any notion of sustainability' (Fisher 2009: 18–19). Repairing the environment, therefore, should be seen as a collective endeavour that is aimed at the transformation of the operating system that generated the damage in the first place.

## Media contamination: framing and polluting the environment

To what extent are the media implicated in reproducing or challenging existing environmental norms? In what ways have communication flows improved or further polluted our physical and symbolic landscapes? I want to highlight two areas: the media's recent framing of climate crisis and their environmental cost, including their dependence on dirty energy sources and their generation of 'digital rubbish' (Gabrys 2011), the material build-up of discarded and obsolete electronic devices.

For many years, mainstream media outlets were complicit in fostering largely trivial narratives about climate and environment that provided snapshots of extreme weather events without systematically exploring their causes and consequences. For example, in a traditionally rainy United Kingdom, hot weather has long been greeted with front-page pictures of crowded beaches, sunbathers and children eating ice creams; in the United States, news bulletins covered tornadoes and hurricanes as they happened, often providing useful information about escape routes for local communities but rarely displaying a curiosity as to *why* they might be happening with increasing ferocity and regularity. Coverage largely echoed the ahistorical, fragmented and descriptive tendencies of commodified news systems. A study by Media Matters found that of 127 stories on network news covering the 2017 heatwave in the United States, only one referred to climate change; Media Matters also researched television coverage of Hurricane Harvey the same year and found that two of the main news networks, ABC and NBC, failed to mention climate change at all in their reports (Al Jazeera 2018). In Ireland, there was scarcely any coverage of climate change in its leading national newspaper, with the *Irish Times* devoting just 0.84 per cent of coverage to the issue between 1997 and 2010, well below European norms (Robbins 2015).

Given that the ten warmest years in historical records have all occurred in the past decade (Lindsey and Dahlman 2025), there has been, perhaps not surprisingly, a change in the volume and seriousness of climate news. Wang and Downey studied the coverage of heatwaves in six countries and identified a 'tipping point' in 2018, a year marked by extreme heat in Europe, South Asia, North America and Japan. They found evidence of 'a growing international consensus in mainstream newspapers at least with respect to the existence and consequences of climate change if not policies to tackle climate change' (Wang and Downey 2024: 14). Others remain less sanguine:

Batziou (2022: 689) studied UK newspaper coverage of the 2018 heatwave and found that 87 per cent of articles treated it as an isolated phenomenon that was 'unlinked to the issue of climate change'. A further study found that the word 'cake' was referred to ten times as often on UK television in 2020 than the phrase 'climate change', and that there were more references to banana bread than there were to wind power and solar power combined (Carrington 2021). The research concluded that 'individual action, such as recycling, was far more frequently featured than issues that are much bigger drivers of the climate crisis such as energy and transport.'

Indeed, there is some evidence that, in some places, coverage is deteriorating. Analysis by Media Matters found that US broadcast coverage of Earth Day has steadily declined since 2022, and that 'segments promoting lifestyle changes, product swaps, and green shopping tips often displaced deeper analysis of structural drivers of climate change or systemic accountability' (Cooper 2025a). A further study (Cooper 2025b) revealed that despite 2024 being a year with 27 billion-dollar major weather events, there was a 25 per cent decline in broadcast television coverage of climate issues. Only 9 per cent of climate-related stories even mentioned 'fossil fuels', while the most frequently cited climate impact concerned economic disruption and insurance costs, well above the consequences for public health and the natural environment. As expressed in the election in 2024 of Donald Trump as US president for the second time, a political backlash that is hostile to the very notion of systemic climate change would appear to have had a significant impact on the willingness of key media outlets routinely to cover major weather events in a joined-up way, to acknowledge the impact of a rapidly warming planet and to call for meaningful preventative measures such as the pursuit of net-zero emissions and implementation of the Paris Agreement at the very minimum. This has contributed to the mainstreaming of climate misinformation and disinformation; climate denialism and climate delayism are not problems confined exclusively to social media platforms[4] but are reproduced in mainstream news. Indeed, one study found that climate disinformation 'was routinely broadcast in news programmes across French TV and radio in the first three months of 2025' (Grostern 2025), with nearly 400 'discourses of delay', aimed at discrediting proponents of net zero, evident in French news broadcasts.

Donald Trump's shadow is all over Hannah Morris's book on climate journalism, which examines US media coverage of key environmental battles between 2015 and 2023, including the Dakota

Access Pipeline protests in 2016 and the movement for a Green New Deal. In the face of a growing 'apocalyptic authoritarianism' that denigrates environmental activists and celebrates climate deniers, Morris finds that journalists are rarely able to convey the complexities of climate change and instead fall back on tried and tested routines of liberal journalism. 'For example', she argues (Morris 2025: 12), 'the claim that "fairness" and "balance" in reporting are key for a thriving democracy is made suspect when fossil fuel industry-backed climate deniers were for decades given equal access and attention in news reports along with climate scientists in the name of journalistic professionalism and objectivity.' This is evident even in public service journalism, where the BBC acknowledged back in 2011 that climate change deniers, who were marginal to the growing scientific consensus on climate change, were afforded unprecedented and unnecessary levels of coverage because of an 'over-diligent search for due impartiality – or for a controversy' (BBC 2011: 72). Seven years later, the Corporation admitted that it was still getting it 'wrong too often', telling its staff in a leaked briefing note that '[y]ou do not need a "denier" to balance the debate' (Carrington 2018).

Back in the United States, Morris argues that a typical journalistic response to the need to address climate issues is to celebrate the role of the 'visionary sage', the technocrat (mostly older white men like the internet pioneer Stewart Brand and Amazon owner Jeff Bezos) who is 'represented as a God-like genius in possession of an unmatched ability to bring *back* national and climatic stability through all-encompassing "fixes" of the sage's own design' (Morris 2025: 2). This is an example, drawing on Stuart Hall and colleagues' earlier work (1978), of the media's role in attempting to 'police' the climate crisis in such a way as to deflect attention from the source of the problem, to control the mitigation strategies and to dismiss those who are seeking collective solutions. Like many of the pro-market strategies described earlier in the chapter, much of the media coverage on the climate continues to minimize, monetize and individualize a problem that is intimately associated with capitalism's fetish for unplanned and unrestricted accumulation.

The problem, however, runs far deeper than distorted framing and rampant disinformation. While mainstream media have long been accused of polluting the information environment, communications infrastructures and technologies are polluting the physical environment. Far from being intangible and immaterial, communication technologies draw on a vast network of energy sources, extracted minerals and physical components, many of which are routinely discarded at great cost to the planet. When Nancy Fraser (2022: 83) talks of capitalism as 'a cannibalistic, extractive relation which consumes ever more biophysical wealth in order to pile up ever more "value" while disavowing ecological "externalities"', she could easily be describing a social media universe whose material footprint is too often overlooked. For example, the annual carbon footprint of TikTok is reckoned to be larger than that of the whole of Greece (O'Brien 2024), while YouTube's annual streaming emissions amount to the equivalent of 32.5 million flights from Paris to New York or the total annual emissions of some two million UK residents (Greenly 2025). Meanwhile, every iPhone contains dozens of chemicals and rare metals – such as lithium for the battery, yttrium for the screen and neodymium for the speaker – that have to be sourced, extracted and shipped to Apple's giant factories in China and India. Personal consumption plays a tiny role in emissions as compared to the carbon-intensive manufacturing phase that is constantly stepped up simply because consumers are encouraged to upgrade their phones on a regular basis.

Maxwell and Miller (2012) open their prescient book *Greening the Media* by noting 'the myriad ways that media technology consumes, despoils and wastes natural resources' (2012: 1). They argue that corporate greed seeks to naturalize a routine obsolescence that has potentially lethal consequences for the planet and highlight the materiality of media infrastructures and technologies that are often seen as enchanting (or 'sublime') rather than as harmful and polluting. Similarly, Gabrys, in *Digital Rubbish*, suggests that obsolescence is built into the business model of producing digital devices that are 'programmed for failure. These machines are self-propagating and self-obsolescing' (2011: 115) – a claim that was found to be true when, in 2017, Apple admitted to using software updates to slow down their phones and drive consumers towards a newer model (BBC 2017). At the same time as artificially stimulating demand for hardware before it reaches the end of its 'useful' life, there is little consideration of the ecological implications of generating some 62 million tons of e-waste a year, less than a quarter of which is recycled (Sandhu 2025). The vast majority of discarded tech goes into landfill or is stripped down further, potentially exposing 'workers and ecosystems to a morass of toxic components' (Maxwell and Miller 2012: 3).

This situation is likely to get worse with the roll-out of artificial intelligence that requires enormous amounts of energy to power its computers and cool its data centres. The typical AI-focused data centre consumes as much electricity as 100,000 households, although the largest ones account for the equivalent consumption of two million households – with the largest announced, although not yet built at the time of writing, set to consume the same as *five million* households (International Energy Agency 2025: 38). Data centres currently account for approximately 1.5 per cent of world electricity consumption but this is expected to double by 2030 when the United States, for example, is expected 'to consume more electricity for data centres than for the production of aluminium, steel, cement, chemicals and all other energy-intensive goods combined' (2025: 14). Given that these sectors are already the drivers of unsustainable levels of carbon emissions and given the slow pace at which industries are turning to renewables, AI is a long way from being a sustainable technology.

Yet innovations like ChatGPT and DeepSeek are presented as immaterial embodiments of human ingenuity and machine learning where the labour is performed by non-human actors and the data stored in a distant cloud. Kate Crawford confronts this myth in her account of the 'planetary infrastructure of AI', in which she argues that the cloud is actually 'made of rocks and lithium brine and crude oil' (2021: 31), resources that have to be extracted and processed, whether in Nevada, Bolivia, Congo, Indonesia, China or Mongolia. As discussed in chapter 4, capitalist innovation relies on the exploitation of multiple forms of labour across the globe, and this is as true for AI as it was for the laying of the first submarine cables two hundred years ago – and with similar consequences for the environment. 'Just as Victorians precipitated ecological disaster for their early cables,' writes Crawford (2021: 39), 'so do contemporary mining and global supply chains further imperil the delicate ecological balance of our era.' Meanwhile, technology companies – often aided by breathless journalists – conceal the real costs of AI and mask the manipulation of their carbon footprints by focusing instead on AI's 'revolutionary' transformation of sectors like health care, education and e-commerce, whatever the likely damage to the environment.

## Conclusion

Nature and environment have been key victims of capitalism's need for constant renewal and relentless accumulation. Capital has super-exploited the natural world in order to furnish itself with the raw materials and energy sources that fuel its profits, but it has paid minimal attention to issues of sustainability and care. Media and tech companies have made the problem worse: first, by failing to address the full implications of an ongoing climate crisis with individualistic and often trivial reporting of climate issues and, second, by further polluting the environment with their circulation of 'digital rubbish' and promotion of energy-intensive platform infrastructures that will stress planetary resources. Far from holding power to account, AI-generated media are going to have to account for their use of power; without a major structural challenge to capitalist priorities, far from informing and educating the planet, the media are more likely to assist in its destruction.

# 14

## Contradiction and Crisis

*Overview* This chapter highlights the structural contradictions that are a key part of capitalism's DNA and that render it both highly dynamic and prone to the crises that have routinely featured throughout its history. It evaluates Gramsci's concept of 'contradictory consciousness' and discusses the tech booms, slumps and bubbles, as well as the ongoing journalism crisis, that stem from capitalism's chaotic pursuit of short-term profits over long-term sustainability.

### Contradiction: a serpent eating its own tail

The world appears to be a very confusing place. The fact that capitalism is destroying the environmental conditions for its very existence is just one – although the most pressing – of the many paradoxes that characterize contemporary life. We are also led to believe that increased defence spending is the only way to keep us safe, that nuclear weapons are 'deterrents' rather than risks, that surveillance will protect our freedoms, that sometimes you need to invade or occupy a country to free its people, that the generation of wealth is totally separate from the production of poverty, and that only private property can deliver public benefits.

These paradoxes are neither accidental nor incidental but the outcomes of contradictions that are fundamental to capitalism's operating system. They are contradictions not in the purely logical sense – related to the mutual exclusivity of two opposing statements (such as 'the world is round and it is also not round') – but are instead connected to the underlying antagonism of capitalist social relations that I have addressed in earlier chapters. This includes the contradiction between, for example, capital's exploitation *of* but dependence *on* labour, the individual and social aspects of production, use value and exchange value, accumulation and sustainability, 'free markets' and state protections, centralization and decentralization, monopoly and competition, risk and caution, and innovation and stagnation.[1] For Nancy Fraser, these contradictions arise from capitalism's addiction to exploitation and expropriation that means that it inevitably undermines its ideological legitimacy and material prospects: 'capital persistently devours the very supports on which it relies. Like a serpent that eats its own tail, it cannibalizes its own conditions of possibility' (2022: 24).

Perhaps the most famous expression of contradiction is Marx's formulation that an era of social revolution emerges when 'the material productive forces of society come into conflict with the existing relations of production' (1970 [1859]: 21) – in other words, when possibilities for human development are held back by the prevailing economic and social structure of society. This has been criticized for being overly mechanical, yet the outcome of this clash is never predetermined; the contradiction does not *cause* the collapse of capitalism but rather creates the circumstances in which change can occur. This is why, far from referring to a linear or predictable process, contradiction, according to John Rees (1998: 7), is a highly dynamic principle: 'two elements that are in contradiction cannot be dissolved into one another but only overcome by the creation of a synthesis that is not reducible to either of its constituent elements.' Contradiction is neither about the mere existence of 'opposites', where an understanding can be reached through logical reflection, nor is it a wholly ideological exercise where one conception eventually triumphs over the other. It is, rather, the source of transformation and political action where the shape of the 'synthesis' depends on the balance of power between contending forces at any given time. Contradiction – understood in relation to the material conflict between antagonistic tendencies – animates capitalist society as well as the struggles against it. As Ellen Wood argues (2002b: 278), contradiction is 'capitalism's basic operating principle, in a way that is true of no other social form. It is the source, at one and the same time, of both the capitalist system's dynamism and its constant self-subversion.'

Many theorists have their own preferred 'central' contradiction of capitalism. For Thomas Piketty in *Capital*, it is the fact that accumulated wealth grows faster than output and wages, which turns entrepreneurs into rentiers and produces unsustainable inequality;

this is a situation in which 'the past devours the future' (2014: 571). For Joseph Schumpeter – much loved, as noted in chapter 6, in Silicon Valley for his theories of innovation and 'creative destruction' – it is the inevitable rationalization and routinization of innovation that will prove to be capitalism's undoing. The source of capitalism's dynamism is a risk-taking and shibboleth-breaking approach to technological development that is at odds with its tendency to consolidate and bureaucratize: 'Since capitalist enterprise, by its very achievements, tends to automatize progress, we conclude that it tends to make itself superfluous – to break to pieces under the pressure of its own success' (Schumpeter 2010 [1942]: 119). For David Harvey (2014: 4), the most important contradiction of all is 'that between reality and appearance in the world in which we live', the fact that empirical observations and surface perceptions do not match the underlying structures that shape our experiences – a process in which, as I have already argued, the media play a key role. And, finally, for Ellen Wood, reflecting on how competition is both the driver and the major source of risk for firms, capitalism is caught between the 'need to impose its imperatives as universally as possible, and the need to limit the damaging consequences that this universalization has for capital itself' (Wood 2002a: 155).

These are all valuable insights that dramatize the multiple tensions that both underpin and stimulate capitalism as it seeks constantly to transform itself to deal with the challenges of these contradictions. For example, datafication and machine learning are just two of the more recent processes that capitalism hopes to mobilize in search of growth and stability, even though there is no reason to believe that, in themselves, they can avoid or overcome the antagonisms that have marked earlier innovations. This is especially the case in light of the argument that *labour* remains key to the securing of profits, even if (and it remains an *if*) generative AI is able significantly to increase productivity and restructure labour markets. After all, despite myths to the contrary, AI – as discussed in chapter 4 – depends on a labour-intensive infrastructure and a complex chain of production based on highly exploitative and precarious conditions. This makes it vulnerable to the very contradictions that Marx highlighted long ago in relation to what he called 'the capitalist application of machinery' and its intensification of some fundamental tensions in relation to labour itself:

> since machinery in itself shortens the hours of labour, but when employed by capital, it lengthens them; since in itself it lightens labour,

but when employed by capital it heightens its intensity; since in itself it is a victory of man over the forces of nature but in the hands of capital it makes man the slave of those forces; since in itself it increases the wealth of the producers, but in the hands of capital it makes them into paupers. (Marx 1977 [1867]: 568–9)

Marx makes the point even more concisely in the *Grundrisse*: 'Capital itself is the moving contradiction, [in] that it presses to reduce labour time to a minimum, while it posits labour time, on the other side, as sole measure and source of wealth' (1973 [1857–61]: 706).[2] This is a perfect illustration of the bind in which capitalism finds itself: simultaneously dependent on and antagonistic to the labour that is decisive for the commodity exchange from which it derives its meaning and value.

Yet while capitalist contradictions animate everyday activities at a material level, they also resonate in ideological terms and are especially relevant to forms of popular consciousness at any given time. I have already discussed in chapter 8 how sets of ideas, to be widely accepted, need to connect at some level with the experiences of ordinary people, even as they emanate from powerful institutions that have an interest in mystifying social relations. Most people are not part of a 'bewildered herd', nor are they passive victims of capitalist brainwashing processes. Instead, they negotiate their world views drawing not only on their own material circumstances, often rooted in exploitation, alienation, poverty and discrimination, but also on the dominant ideas of the time inherited from ruling elites. Given that people's beliefs do correspond, at least in part, with the objective conditions in which they find themselves, it is then far from surprising that they might hold contradictory ideas in their own heads: for example, that high taxes are undesirable but that wealth taxes are justified; that immigration is a threat to 'home' populations but that economies also need immigrant labour to prosper; that competition is natural but that cooperation is required in order to survive; that the 'nanny state' is a bad idea but that welfare protection should always be provided for the most vulnerable in society.

This is precisely what Gramsci was trying to highlight in his conception of a dual consciousness, torn between 'common sense', the prevailing ideas instilled by the ruling class, and the 'good sense' that is fostered in the course of struggles against that class.

The active man-in-the-mass has a practical activity, but has no clear theoretical consciousness of his practical activity, which nonetheless involves understanding the world in so far as it transforms it. His theoretical consciousness can indeed be historically in opposition to his activity. One might almost say that he has two theoretical consciousnesses (or one contradictory consciousness): one which is implicit in his activity and which in reality unites him with all his fellow-workers in the practical transformation of the real world; and one, superficially explicit or verbal, which he has inherited from the past and uncritically absorbed. (Gramsci 1971: 333)

We can argue about the extent to which people 'uncritically absorb' establishment narratives, especially in the context of Gramsci's own conception of hegemony as a highly unsettled and contested process (see chapter 8). The key point, however, is that capitalism generates contradictory consciousness as a matter of course because of its own internal antagonisms. Lukács, too, writes about a 'consciousness divided within itself' (1971 [1923]: 70) as a result of the reification that distorts our sense of self and hides our objective interests. For both theorists, the only way of resolving this tension between contradictory consciousness and objective class interests is through collective struggle – the 'practical transformation of the real world' to which Gramsci refers above.

I have drawn on this highly productive approach to consciousness and ideology in my formulation of a 'contradiction paradigm' of media power (Freedman 2014). This was designed to avoid both the idealism of the liberal pluralist account of the media's role as well as the functionalism and pessimism of some radical critiques that see the media simply as a straightforward transmission belt for the ruling class, generating content that is gobbled up and internalized by unquestioning audiences. As I hope this book has made clear, this is an ambition that ruling elites would *like* to realize but for a number of reasons – including the antagonisms discussed in this chapter and the divisions within the elites themselves (further discussed in chapter 8) – cannot be guaranteed. One only has to look at the declining levels of trust across all media platforms (see Reuters Institute 2025) and the growing interest in independent media outlets to get a sense that the mainstream media's grip is not at all what establishment voices would like it to be. Instead of a seamless exercise of media power, there are multiple contradictions within the capitalist media:

a simultaneous desire for a narrow consensus and yet a structural imperative for difference; a situation in which audiences are treated as commodities but in which they do not always play this role; a tendency for those who work within the media not to rock the boat (for self-protection and advancement) but, in exceptional periods, to do precisely this. (Freedman 2014: 28)

This has some bearing on the kind of mainstream content that is commissioned. Even though most output continues to reproduce the ideological frameworks of powerful groups – a tendency most obviously reflected in news and current affairs where the policing of dissent is at its most visible – the media are not wholly monolithic and immune to wider public sentiment. Just as they are more likely to articulate the strategic interests of the elites with whom they are intimately connected, neither can they afford to be completely oblivious to the concerns that preoccupy their audiences. This means that at moments of social struggle and political division, there may be opportunities for counter-hegemonic content to appear that, albeit in a fragile way, expresses the prevailing tensions in society (see Saha 2018 for examples of how this has impacted on Black audiences, generating both new possibilities for representation as well as old problems of exclusion and commodification). Anti-capitalist sentiment, such as the titles I mentioned in the opening chapter, while incredibly rare, exists 'not because of an inherent pluralism inside the mainstream media, but because there is currently a business model that rewards critical output at a time when millions of viewers are themselves increasingly aware of capitalism's shortcomings' (Freedman 2014: 125). An analysis of the media that is informed by an understanding of contradiction, rather than one of uninterrupted control and irresistible domination, allows users and audiences not only to challenge media systems that fail to reflect the aspirations and experiences of ordinary people but also to imagine and build new and democratic media institutions as part of wider struggles for social justice.

## Crisis: capitalism 'inhaling and exhaling'

The world is afflicted by constant crises including climate crisis, financial crisis, military crisis, humanitarian crisis, food insecurity crisis, cost-of-living crisis and a more recent disinformation crisis. To what extent are these one-off or disconnected phenomena caused by bad luck, bad weather or bad government or are they, as this book suggests, related to deeper systemic failures that are rooted in capitalism's very DNA? Crises are often attributed, at least by pro-market commentators, to specific failures in the 'business cycle', for example related to rising debt, loose credit, falling investment and excessive and intrusive government regulation. As Wolfgang Streeck notes (2011: 9), for mainstream economists, 'crises appear as punishment for governments failing to respect the natural laws that are the true governors of the economy'. There is a harsh price to pay, apparently, for anyone who messes with Adam Smith's 'invisible hand' guiding the circulation of capital.

More astute bourgeois economists, however, note that crisis is a necessary, if at times painful, deviation from 'business as usual' because of its stabilizing impact on capital itself. Schumpeter, as I identified in chapter 6, highlighted the 'creative destruction', most evident during periods of crisis, that is necessary for capitalism to reinvigorate itself and reproduce the dynamism that is undermined by an inevitable drift towards monopoly and stagnation. Creative destruction, he argues, is required to produce the boom that would follow the occasional slump. The free-market economist Milton Friedman is also clear both about the cathartic nature of economic trauma and the ideological way in which it is interpreted and acted on: 'Only a crisis – actual or perceived – produces real change. When that crisis occurs, the actions that are taken depend on the ideas that are lying around.' Crisis is essential, he argues, to overcome bureaucratic inertia so that 'the politically impossible becomes politically inevitable' (Friedman 2002 [1962]: xiv). This was the approach taken by his supporters in implementing and naturalizing the neoliberal policies that sought to hollow out the public sector and enshrine markets as the only dependable regulator of economic and social relations.[3]

Radical critics of capitalism, on the other hand, argue that economic and social crises are hard-wired into capitalism because of the contradictions embedded in the system's compulsion endlessly to generate profit. Focusing on the economy, Streeck sees crisis not as a one-off event but as 'a manifestation of a basic underlying tension in the political-economic configuration of advanced-capitalist societies' (2011: 5). Crises are caused by a rupture between market logic and social priorities where the interests of capitalists and the majority of the population most clearly diverge. So, for example, Streeck suggests that the 2008 financial crash was caused by the widespread roll-out of highly precarious and unsustainable subprime mortgages that were provided in place of wage rises or stable welfare entitlements as a new, and highly individualized, type of social policy. 'Instead of the government borrowing money to fund equal access to decent housing, or the formation of marketable work skills, it was now individual citizens who, under a debt regime of extreme generosity, were allowed, and sometimes compelled, to take out loans at their own risk' (2011: 17).

The 2008 crash, however, was only the latest in a very long line of economic crises that has marked capitalism's genealogy. In the *Grundrisse*, Marx specifically addresses both the destructive and cathartic qualities of crises, later recognized by writers like Schumpeter and Friedman, which were caused by the explosive tensions at the heart of capitalism. 'The growing incompatibility between the productive development of society and its hitherto existing relations of production expresses itself in bitter contradictions, crises, spasms. The violent destruction of capital not by relations external to it, but rather as a condition of its self-preservation, is the most striking form [of this tendency]' (Marx 1973 [1857–61]: 749–50). He goes on to talk about the fact that crises provide capitalism with a means whereby it can go 'back to the point where it is enabled [to continue] fully employing its productive powers without committing suicide' (1973 [1857–61]: 750). Crises are, therefore, 'violent' and painful episodes for those most affected, but they are necessary and inevitable outcomes of underlying contradictions. As Trotsky puts it (1973: 52), 'capitalism does live by crises and booms, just as a human being lives by inhaling and exhaling. First there is a boom in industry, then a stoppage, next a crisis, followed by a stoppage in the crisis, then an improvement, another boom, another stoppage and so on.' He concludes that '[c]risis and booms were inherent in capitalism at its very birth; they will accompany it to its grave' (1973: 52).

If crises are inevitable outcomes of capitalist contradictions, to what extent can we talk of a particular trigger for them? John Maynard Keynes provided a famous explanation in his *General Theory of Employment, Interest and Money* (Keynes 1936) – written during the Great Depression of the 1930s – that dramatic falls in expected rates of return on investment take place when supply and demand are out of kilter, in other words when there are too many goods in circulation at the same time as a decline in what he describes as the 'propensity to consume' (1936: 96). For Keynes, the modern economy is dominated by wanton speculation and 'animal spirits' (1936: 161), rather than rational planning and mathematical modelling. His recipe to counter the regular, but nevertheless traumatic, lapses in business confidence was to use the powers of government to stimulate consumption and restore economic equilibrium – a policy approach that underpinned many western welfare regimes up until the 1970s and the onset of neoliberalism.

Marx, however, had already argued that underconsumption is common to *all* periods of capitalism and that the system's innate anarchy – caused by its drive to allocate goods and services on the basis of profit and not need – meant that there was little scope for enduring stability. In particular, he insisted that there was a tendency for the overall rate of profit – the proportion of surplus value to capital investment – to fall that is built into the very architecture of capitalism. The more capitalists are forced to spend on technology and infrastructure in proportion to the labour that delivers their profits – caused by their compulsion to beat off the competition – the less profit proportionately they are likely to make in the long term. This contradiction then generates the momentum behind both booms and slumps. For Marx, this was 'in every respect the most important law of political economy and the most essential for understanding the most difficult relations' (1973 [1857–61]: 748). This assertion has been widely contested by mainstream economists and may seem counter-intuitive today, given the vast profits of, for example, tech companies and oil giants – little wonder that Thomas Piketty describes this in *Capital* as a 'historical prediction that turned out to be quite wrong' (2014: 52).

But Marx's point was not that profits were going to disappear entirely; instead, he argues that the falling rate of profit is a structural *tendency* within capitalism as opposed to a steady, persistent or apocalyptic decline. In fact, he devotes an entire chapter in the third volume of *Capital* to identify what he calls the 'counteracting influences' or 'counterbalancing forces' designed to address this tendency. Measures such as stepping up the rate of exploitation by lengthening the working day, forcing workers to take on additional unpaid roles and intensifying precarity, together with ensuring that wages never compensate for the full value of the goods and services that labour produces, taken together, 'hamper, retard and partly paralyse this fall [in the rate of profit]' (Marx 1971 [1894]: 239). Interestingly, Marx continues, such is the effectiveness of such countermeasures that it is 'only after long periods that its effects become strikingly pronounced' (1971 [1894]: 239) in the occasional but regular crises with which capitalism is associated. Indeed, precisely because so many of these countermeasures are familiar to us today in the gig economy and in ongoing attacks on labour organization, it's worth emphasizing that profitability – although astonishingly high in terms of absolute profits at the top levels of the world economy – remains extremely volatile (see Carchedi and Roberts 2018 for contemporary case studies). As Corey Robin notes (2025), while it used to be the case, at least in the wealthiest economies, that there were long and drawn-out upturns followed by short recessions, 'now it is the booms that are brief, the busts that are long.'

Indeed, for some theorists like Streeck (2014), it's possible to consider the idea of capitalism collapsing as a result of its own economic contradictions in a long, drawn-out and painful process. After all, neoliberalism seemed so unassailable and deeply rooted in all areas of life until popular opposition, financial disaster, global pandemic and rising protectionism together signalled its imminent demise as a hegemonic system. Streeck claims that 'it is high time, in the light of decades of declining growth, rising inequality and increasing indebtedness – as well as of the successive agonies of inflation, public debt and financial implosion since the 1970s – to think again about capitalism as a historical phenomenon, one that has not just a beginning, but also an end' (2014: 45).

While admitting that this is a prognosis that is more likely to be confined to the West and not to areas of the world where there is continued economic growth, for example China, India and Brazil, he insists that contemporary capitalism is characterized by a series of disorders and crises that have left it in critical condition. Capitalism, he claims, is too discredited and morally bankrupt to be able to resuscitate itself, even though he admits that it is not at all clear what kind of system will replace it.

Streeck's apocalyptic scenario highlights the vulnerability of all social systems and provides a valuable reminder that technological solutions – such as the one provided by generative AI – designed to improve productivity and restore long-term profitability, cannot be taken for granted. However, as Streeck recognizes, he is by no means the first theorist to talk about the impending end of capitalism under the weight of its own contradictions; capitalism is still with us (albeit limping along in some of its oldest locations) and unlikely to vanish without a conscious and systematic challenge. The question for capitalism's opponents is whether they can exploit the system's increasingly visible weaknesses and glaring lack of alternatives by offering a coherent and popular vision of an entirely different world – one that is not predicated on the unsustainable pursuit of profit and the repeated experience of crisis.

## Communications crisis

### Booms, slumps and bubbles

The communications landscape is as prone to crisis and as susceptible to feverish financial speculation as any other sector of the global economy. In fact, it is especially vulnerable to technological developments, regulatory interventions and changing consumption habits that can positively or negatively affect entire sectors. Consider the impact of the development of television on the film industry or of the internet on the music and news industries where there was tremendous disruption before many of the dominant players were once again able to enforce their power and to stabilize their role in the newly modified industries (see deWaard 2024: 85–9 for a discussion of how the music industry exploited this crisis). There is also the constant threat of economic uncertainty so that, for example, in more challenging times, companies often cut back on advertising – a crucial source of revenue for digital platforms just as it was for analogue enterprises – while anxious consumers may well revisit their subscription commitments,[4] leading to more cancellations and therefore less cash for investment in infrastructure and content. This then leads to a spiral in which both content creators and audiences are faced with further cuts and increased cultural austerity. I described in chapter 7 how, in the downturn following the Covid-19 pandemic, previously free-spending streaming companies and tech giants slashed their workforces, cut back on original spending and rationalized their entire organizations – a programme of corporate retrenchment that saw them once again earn significant profits as economies started to recover in 2023.

It is also the case that the communications sector can sustain a *simultaneous* boom and slump. For example, at the time of writing, there is both an upturn and a depression in the United Kingdom's film and television sector. Actually, this is less of a logical contradiction than it might first appear to be as it is more a question of who is 'winning' and who is losing out. Largely US streamers are exploiting a favourable exchange rate, generous tax relief and strong pools of talent to produce 'high-end' content in the United Kingdom that is aimed at global audiences. Huge companies like Amazon Studios, Netflix and Warner Bros have embarked on a post-pandemic spending spree that has driven up domestic production costs and increased pressure on smaller UK independent companies; many of these have either gone out of business or are unable to earn commissions from underfunded UK-based broadcasters who are already reeling from declining advertising revenue and, in the case of the BBC, a shrinking amount of licence fee income. 'As is often the case', notes one media analyst, 'it is individuals and organisations lower down the ladder who are bearing the brunt of the sector's adjustment' (Meyrick 2025). They quote one survey of UK screenworkers, carried out in February 2024, which found that 68 per cent were not working at the time of the poll and that nine in ten were worried about their financial security in the coming months, with more than one third planning to leave the sector within the next five years.

The situation, however, does bear out some of the underlying contradictions and inequalities of capitalist cultural production. While total investment in high-end film and television in the United Kingdom is nearly at an all-time high and while blockbuster movies are being filmed using UK-based labour, *Variety* reports that for the 'grips, cinematographers and production designers who once made their living on British-produced content, it's never been harder to get a gig' (Ritman 2025). The economic logic of commercial screen production means that it is now more viable to invest in expensive franchise movies and formulaic sequels than to support lower-budget domestic output with specific relevance to UK audiences. This has, of course, consequences both for cultural diversity and for employment stability, given that the biggest productions rely on specialist teams working on short-term contracts. Creative workers have already been unsettled by the competition posed by generative AI – and the reluctance thus far by AI companies fully to compensate for everything from the cloning of voices to the mining of creative content – so it is far from surprising that commentators are describing what ought to be a boom time for UK creatives instead as a 'perfect storm' for the sector (Meyrick 2025).

This kind of simultaneous boom and bust and episodic crisis sits alongside the more dramatic phenomena of 'bubbles', speculative frenzies that fuel the often meteoric rise and equally speedy collapse in value and investment in specific technologies. One relatively recent example is the dotcom bubble of 1998–2000, a period in which venture capitalists and investment bankers poured money into internet start-ups in the hope of owning the 'next big thing'. Many of these tiny companies with short histories and no discernible records of profit making were then floated on the US Nasdaq, where ordinary investors joined in the fun. Famous examples that illustrate the scale of the frenzy include Priceline.com, a loss-making airline ticket site that came out of nowhere to be valued at US$10 billion in 1999, more than the entire US airline industry; two years later, the stock was virtually worthless. Then there was Webvan, another unprofitable online grocery store that was valued at its 1999 public offering at US$8 billion and which also collapsed two years later after having spent US$1.2 billion on building a nationwide distribution system. And let's not forget Kozmo.com, an online food delivery company with an impossibly ambitious business model that barrelled through US$150 million in its short life before going out of business in 2001. The 'dot.con data bank' in the appendix to John Cassidy's excellent book on the bubble (Cassidy 2002) lists the share price and market capitalization of literally hundreds of online companies – most of which have entirely disappeared – and highlights their astonishing collapses in value.

Backed by free-market zealots like the US Federal Reserve chairman Alan Greenspan, one of the most vocal proponents of the idea that a 'new economy' was being built along an information superhighway, Cassidy argues that 'the Internet provided fresh confirmation of capitalism's infinite capacity to re-create itself' (2002: 162), not in terms of actually overcoming systemic contradictions but simply to create more wealth for the entrepreneurs, banks and shareholders who might benefit (before losing out). The media themselves were a key element of the charade, celebrating the 'bull markets' on cable news, and failing forensically to investigate either specific business plans or the basis of the emerging 'information economy'. Cassidy argues that the vast majority of start-ups failed because they celebrated a revolutionary new business model which didn't actually exist. Claims of huge productivity gains were inflated, with the internet contributing to only a modest increase in productivity in the second half of the 1990s, while the notion that information-based processes would supplant physical production turned out to be something of an exaggeration: 'Wings have to be attached to planes; roofs have to be put on houses; airbags have to be installed in SUVs' (Cassidy 2002: 319).

Cassidy argues that the bubble was caused by some of the 'animal spirits' that Keynes had referred to in the 1930s and that, while Silicon Valley, Wall Street, Alan Greenspan and the media were partly responsible, 'when all is said and done it was primarily a story of greed and gullibility on the part of the American public' (2002: 323). The financial journalist Roger Lowenstein agrees that the bubble was a kind of 'mass conspiracy, or mass delusion' (2004: 218), in which the market went into an inexplicable fever. Yet others argue that bubbles are actually the logical outcomes of an irrationality that is built into capitalist business models. Just as with tulip mania in seventeenth-century Netherlands or bicycle mania in nineteenth-century Britain, the rapid rise and decline in value is a product of a system that relentlessly chases short-term profits at the expense of long-term stability. Quinn and Turner (2020: 6) argue that bubbles are not simply the result of irrational and crowd-like behaviour but are instead generated by low interest rates and loose credit conditions where investors are looking (and able) to secure higher rates of return, no matter the risk. They acknowledge that the media did play a significant role in the dotcom bubble – not least in perpetuating a '"new era" narrative, in which the world-changing magic of the new technology renders old valuation metrics obsolete, justifying very high [and unsustainable] prices' (2020: 8) – but the real fuel for the bubble is, as always, money and credit.

The dotcom crash is far from the last bubble that will affect media and communications. Indeed, we have already witnessed the bursting of the podcasting bubble in the late 2010s, a situation in which some of the largest podcasting companies, having invested millions of dollars buying innovative start-ups earlier in the decade, resorted to layoffs and cancellations following the plateauing of audiences. This was not because – as with CB radio in the 1970s – podcasting was in terminal decline but simply because the rate of return was not sufficient to impress the giant new entrants to the sector, including Spotify and Amazon. As the veteran podcaster Max Linsky remarked at the height of the bubble in 2015, 'the level of investment is about to get higher than it's ever been. And someone, somewhere, is going to want to see a return on that' (quoted in Friedman 2015). Meanwhile, the scale of both investment in and claims that are currently being made about both generative AI and artificial general intelligence would suggest that this is a sector that is subject to the same risk of boom and bust. The business magazine *Forbes* has run a series of articles on the volatility of the AI sector, with one article, headlined 'Are We at Peak AI Bubble and the Cusp of "AI Moment"?' (Press 2025), noting that the bubble is likely to burst soon. For investors, it suggests that this is a necessary and productive part of the economic cycle – yet more Schumpeterian 'creative destruction' – in order to pave the way for a more stable and sustainable AI sector; for its critics, it is a symbol of the waste and inefficiency at the heart of capitalism's drive to accumulate.

### A crisis (partly) of its own making: western journalism's fall from grace

Nowhere is the language of crisis more evident than in what has happened to mainstream journalism since the 1980s. Newsrooms have been hollowed out, jobs slashed, titles shut down, specialist areas of reporting deemed to be too expensive, local journalism often turned into a patchwork of news 'deserts, oases and drylands'[5] and the remaining news culture marked by hypercommercialism, misinformation and precarity (Miller 2024). This leads to a type of diminished clickbait journalism that, according to Victor Pickard, paved the way for Donald Trump's initial election as US president in 2016 and that highlights the 'slow-but-sure structural collapse of professional journalism' (Pickard 2020: 4). Journalism is facing a crisis of jobs, engagement, relevance (Carlson, Robinson and Lewis 2021), trust, confidence and funding. While digital subscriptions are now stagnating, while increasing numbers of people report that they actively 'avoid' the news (some 40 per cent, according to the Reuters Institute [2025]) and while younger audiences are turning to digital platforms like TikTok and YouTube where news-like content is as likely to be generated by influencers and celebrities as it is to be provided by professional reporters, journalism is facing an existential crisis.

Of course, the most 'common sense' explanation for this sense of crisis is a technological one: that the internet broke apart journalism's monopoly both of classified advertising and attention, and, as such, there was little that news organizations could do fully to offset the damage. Digital revenue could never compensate for the money lost as a result of classified ads shifting over to, for example, Craigslist (at the start of the millennium), the depreciated value of display advertising in a more competitive climate and the collapse in the circulation of, especially, paid-for print newspapers. According to this logic, the best that news organizations can hope for is that slimmed-down newsrooms, a more emaciated type of journalism and a more aggressive relationship to audiences based on the relentless use of metrics (Petre 2021) might yet yield the revenue necessary to continue performing such an important democratic role. For some commentators, this is simply part of the cut and thrust of capitalism as it goes through different economic and technological cycles: 'Metaphors and phrases such as "perfect storms" and "disruptive innovation" implicitly construct the crisis as something beyond our control and outside the realm of public policy' (Pickard 2020: 6).

There is an entirely different way of approaching the crisis. It is not at all the case that there is neither the appetite nor the capacity to support accurate and relevant journalism but simply that the business model that has long underpinned commercial journalism has crumbled. This cannot simply be blamed on Craigslist, TikTok or YouTube – not least because decline pre-dates the internet – but on the industry's insatiable lust for profits which, according to Caitlin Petre (2021: 23), 'reached a high point in the 1980s, when publishers joked that newspapers were a business in which "even the brain dead could make money".' A decade later, when the threat of online disruption was becoming clear, news was still a highly profitable industry with many newspapers continuing to generate impressive profit margins. The situation changed with the 2008 financial crash that decimated advertising revenue and accelerated the layoffs and closures that characterize the contemporary news landscape.

Yet, even in this context, Pickard argues that 'the news industry suffered from self-inflicted wounds' (2020: 43). Companies were often loaded with unsustainable amounts of debt accrued from earlier purchases and were wedded to opportunistic, short-term strategies that focused on asset acquisition rather than modernizing and transforming newsrooms to meet the digital challenge. 'Making matters worse', according to Pickard, 'newspapers ruthlessly disinvested in news and cut costs as they chased the increasingly elusive goal of maintaining obscene profits' (2020: 44). This situation was then exploited in a post-crash spending spree by private equity firms and hedge-fund companies like Alden Global Capital that see newspapers as lucrative investment opportunities and potential 'cash cows'. Rubbishing the 'myth of newspaper insolvency', Margot Susca, who has comprehensively investigated newspaper chain ownership by private investment firms, insists that '[w]hat we have is not a crisis of profit. What we have is a crisis of greed and growing inequality' (Susca 2024: 9). This is not an organic crisis but one brought about by the industry's zealous adherence to core capitalist principles.

## Conclusion

Communication crises are neither preordained nor irresistible 'acts of God' in which the natural equilibrium of the market is disrupted but then restored. Rather, crises are often the direct result of capitalism's privileging of private profits over public benefits, short-term gain over long-term sustainability, and proprietorial control over creative autonomy. Crises are neither harmless nor necessary acts of 'creative destruction' but clear-outs with very real and damaging human and societal consequences. Instead of bowing down to the instrumental logic of capital or looking for market solutions to crises generated by the very contradictions of market orientations, there is an urgent need – both within journalism and the wider technology and communications landscapes – to develop non-market forms that serve publics according to their needs, not their investment portfolios.

# 15

# Conclusion

***Overview*** This final chapter summarizes capitalism's enduring structural imperatives and foundational principles, in
particular as they apply to media, communications and technology. It identifies and rebuts three possible criticisms of the
book's approach: that it underestimates the full implications
of technological transformation, unduly homogenizes capitalism
and fails to explore contemporary media landscapes in sufficient
detail. The chapter ends by highlighting capitalism's vulnerabilities and contradictions and suggests that, for all its apparent
and superficial invincibility, capitalism has long lost its veneer of
immortality, rendering it open to challenge.

## Pessimism of the intellect

As I hope will be clear from the preceding chapters, capitalism is a
complex, contradictory and crisis-ridden socio-economic system that
is nevertheless subject to a series of broad, underpinning imperatives.
It was revolutionary at birth but now seeks fiercely to protect its own
privileges and to secure the private property relations on which it has
long depended. It has extended exploitation and commodification
to all corners of the globe and, in so doing, generated huge wealth
for a tiny minority of asset holders on the backs of a global majority.
It has imposed a monetary value on virtually every aspect of human
activity while any continuing innovations are predicated on their
ability to generate profit rather than to serve the public interest. It
boasts about unleashing meaningful competition and facilitating a
level playing field for entrepreneurial skills but, in its relentless drive

to accumulate, has paved the way for giant concentrations of capital that dominate their respective sectors.

Capitalism has also fostered a series of powerful institutions that circulate and attempt to normalize its foundational principles and to generate a 'common sense' that reproduces its culture and values. It celebrates the importance of freedom and democracy but, at the same time, restricts their application, hollows out their meaning and insulates them from the economic sphere where crucial decisions are made that shape the life chances of its citizens. Capitalism continues to depend on state formations that provide it with resources and infrastructures to help defend itself against rivals and to suppress domestic challenges to its domination. It has long sought to internationalize its operations, whether through forceful expropriation or allegedly more benign forms of 'free trade' which further intensify global inequalities. It has weaponized the different backgrounds and identities of its populations and profited from the discrimination that is embedded within capitalist societies. In place of a productive and sustainable relationship with nature, it has embraced – and still refuses to give up – the fossil fuels that have polluted the environment and that threaten to rip up any remaining possibility for ecological balance. And instead of purposeful planning and careful coordination of society's resources to meet the needs of all, capitalism prioritizes short-term rewards that render it liable to repeated economic and social convulsions.

These structural imperatives and associated developments provide essential context for understanding the current trajectory of the media and technology sectors. Capitalism's privileging of private property was initially conceived as a protection from state control but has now been rationalized in the paywalls, chokepoints and 'walled gardens' that dominate the online world and that constitute a new form of digital enclosure. Far from reducing exploitation, digital technologies rely on the wage labour of the miners, moderators, annotators, scrapers and many more workers who populate the circuit of production, while class, far from disappearing in an 'information age', remains a central determinant of employment prospects, investment decisions and on-screen representation. Few areas of human creativity remain off-limits to rampant marketization – witness, for example, the fetishization of brands and the implantation of a commodity logic into practices like journalism, where context and connection are routinely sacrificed on the altar of clickbait, sensationalism and the pursuit of a 'phantom objectivity'. The entire communications landscape is dominated by giant concentrations of capital and influence that make a mockery of the claim that 'mass media boulders' would be replaced by 'digital pebbles'. Instead of a communications cornucopia, we are instead witnessing the consolidation of a 'tech-industrial complex' which effortlessly bats off the occasional antitrust challenge to its power and relentlessly pursues accumulation strategies – usually based on cost cutting and the acquisition of rivals – that prioritize profit seeking (and not simply rent seeking) as a key objective.

The media also continue to furnish populations with a set of values that articulate the broad interests of the most powerful social groups and that seek to secure consent to existing capitalist formation of power. They draw on and regularly foster well-established myths that a 'free media', independent of the state or indeed of any special interests, is necessary to guarantee individual liberty and to safeguard liberal democracy and 'hold power to account', even if the media themselves are a key component of those very power structures. Indeed, the state remains a central actor in the operation, regulation and policing of the digital landscape and has embraced a variety of roles – including as propagandist, bully, data controller and sponsor – that mitigate against the gradual diminution of its influence in the face of increased corporate power.

Media technologies and content have long been central to capitalism's desire to circulate across national boundaries and to internationalize its footprint; imperialism, colonialism and more recent forms of neo-liberal globalization have all fostered asymmetrical communication flows, and we continue to see highly unequal practices of expropriation and commodification underpinning the global circulation of text, data, images and sounds. Furthermore, just as media have long been involved in producing specific conceptions about marginalized social groups that reflect hegemonic interests, they retain the ability to disseminate damaging stereotypes and to pit communities against each other in their construction of norms around, for example, race, gender and sexuality. These distortions also relate to the media's ongoing preoccupation with superficial and individualistic accounts of climate change and the more general environmental risks posed both by the 'digital rubbish' of discarded devices and the unsustainable energy requirements demanded by the newest forms of AI. Finally, the communications sector is far from immune from the booms, slumps, bubbles and episodic crises that mark the wider economy as a direct result of its underlying tensions. Media, communications and technology are, after all, not isolated or utterly unique economic sectors but ones that are both constituted by and, in turn, constitutive of the wider society in which they are located.

I want briefly to address three possible criticisms of the structural imperatives laid out above and of my approach more generally.

First, to what extent does the book's focus on capitalism make it obsolete on the basis that it refers to an allegedly outdated mode of production that has been – or is in the process of being – replaced by new, digital regimes of accumulation? I have already critiqued arguments made by Zuboff on surveillance capitalism, Wark on vectoralism and Varoufakis on technofeudalism and suggest that they underestimate the resilience of traditional economic levers and exaggerate the extent to which capitalism has been eclipsed by new social forces based on unaccountable networks and pre-capitalist value systems. Jodi Dean, a sharp critic of the role played by communication technologies under capitalism, has recently suggested that, given the unprecedented rise of datafication, financialization and rentierism, we are seeing a new type of 'neofeudalism' marked by strategies of 'rent-seeking, plunder and political control' (Dean 2025: 3) that are quite different to the traditional pursuit of profit. This is a wholly regressive development (in other words, capitalism is being superseded by something even worse), but she is quite clear that '[c]apitalist laws of motion are reflexively folding in on themselves and becoming something no longer capitalist' (2025: 3).

Yet, as I have repeatedly emphasized, one of capitalism's fundamental laws of motion is that it is vulnerable to its own internal contradictions and that much of capitalism's history relates to the strategies and coping mechanisms adopted by its most powerful agents in the face of its underlying antagonisms. Capitalism has always been a victim of its own contradictory tendencies – at once elastic and rigid, dynamic and stagnant, productive and destructive, creative and parasitical – which has seriously undermined its own coherence, logic and credibility. Moreover, where Dean sees 'lords', I see 'oligarchs'; where she sees 'serfs' and a new sector of 'servants', I see a growing and diverse international working class that emerges out of the new sectors – including the rapidly expanding service sector – developed by capital to take advantage of digital innovations; where she sees neofeudalism, I see a very old kind of capitalism forced to adapt to and shape the new circumstances in which it finds itself. The fact that increasing numbers of workers may *say* that they are being treated like 'peasants' by unaccountable or unassailable 'barons' does not mean that commodity production has been replaced by a rentierism that is independent of wage labour. Rather, it points to the continuing experience of exploitation at the heart of a system that has long demonstrated a knack for shape shifting when necessary and reminds us that capitalism is not defined by its dependence on cotton, oil, coal or data at any one time but by the social relations that seek to exploit their possibilities.

The second potential criticism is that the book runs the risk of treating capitalism as a homogeneous and singular entity when it might instead be seen as a fluid and multidimensional combination of forces. As I argue in the opening chapter, the fact that capitalism has many distinct iterations across the globe and many different – and often conflicting – features of its personality does not mean that it lacks commonalities which allow us specifically to refer to capitalism (and not to another social formation) in the first place. Indeed, one of capitalism's strengths is that it can accommodate contrasting variations of its constituent elements without losing sight of the overall operating system to which it is attached. China, for example, practises a very different form of capitalism to that of Norway, but this does not negate the fact that both countries are in thrall to many of the imperatives discussed in this book; Trump's America is not the same as its neighbours to the north and south, and yet all of them are accountable to the same pressures of capital, even if their political responses and economic strategies do not converge. Capitalism is certainly complex and multidimensional, but that does not mean it lacks an overarching set of disciplines which, together, constitute a 'totality' as opposed to the appearance of a discrete set of variables.

To the extent that the book treats capitalism as a singularly decisive analytical category, does it then suggest that capitalism provides a lens with which to make sense of *all* areas of human experience? Or to put it another way, is capitalism responsible for *all* social problems and grievances? Of course, not every activity that takes place is capitalist in the sense that it is organized solely for the purposes of exchange, and it is equally true there are areas of human life – from publicly held resources like parks and libraries to the sphere of social reproduction – in which commodity production is not the overarching motivation. But the contention of this book is that capitalist imperatives are never too far away and that the operation of these spheres is never insulated from the expansive logic of capital accumulation. Public services are constantly subject to market creep while, as I argued in chapter 5, care and affective labour are intertwined with 'core' economic structures in the sense that production and social reproduction are mutually interdependent. The same is also true of creative activities, whether making a TikTok video, posting a photograph on Instagram or uploading a track to SoundCloud, given that such endeavours are ultimately integrated into vampire-like accumulation processes.

This is part of capitalism's unique ability to universalize commodity relations and thus to objectify all areas of life such that 'the whole of society is subjected . . . to a unified economic process' (Lukács 1971 [1923]: 92). Capitalism, like the sun, casts its shadow across the whole of the globe, even as that shadow covers different countries at different times and with different intensities.

This helps to explain both capitalism's enduring power as well as the advantages it offers as a critical framework for understanding the multiple and connected grievances experienced by members of a capitalist society. Far from suppressing difference and smoothing over conflicts, a perspective focused on the imperatives identified in this book can highlight the ways in which what appear to be disconnected phenomena – for example of discrimination, exploitation and alienation – may instead have a common and systemic source. Rather than accepting these grievances as natural, immutable or isolated, a focus on capitalism can help to generate forceful and impactful forms of resistance and redress.

The third potential criticism is that the book is overly preoccupied with the systemic imperatives of capitalism and fails to spend sufficient time evaluating their impact on media, communications and technology. To the extent this is true (in absolute terms), this reflects a determination on my part to challenge an often dominant media centrism in which, for example, social media are held responsible for generating political polarization and disinformation as if there were no pre-existing socio-economic factors outside the media that may have had an impact on their genesis. It's also the case that the book's emphasis on the broader operation of capitalism is designed to mitigate against an increasingly widespread technological determinism (discussed in chapter 2) in which particular innovations are endowed with almost biological affordances and where there is no room for policy alternatives or popular resistance to their impacts. Technological determinism is neither an innocent expression of 'geekiness' nor a necessary incentive for innovation but a political and industrial strategy to close down public debate and dissent in the light of a widespread fetish for, for example, smartphones and artificial general intelligence (widely promoted by the media themselves). The aim of the book, therefore, is to equip readers with a critical vocabulary of capitalism in the hope that they will more effectively analyse and challenge the structures, policies and behaviours of the digital landscape in its current and future iterations.

## Optimism of the will

That capitalism is still dominant and has some highly durable characteristics doesn't mean that it is impregnable, and the fact that our communications systems are dominated by oligarchic forces doesn't mean that they are irresistible. In the turbulence of Italian politics in the 1920s, Gramsci's formulation for evaluating 'the various levels of the relations of force' in order to produce 'more rigorous and more vigorous political insights' (1971: 175–6) was based on what is now the famous maxim, 'pessimism of the intellect, optimism of the will'.[1] I read this not just as a desperate plea to keep your spirits up in dark times but as confirmation that human agency is necessary to challenge capitalist hegemony and that only practical activity can break the logjam between the resilience of the old and the possibility of the new.

Capitalism is riddled with internal tensions that, at times of profound crisis, both destabilize and diminish it in the eyes of its populations. This is an opportunity for progressive forces to exploit the contradictory consciousness (discussed in chapter 14) that emerges out of this volatility and to contest the capitalist 'common sense' that, in less turbulent times, is bound to dominate. This is not an idealist exercise in the sense of hoping that all that is required is to press for *better* education, *fairer* media policies, *sharper* memes or *improved* levels of media literacy to shift established relations of power. Gramsci's point was that an anti-capitalist 'good sense' can only be nurtured through practical efforts to resolve social and economic contradictions through the building of mass social movements – for example over austerity, war, climate, racism, misogyny and exploitation. Once people are mobilized in and exposed to collective struggles against capitalism's injustices and failures, they are far more likely to search for new explanations and far less likely uncritically to accept the 'received wisdom' of mainstream media narratives and mystifying explanations.

As demonstrated in multiple opinion polls, capitalism's vulnerabilities have already seen the emergence of a gap between mainstream media agendas and the concerns of its audiences. They have also generated an increased willingness not to trust established institutions – including the media – and stimulated an appetite for content and perspectives that deviate from a previously carefully cultivated consensus. For example, journalists inside Gaza, using a range of low-cost communications devices, have been able partially to offset the impact of the Israeli government's ban on foreign journalists operating in the region, while social media channels have provided an opportunity to forge solidarity between pro-Palestinian voices outside Gaza and those inside the territory (although of course they have also been used to circulate pro-Israeli material as well). However, the extent to which 'good sense' about the world can be circulated depends above all on the breadth and depth of the social movements that breathe life into alternatives and challenges to capitalism; in order to intensify and generalize anti-capitalist sentiment, there needs to be an organic relationship between collective organization and the information channels that can publicize and solidify these movements.

That is the lesson also of previous struggles against inequality and injustice in which virtually every major campaign for social change has had its own media infrastructure. Illegal pamphlets helped to cohere the disparate forces of the Leveller Revolution during the English Civil War in the 1640s, while newspapers like *Le Père Duchesne* were central to publicizing the insurrectionary events of the 1789 French Revolution; the Chartists had the *Northern Star*, the suffragettes had their own self-titled newspaper, while the Bolsheviks relied on 'worker-correspondents' writing in *Pravda* to cement the Russian Revolution. Mahatma Gandhi founded *Harijan* to help build his anti-colonial struggle in India, *Vanguardia* championed the Republicans in the Spanish Civil War, while pro-independence forces in Algeria relied on the underground Voice of Fighting Algeria radio network (mentioned in chapter 11) to inspire the Indigenous population and demoralize the French occupiers. The Shah of Iran was toppled by a movement in the late 1970s that used cassettes to circulate its anti-regime messages, while the 2011 Arab Spring used a variety of digital platforms to organize its protests and delegitimize the rulers it sought to bring down.

Precisely because capitalist society is so riven by contradictions, it is never fixed, stable or predictable. There is always the possibility of friction, resistance and change – a situation in which media and communications are bound to play significant roles. Writing about new electronic media in the political turmoil of the 1970s, the radical German theorist Hans Magnus Enzensberger embraced the idea that every receiver could now be a potential transmitter, a statement that applies to people as well as machines. 'For the first time in history, the media are making possible mass participation in a social and socialized productive process, the practical means of which are in the hands of the masses themselves. Such a use of them would bring the communications media, which up to now have not deserved the name, into their own' (Enzensberger 1976: 22). This is even more true of a digital era in which a plethora of tools is available to drama-tize, publicize and organize against the injustices we face.

This is not a call for a narrow programme of media reform and repair. Any radical communications-centred programme or media strategy needs to complement and feed into wider political move-ments that have an explicitly anti-capitalist focus. Neither is this a pipe dream. Given capitalism's own crisis of legitimation and its increasingly brittle and fragile support, there exist today the tech-nological infrastructures, political opportunities and economic incentives to realize this scenario and to both envisage and struggle for the replacement of a system that has lost its veneer of immortality. Capitalism has generated the conditions for its own destruction, and therein lie both the hope and the great challenge.

# Notes

**Chapter 1  Capitalism Shouldn't Need an Introduction**

1  https://www.wsj.com/about-us; https://www.economistgroup.com/about-us; https://asia.nikkei.com/about; https://www.bloomberg.com/company/what-we-do/

2  According to the Lexis Nexis database, there were 48,510 articles referring to 'capitalism' from 2005 to 2007 and 80,150 in the period from 2008 to 2010.

3  These communications and digital-related titles often draw on and sit alongside a whole raft of other 'X-capitalism formulations', including 'cotton capitalism', 'racial capitalism', 'monopoly capitalism', 'crony capitalism', 'emotional capitalism', 'rentier capitalism' and 'extractive capitalism', to name just a few.

4  Data derived from the World Inequality Index, https://wid.world/

5  The US magazine *Current Affairs* described Norberg's book as a 'manifesto you can detesto'; https://www.currentaffairs.org/news/the-capitalist-manifesto-is-manifestly-wrong

6  Braudel (1983: 433) makes a similar point about what he describes as 'an essential feature of the general history of capitalism: its unlimited flexibility, its capacity for change and *adaptation*' (italics in original). This is manifested in capitalism's 'capacity to slip at a moment's notice from one form or sector to another, in times of crisis or of pronounced decline in profit rates'.

7  This is precisely why some pro-capitalist writers are more reluctant to use the term. For John Kay (2024: 23), capitalism has simply 'become a term of disapproval, or more rarely approbation without specific content. Mostly "capitalism" is something that the speaker blames for an outcome that he or she dislikes.' Norberg, on the other hand, as a true evangelist, still wants to rescue it from any negative connotations: 'no matter what we think of it, and no matter which word we would prefer for a system of

private property and free markets, this is the word that has become inextricably linked to it and if its supporters don't fill that word with meaning, its opponents will' (2023: 16).

## Chapter 2 Technology and Revolution

1 The *Cambridge Dictionary* actually notes both meanings of revolution: 'a sudden and great change, esp. the violent change of a system of government', as well as 'a movement in a circle'; https://dictionary.cambridge.org/dictionary/english/revolution

## Chapter 3 Private Property and Enclosure

1 Land, however, still remains a major generator of revenue and a significant part of the privatization process. Brett Christophers' book on the 'new enclosure' notes that since 1979, 10 per cent of all land in the United Kingdom has been privatized, an astonishing transfer of assets from the public to the private. He argues that privatization 'is indubitably a form of enclosure; and it epitomizes key developments in late capitalism more generally' (Christophers 2018: 13).
2 Such was the impact of the protests that they provided the setting for a major Spanish film, *También la lluvia* (*Even the Rain*), in 2010, directed by Icíar Bollaín and starring Gael García Bernal, which was nominated for an Academy Award.
3 Theine and Sevignani (2024: 417), in a welcome special journal issue on 'media property' that they edited, speak of 'two crucial and intertwined trajectories in digital media capitalism: First, from private property to access . . . and, in connection with this, a second trajectory from profit to rent.' While it's true that the political economy of digital media needs to prioritize issues of access and rent, the 'trajectory' is not away from private property per se but towards its incorporation into the changing dynamics of the digital landscape.
4 This is very similar to the evolution of broadcasting where 'content' was an afterthought to the more important need to sell the hardware. As Raymond Williams notes, 'radio and television were *systems primarily devised for transmission and reception as abstract processes, with little or no definition of preceding content*' (1974: 25; emphasis in original).

## Chapter 4 Labour, Exploitation and Class

1 Not all labour is 'productive' in this specific sense because 'unproductive' labour, which is not subject to the same wage relationship, is crucial for the sustainability of capitalism, including the highly gendered areas of childcare, social care and other formally non-commodified activities. It is not that 'productive' labour is objectively more important as the two

spheres are intertwined but that it has a different relationship to the 'point' of production. Ursula Huws (2013) discusses this relationship and recommends the use of 'reproductive' and 'directly productive' forms of labour as a more appropriate typology.

2  Some editions translate this as the '*dull* compulsion of economic relations', which I feel is a more appropriate way of describing the monotonous and routine forms of exploitation that are imposed on 'free labour'.

3  See, for example, the *New Statesman* quiz on 'What class are you?', https://www.newstatesman.com/politics/society/2023/08/quiz-which-social-class-are-you-working-middle-upper . Rather more seriously, the National Centre for Social Research regularly surveys people on which class they believe they belong to. In 2021, 52 per cent of the UK public described themselves as working class, while over three-quarters of those polled argued that social class significantly affects life opportunities, leading the authors to talk of the 'myth of a classless Britain'. https://natcen.ac.uk/publications/bsa-40-social-class

4  David Hesmondhalgh (2010) has written a comprehensive critique of 'free labour' in digital conditions. Not only does he discuss how this relies on an imprecise understanding of exploitation, but he also argues that it elides wage labour with other kinds of activities and overstates the acquiescence of ordinary people: 'it would surely be wrong to imply that any work done on the basis of social contribution or deferred reward represents the activities of people duped by capitalism' (2010: 278).

5  The 2023 British Social Attitudes survey found that 52% of the UK population described themselves as working class, while 77% agreed that social class affects life chances either 'a great deal' or 'quite a lot', up from 70% in 1983. The perception is that society is becoming more, not less, unequal and that this is related to class (Heath and Bennett 2023: 2).

### Chapter 5  Commodification and Marketization

1  See, for example, Pollock (2020) on the commodification of health care, Giroux (2019) on the neoliberalization of universities and Bergström (2021) on the privatization of intimacy.

2  This doesn't mean that we are seeing 'a more extreme degree of alienation' as claimed by Couldry and Mejias (2019: 84) on the basis that, through digital colonialism, 'subjects are estranged not only from the products of their labour, but from their own personhood, their basic realities as human beings' (2019: 84). As we saw in the last chapter, it is problematic to equate the loss of control over one's own labour power with the dispossession of data where it is generated voluntarily. I discuss this further in chapter 11.

3  Arturo Toscanini was an Italian conductor who moved to the United States from Italy after the rise of fascism in the 1930s to lead the New York Philharmonic, followed by the in-house orchestra of the commer-

cial broadcaster NBC. The latter's concerts were broadcast live on the network from 1937.
4 Smythe's argument also depends on a generous definition of the work carried out by an audience as labour that is equivalent to core productive activity – a debate I referred to in relation to social media audiences in chapter 4. For example, according to Smythe (1977: 6), 'The work which audience members perform for the advertiser to whom they have been sold is to learn to buy particular "brands" of consumer goods, and to spend their income accordingly.' This appears to reduce labour to a form of education and behavioural change that lacks explicit criteria of exploitation and suffocates any sense of agency.

## Chapter 6  Competition and Monopoly

1 See https://tracxn.com/sectors
2 In the United Kingdom, 'market exit' is now the official euphemism for what happens if a university goes bankrupt or ceases to exist as a result of the turbulence of treating higher education as a competitive market and not a public good. A 'market exit' plan is now required by the regulator, the Office for Students, as a condition for registration. A market 'exit' would obviously have huge implications for staff, students and the local community who depend on the institution for jobs and revenue far beyond the idea that the university is simply leaving the stage.
3 Schumpeter's work resonates with the more recent arguments of Peter Thiel, the co-founder of PayPal and prominent Silicon Valley libertarian. Thiel describes the fetish for competition as a 'relic of history' that underestimates the contribution of dynamic entrepreneurs who build monopolies on the back of strong products: 'the history of progress is a history of better monopoly businesses replacing incumbents. Monopolies drive progress because the promise of years or even decades of monopoly profits provides a powerful incentive to innovate' (Thiel 2014).
4 It is revealing that the villain of a major 2025 Netflix production, *Zero Day*, starring Robert De Niro, is a fictional tech mogul who launches a devastating and murderous cyber attack on the United States, fuelled in part by an impending investigation into her business by the Federal Trade Commission.
5 See the excellent book series on 'Global Media Giants', edited by Ben Birkinbine, Rodrigo Gómez García and Janet Wasko. Available at: https://www.routledge.com/Global-Media-Giants/book-series/GMG?
6 Brett Christophers argues that rentierism, understood as the 'exclusive control of assets' (2020: 474), is prevalent both in the platform economy but also across the wider economic landscape, especially in relation to the exploitation of intellectual property. Subway and McDonalds, for example, aren't fast-food operators but rentiers that license their

intellectual property to franchisees: 'Economic rent, not food, is Subway's business' (2020: 143).

7 This is calculated using a regularly updated tool, originally featured in Welsh and Randewich (2024). The biggest increases in stock market share during Joe Biden's administration were seen by Microsoft, rising from 5.2% to 6.4% and by NVidia – on the wave of the 'AI revolution' – from 1% to 6.8% of the entire S&P 500.

8 Data gathered from https://www.businessofapps.com/data/

## Chapter 7  Accumulation and Profit

1 Spending on luxury goods remains a small percentage of total consumer expenditure but, at US$1.6 trillion in 2024 – according to the Bain-Altagamma Annual Luxury report available from bain.com – it is nevertheless half of the entire gross domestic product of the continent of Africa.

2 A typical example of this was an NBC report in 2011, reflecting on whether editorial failures were confined only to News International titles, headlined 'Has Murdoch's bad apple spoiled the barrel?' (https://www.nb cnews.com/id/wbna43762510).

3 Robert McChesney (2004: 27) notes that 'the press in the early [US] republic was not seen as an engine of capital accumulation, as merely one of many areas in which investors might put their capital to generate maximum returns in the marketplace. The press was highly partisan and integrally linked to the political process.' His argument is that the American media system was 'not "naturally" profit driven' (2004: 25) but had to be designed that way and legitimized as such.

4 After being successfully sued by a private individual in the United Kingdom courts for abusing her right to privacy, Meta, the owner of both Facebook and Instagram, agreed to stop targeting the individual with personalized adverts 'in a landmark privacy case that could set a precedent for millions of social media users' (Milmo 2025). In response, Meta stated that it might introduce a paid, ad-free version of its platforms demonstrating the fragility of surveillance-based advertising models.

5 *New York Times* reporters Kate Conger and Ryan Mac provide a detailed account of the brutality and irrationality of the layoffs at Twitter in their book *Character Limit* (Conger and Mac 2024). They reveal that one person reacted to being sacked by posting on Slack 'an image of a scene from *Avengers: Infinity War* (2018), in which Thanos, the main antagonist, gains powers that allow him to eliminate half of all life in the universe with the snap of his fingers. This was Twitter's own mass extinction event. Employees began referring to it as their "snap"' (2024: 305).

6 This was not designed to actually save Spotify money, given that it did not affect the total amount of money the company would pay out in royalties to rights holders. Instead, it was aimed at reducing fraud, 'declutter-

ing' the site and presumably appeasing the largest music companies who would benefit most from a more favourable redistribution system.

## Chapter 8 Ideology and Hegemony

1 Garnham seeks, in particular, to highlight the significance of the social relations of production without removing all agency from the ideological sphere. While noting that Marx claims that capitalism involves 'the pressure to reduce everything to the equivalence of exchange value', Garnham argues that 'ideological forms can never be simply collapsed into a system of exchange values, precisely because they are concerned with difference, with distinction, they are by definition heterogeneous; whereas exchange value is the realm of equivalence' (1990: 30–1).

2 There is a popular museum on the Royal Mile in Edinburgh called Camera Obscura and World of Illusions that promises 'five floors of optical illusions' under the banner that 'Nothing Is What It Seems'. See https://camera-obscura.co.uk/attractions/ground-floor

3 The French structuralist philosopher Louis Althusser attempted to provide this in his depiction of 'ideological state apparatuses' (Althusser 2014), institutions such as the Church, education, mass media and family, which integrate individuals into capitalist social relations. However, Althusser provides ideology with an autonomy and permanence that effectively insulates it from the economic basis of society.

4 Laclau and Mouffe's influential book, *Hegemony and Socialist Strategy*, attempts to move hegemony beyond what they see as an 'orthodox essentialism' (2001: 76) that privileges economic questions and exaggerates the significance of class. Instead, they propose a new hegemonic project based on 'the need to create a chain of equivalence amongst the various democratic struggles against different forms of subordination' (2001: xviii) in a way that effectively displaces class as a decisive variable.

5 We can see the same ideological slant in much of the media's business coverage, for example its support for privatization (Silke and Graham 2017), austerity (Berry 2019) and tax cuts (DiMaggio 2017). Laura Basu (2018: 69) writes persuasively about a more general 'media amnesia' that dominated economics coverage before the 2008 financial crash and that was epitomized by 'the lack of historical context, the narrow range of elite perspectives and the lack of global context'.

6 None of the main UK news outlets investigated the growing allegations that genocide was taking place in Gaza and only changed their tune (and only for a short time) once South Africa had successfully taken its case to the International Court of Justice in January 2024 (Freedman 2024a).

## Chapter 9 Freedom and Democracy

1 Capitalism, argues the Russian revolutionary leader Leon Trotsky, 'needs the distinction between political power and economic power. But it is precisely for this reason that we must reject this terminological trap. "Economic power," as such, does not exist. There is [only] *property*, different forms of property' (Trotsky 1977: 95; emphasis in original).

2 Milton Friedman argues that capitalism is a 'necessary' but not a 'sufficient' condition for political freedom and democracy, noting the rise of fascism in Italy, Spain and Germany as well as authoritarian rule in Japan and Tsarist Russia. 'It is therefore clearly possible to have economic arrangements that are fundamentally capitalist and political arrangements that are not free' (2002 [1962]: 10).

3 Paul Foot provides an apt reminder of the shortcomings of this approach to democracy.

> British representative democracy is founded on the notion of one person, one vote. An industrial magnate has one vote, and so does each worker he can sack or impoverish. A millionaire landlord has one vote, and so does every person he evicts. A banker has one vote, so does every person impoverished by a rise in the bank rate or a financial takeover. A newspaper proprietor has one vote, so does each of the readers he deceives or seduces every day of the week. Are all these people really equally represented? (Foot 2024: conclusion)

4 Power asymmetries also shape contemporary debates on 'free speech' where right-wing columnists, broadcasters and politicians use their substantial influence to claim that their views – for example on immigration, the economy, sexuality and morality – are being silenced by 'woke' voices. 'The capture of free speech', writes Gavan Titley (2020: 104), 'aims to create space for racist speech as a beleaguered expression of liberty, and positions the dissemination of racist discourse as a contribution to democratic vitality.'

## Chapter 10 Capitalism and the State

1 This chapter draws on work previously published in Freedman (2020).

2 Smith is disarmingly honest about the need for administrative oversight over a system of *unequal* property relations.

> Wherever there is a great property, there is great inequality. For one very rich man, there must be at least five hundred poor, and the affluence of the few supposes the indigence of the many. The affluence of the rich excites the indignation of the poor, who are often both driven by want, and prompted by envy to invade his possessions. It is only under the shelter of the civil magistrate, that the owner of that valuable property, which is acquired by the labour of many years, or perhaps of many

successive generations, can sleep a single night in security. . . . The acquisition of valuable and extensive property, therefore, necessarily requires
the establishment of civil government. (2012 [1776]: 709)

3  We have had the laissez-faire, warfare state, the welfare state and, more
recently, according to Mariana Mazzucato (2015), the 'entrepreneurial
State' which, through its coordination of public–private partnerships,
military spending, government contracts and, crucially, state-funded
research, has helped to play an important role in technological innovation.
See a fuller discussion later in this chapter.
4  See Committee to Protect Journalists, https://cpj.org/
5  For a full list of prosecutions under the Espionage Act, see a list published
in September 2024 by the Knight First Amendment Institute; https://kni
ghtcolumbia.org/documents/whq7babj86
6  Trump stepped up his attack on Voice of America (VoA) in his second
administration by issuing an executive order in March 2025 dismantling
the US Agency for Global Media that funds not only VoA but other international news services. The likely result of this defunding is that other state
broadcasters, in particular Chinese services, are likely to fill the ensuing
gap in what is becoming an increasingly fierce international propaganda
battle. Trump followed this up with a further executive order in May 2025
that slashed federal funding to public media networks PBS and NPR.

## Chapter 11  Imperialism, Colonialism and Globalization

1  The same is true for colonialism in that, as Ellen Wood argues (2002a:
147), 'colonial ventures, conquest, plunder and imperial aggression' all
preceded capitalism. For example, Spain was a crucial colonial power
that conquered huge parts of Latin America from the early sixteenth
century and yet did not initially develop in a capitalist direction. Colonial
exploitation was therefore not a precondition for capitalism, though it is
impossible to imagine how capitalism could have developed later without
it.
2  Writing shortly before the outbreak of the First World War, the Marxist
economist Rudolf Hilferding also argued that it was unimaginable to
detach violence from colonialism.

Violent methods are inseparably bound up with the essence of colonial
policy, which without them, would lose its capitalist meaning . . . To be
in favour of a colonial policy and at the same time to talk about eliminat-
ing its violent methods[,] is a dream which cannot be treated with more
earnestness than the illusion that one can eliminate the proletariat while
retaining capitalism. (Hilferding 1981 [1910]: 319)

3  These writers – and many more – are included in the two-volume anthol-
ogy on *Communication and Class Struggle*, edited by Armand Mattelart and
Seth Siegelaub, published in 1979 and 1983 respectively.

4 Netflix's own list of its most popular non-English shows is at https://www.netflix.com/tudum/top10/most-popular/tv-non-english; its list of the most popular English-language shows is at https://www.netflix.com/tudum/top10/most-popular/tv

5 Jin (2015) provides a detailed analysis of imperialism in his conceptualization of 'platform imperialism'. The book considers the extent to which platforms offer a strategic advantage for the United States to extend its domination of world trade and services as part of its overall imperial ambitions.

## Chapter 12 Oppression

1 Williams notes that the incentive for both the founding and the abolition of slavery 'was not a moral question but an economic one' (1964 [1944]: 169). He concludes that the 'decisive forces . . . are the developing economic forces', and that the liberation of subjugated people from colonialism and imperialism will be resolved not simply by independence struggles but in relation to 'the necessities of production' (1964 [1944]: 210).

2 In his wonderful book *The Black Jacobins* (James 1963), the title of the chapter on the background of the slaves who eventually rose up in the Haitian Revolution is simply this: 'The Property'.

3 Even though Du Bois referred at times to African Americans as a 'race', he also acknowledged that the division of the world into race 'is nothing more than an acknowledgment that, so far as purely physical characteristics are concerned, the differences between men do not explain all the differences of their history. It declares, as Darwin himself said, that great as is the physical unlikeness of the various races of men their likenesses are greater' (Du Bois 2007 [1903]: 180). Throughout his famous book *Souls of Black Folk*, he appears to forgo the term 'race' for the lived experience of the 'veil', a way of seeing through a racial lens as opposed to a biological reality.

4 Said's emphasis on critiquing the Occident also means that he spends little time evaluating the 'Orient's' own representation of itself. See Lila Abu-Lughod (2005) for a wonderful analysis of how Egyptian television dramas in the 1990s provided a critical lens through which to understand both official and vernacular perspectives on Muslim life.

## Chapter 13 Nature and Environment

1 Weber (2001 [1930]: 123) famously talked about capitalism prioritizing its instrumental obsession with the accumulation of wealth 'until the last ton of fossilized coal is burnt'.

2 Williams describes 'nature' as 'perhaps the most complex word in the language' (1983: 219), one of whose meanings relates to 'the material

world itself, taken as including or not including human beings' (1983: 219).

3 According to Naomi Klein:

> Coal didn't create structural inequality – the boats that enabled the transatlantic slave trade and first colonial land grabs were powered by wind and the first factories powered by water wheels. But the relentless and predictable power of coal certainly supercharged the process, allowing both human labor and natural resources to be extracted at rates previously unimaginable, laying down the bones of the modern global economy. (Klein 2015: 416)

4 Of course, this doesn't diminish the very real damage caused by online disinformation, mapped out in detail in the comprehensive report by the Center for Countering Digital Hate (2024) on *The New Climate Denial*.

## Chapter 14 Contradiction and Crisis

1 Many of these (and more) are discussed at length in David Harvey's *Seventeen Contradictions and the End of Capitalism* (Harvey 2014).

2 John Rees notes an additional contradiction of capitalism: that although labour power is treated as just another commodity, it is a commodity that cannot be detached from the person who bears it: 'much as the capitalist might wish to, he cannot separate the owner of labor power from labor power itself' (1998: 221).

3 Of course, critics of capitalism are equally vociferous about the 'stabilizing' role that crises can play. 'Crises', according to David Harvey (2014: ix), 'are essential to the reproduction of capitalism. It is in the course of crises that the instabilities of capitalism are confronted, reshaped and re-engineered to create a new version of what capitalism is about. Much gets torn down and laid waste to make way for the new.'

4 The UK communications regulator Ofcom publishes a regular 'affordability tracker' which highlights how significant numbers of households find it difficult to pay for their communications services. For example, in October 2022, 32% of all households (and 56% of those on means-tested benefits) struggled to pay their bills for broadband and streaming services. In January 2025, nearly 10% of all households still struggled to pay for streaming services, while 14% of the most disadvantaged households had either cut their spending on other items or cancelled a communications service. See https://www.ofcom.org.uk/phones-and-broadband/saving-mo ney/affordability-tracker

5 The United Kingdom's Public Interest News Foundation identified that there are 38 local news deserts affecting some 7% of the population, with a further 2% living in 'relative news deserts' without a dedicated provider but with at least some access to local content. See https://www .publicinterestnews.org.uk/local-news-map-report-2024

**Chapter 15 Conclusion**

1 Gramsci's editors note that the original formulation, taken from the French writer Romain Rolland, was actually 'pessimism of the intelligence, optimism of the will'. Either way, they suggest that Gramsci used this as a 'programmatic slogan as early as 1919', in other words, before he was jailed for his radical activity (Gramsci 1971: 175n).

# References

Abu-Lughod, L. (2005) *Dramas of Nationhood: The Politics of Television in Egypt*. Chicago: University of Chicago Press.

Acemoglu, D. (2017) 'Capitalism', in B. Frey and D. Iselin (eds), *Economic Ideas You Should Forget*. Cham, Switzerland: Springer.

Acemoglu, D. (2024) 'The Simply Macroeconomics of AI', NBER Working Paper 32487, http://www.nber.org/papers/w32487

Adorno, T. (2001) *The Culture Industry: Selected Essays on Mass Culture*. London: Routledge.

Adorno, T. and Horkheimer, M. (2002 [1947]) *Dialectic of Enlightenment*. Stanford: Stanford University Press.

Agustin, F. (2024) '"We Are Famously Unprofitable": A 36-year-old Jeff Bezos on Amazon', BBC Culture, 1 July, https://www.bbc.co.uk/culture/article/20240628-a-36-year-old-jeff-bezos-talks-about-losing-money

Ahmad, A. (1994) *In Theory: Classes, Nations, Literatures*. London: Verso.

Al Jazeera (2018) 'Why the Media Need to Turn up Temperature on Climate Change', *Listening Post*, https://www.youtube.com/watch?v=yRFARcaA_7U

Alphabet (2025) 10-K Filing to US Securities and Exchange Commission, 5 February, https://www.sec.gov/edgar/browse/?CIK=0001652044

Althusser, L. (2014) *On the Reproduction of Capitalism*. London: Verso.

Anderson, C. (2009) *The Longer Long Tail: How Endless Choice Is Creating Unlimited Demand*. London: Random House.

Andrejevic, M. (2007) *iSpy: Surveillance and Power in the Interactive Era*. Lawrence: University Press of Kansas.

Anievas, A. and Nişancıoğlu, K. (2015) *How the West Came to Rule: The Geopolitical Origins of Capitalism*. London: Pluto.

Artz, L. and Murphy, B. (2000) *Cultural Hegemony in the United States*. London: Sage.

Arvidsson, A. (2005) 'Brands', *Journal of Consumer Culture* 5(2).

Bagdikian, B. (1983) *The Media Monopoly*. Boston: Beacon Press.

Bagdikian, B. (2004) *The New Media Monopoly*. Boston: Beacon Press.

Baker, C. E. (2007) *Media Ownership and Concentration: Why Ownership Matters*. Cambridge: Cambridge University Press.

Bakir, V., Herring, E., Miller, D. and Robinson, P. (2019) 'Organized Persuasive Communication: A New Conceptual Framework for Public Relations and Propaganda Research', *Critical Sociology* 45(3).

Banet-Weiser, S. (2018) *Empowered: Popular Feminism and Popular Misogyny*. Durham: Duke University Press.

Baran, P. and Sweezy, P. (1968) *Monopoly Capital*. London: Penguin.

Barca, S. (2024) *Workers of the Earth: Labour, Ecology and Reproduction in the Age of Climate Change*. London: Pluto.

Barling, K. (2019) 'How the media failed Grenfell', *Prospect*, 1 November, https://www.prospectmagazine.co.uk/politics/39428/how-the-media-fai
led-grenfell

Barlow, J. P. (1996) 'A Declaration of the Independence of Cyberspace', https://www.eff.org/cyberspace-independence

Barwise, P. and Watkins, L. (2018) 'The Evolution of Digital Dominance: How and Why We Got to GAFA', in M. Moore and D. Tambini (eds), *Digital Dominance: The Power of Google, Amazon, Facebook and Apple*. Oxford: Oxford University Press.

Basu, L. (2018) *Media Amnesia: Rewriting the Economic Crisis*. London: Pluto.

Batziou, A. (2022) 'Climate Change and the Heatwave: Searching for the Link in the British Press', *Journalism Practice* 16(4).

BBC (2006) *Report of the Independent Panel for the BBC Governors on Impartiality of BBC Coverage of the Israeli-Palestinian Conflict*, April, http://
downloads.bbc.co.uk/bbctrust/assets/files/pdf/our_work/govs/panel_repo
rt_final.pdf

BBC (2011) 'BBC Trust Review of Impartiality and Accuracy of the BBC's Coverage of Science', July, https://www.bbc.co.uk/bbctrust/our_work/edit
orial_standards/impartiality/science_impartiality.html

BBC (2017) 'Apple Apologises for Slowing Older iPhones Down', 29 December, https://www.bbc.co.uk/news/technology-42508300

Bellamy Foster, J., Clark, B. and Holleman, H. (2021) 'Marx and the Commons', *Social Research* 88(1).

Beltrán, L. (1978) 'Communication and Cultural Domination: USA–Latin American Case', *Media Asia* 5(4).

Bennett, W. L. (1990) 'Towards a Theory of Press-State Relations in the United States', *Journal of Communication* 40(2).

Bennett, W. L. (1994) 'The News about Foreign Policy', in W. L. Bennett and D. Paletz (eds), *Taken by Storm: The Media, Public Opinion, and U.S. Foreign Policy in the Gulf War*. Chicago: University of Chicago Press.

Bergström, M. (2021) *The New Laws of Love: Online Dating and the Privatization of Intimacy*. Cambridge: Polity.

Berry, M. (2019) *The Media, the Public and the Great Financial Crisis*. London: Palgrave Macmillan.

Bevins, V. (2023) *If We Burn: The Mass Protest Decade and the Missing Revolution*. London: Wildfire.

Blakeley, G. (2024) *Vulture Capitalism: Corporate Crimes, Backdoor Bailouts and the Death of Freedom*. London: Bloomsbury.

Blum, F. (2022) 'Here's a Rundown of Tech Companies that Have Announced Layoffs in 2022', CNBC, 9 November, https://www.cnbc.com/2022/11/09/tech-layoffs-2022.html

Booth, P. (2020) *New Visions: Liberating the BBC from the Licence Fee*, Institute of Economic Affairs Current Controversies 71, https://iea.org.uk/wp-content/uploads/2020/01/CC71_BBC-licence_web.pdf

Borg, J., Sinnott-Armstrong, W. and Conitzer, V. (2024) *Moral AI and How We Get There*. London: Penguin.

Bork, R. (1978) *The Antitrust Paradox*. New York: Free Press.

Bourdieu, P. (1984) *Distinction: A Social Critique of the Judgement of Taste*. Cambridge, MA: Harvard University Press.

Bourdieu, P. (1991) *Language and Symbolic Power*. Cambridge: Polity.

Bourdieu, P. (2014) *On the State*. Cambridge: Polity.

Bowles, P. (2024) *Capitalism*, 3rd edn. London: Routledge.

Boyd-Barrett, O. (1977) 'Media Imperialism: Towards an International Framework for the Analysis of Media Systems', in J. Curran et al. (eds), *Mass Communication and Society*. Milton Keynes: Open University Press.

Boyd-Barrett, O. (2015) *Media Imperialism*. London: Sage.

Braudel, F. (1983) *Capitalism and Civilization, 15th to 18th Centuries, Vol. 2: The Wheels of Commerce*. London: Harper Collins.

Braudel, F. (1984) *Capitalism and Civilization, 15th to 18th Centuries, Vol. 3: The Perspective of the World*. London: Harper Collins.

Braudel, F. (1995) *A History of Civilizations*. London: Penguin.

Brown, W. (2015) *Undoing the Demos: Neoliberalism's Stealth Revolution*. New York: Zone Books.

Brown, W. (2024) 'Foreword' to K. Marx, *Capital: Critique of Political Economy, Volume 1*. Princeton: Princeton University Press.

Bukharin, N. (2003 [1917]) *Imperialism and World Economy*. London: Martin Lawrence.

Burn-Murdoch, J. (2024) 'What the "Year of Democracy" Taught Us in 6 Charts', *Financial Times*, 30 December, https://www.ft.com/content/350ba985-bb07-4aa3-aa5e-38eda7c525dd

Carbon Majors (2024) *The Carbon Majors Database Launch Report*, April, https://carbonmajors.org/site/data/000/027/Carbon_Majors_Launch_Report.pdf

Carchedi, G. and Roberts, M. (2018) *World in Crisis: A Global Analysis of Marx's Law of Profitability*. Chicago: Haymarket.

Carey, H., Florrison, R., O'Brien, D. and Lee, N. (2020) 'Getting in and

Getting on: Class, Participation and Job Quality in the UK Creative Industries', Nesta Policy Review Series 1, https://pec.ac.uk/wp-content/up loads/2024/01/PEC-report-class-in-the-creative-industries-FINAL.pdf

Carlson, M., Robinson, S. and Lewis, S. (2021) *News after Trump: Journalism's Crisis of Relevance in a Changed Media Culture.* Oxford: Oxford University Press.

Carmody, P. R. (2011) *The New Scramble for Africa.* Cambridge: Polity.

Carrington, D. (2018) 'BBC Admits "We Get Climate Change Coverage Wrong Too Often"', *Guardian*, 7 September, https://www.theguardian .com/environment/2018/sep/07/bbc-we-get-climate-change-coverage-wrong-too-often

Carrington, D. (2021) '"Cake" Mentioned 10 Times More than "Climate Change" on UK TV – Report', *Guardian*, 15 September, https://www.the guardian.com/environment/2021/sep/15/cake-mentioned-10-times-more -than-climate-change-on-uk-tv-report

Carrington, D. (2022) 'Revealed: Oil Sector's "Staggering" $3bn-a-day-Profits for Last 50 Years', 21 July, https://www.theguardian.com/environ ment/2022/jul/21/revealed-oil-sectors-staggering-profits-last-50-years

Cassidy, J. (2002) *Dot.Con: The Greatest Story Ever Told.* London: Allen Lane.

CBC (2019) 'CBC President Compares Netflix Influence to Colonialism', 31 January, https://www.cbc.ca/news/entertainment/tait-netflix-coloniali sm-analogy-1.5000657

Center for Countering Digital Hate (2024) *The New Climate Denial*, https:// counterhate.com/wp-content/uploads/2024/01/CCDH-The-New-Clima te-Denial_FINAL.pdf

Centre for News, Technology and Innovation (2024) 'Journalists & Cyber Threats', 11 October, https://innovating.news/article/journalists-cyber-th reats/

Cesaire, A. (2000 [1950]) *Discourse on Colonialism.* New York: Monthly Review Press.

Chakravartty, P. (2019) 'Media, "Race" and the Infrastructures of Empire', in J. Curran and D. Hesmondhalgh (eds), *Media and Society.* London: Bloomsbury.

Chan, K. (2024) 'EU Slaps Meta with a Nearly 800 million Euro Fine for Engaging in "Abusive" Marketplace Practices', Associated Press, 14 November, https://apnews.com/article/meta-facebook-european-union-co mpetition-fine-6886192353a344126a15886d6ca7c627

Chandonnet, H. (2025) 'Streaming Is Finally Profitable. It Offers a Lesson in Patience', *Fast Company*, 11 February, https://www.fastcompany.com /91274473/streaming-is-finally-profitable-it-offers-a-lesson-in-patience

Chang, H.-J. (2011) *23 Things They Don't Tell You about Capitalism.* London: Penguin.

Chomsky, N. (1999) *The Fateful Triangle: The United States, Israel and the Palestinians*, updated edn. London: Pluto.

Christophers, B. (2018) *The New Enclosure: The Appropriation of Public Land in Neoliberal Britain*. London: Verso.

Christophers, B. (2020) *Rentier Capitalism: Who Owns the Economy, and Who Pays for It?* London: Verso.

Coates, D. (2016) *Capitalism: The Basics*. London: Routledge.

Cohen, J. (2019) *Between Truth and Power: The Legal Construction of Informational Capitalism*. Oxford: Oxford University Press.

Conger, K. and Mac, R. (2024) *Character Limit: How Elon Musk Destroyed Twitter*. New York: Penguin Random House.

Cooper, E. (2025a) 'How Corporate Broadcast Networks Covered Earth Month in 2025', Media Matters for America, 7 May, https://www.media matters.org/cbs/how-corporate-broadcast-networks-covered-earth-month -2025

Cooper, E. (2025b) 'How Broadcast TV Networks Covered Climate Change in 2024', 6 March, https://www.mediamatters.org/broadcast-net works/how-broadcast-tv-networks-covered-climate-change-2024

Coppins, M. (2025) 'Growing up Murdoch', *The Atlantic*, 14 February, https://www.theatlantic.com/magazine/archive/2025/04/rupert-murdoch-f amily-succession-james-murdoch/681675

Couldry, N. and Mejias, U. (2019) *The Costs of Connection: How Data Is Colonizing Human Life and Appropriating It for Capitalism*. London: Bloomsbury.

Crawford, K. (2021) *Atlas of AI: Power, Politics and the Planetary Costs of Artificial Intelligence*. New Haven: Yale University Press.

Crenshaw, K. (1989) 'Demarginalizing the Intersection of Race and Sex: A Black Feminist Critique of Antidiscrimination Doctrine, Feminist Theory and Antiracist Politics', *University of Chicago Legal Forum* 1, Article 8.

Criales, J. P. (2023) 'Free Use of Weapons, Privatization and the End of Legal Abortion: Javier Milei's Plan for Argentina', *El Pais*, 18 May, https://english.elpais.com/international/2023-05-18/free-use-of-weapons -privatization-and-the-end-of-legal-abortion-javier-mileis-plans-for-argen tina.html

Crouch, C. (2011) *The Strange Non-Death of Neoliberalism*. Cambridge: Polity.

Cunningham, S. and Jacka, E. (1996) *Australian Television and International Mediascapes*. Cambridge: Cambridge University Press.

Curran, J. (2002a) *Media and Power*. London: Routledge.

Curran, J. (2002b) 'Media and the Making of British Society, c. 1700–2000', *Media History* 8(2).

Curran, J. and Seaton, J. (2018) *Power without Responsibility*, 8th edn. London: Routledge.

Das, R. (2022) *Marx's 'Capital', Capitalism and Limits to the State*. New York: Routledge.

DasSarma, A. and Fisher, L. (2023) 'The Persistence of Indigenous

Unfreedom in Early American Newspaper Advertisements, 1704–1804', *Slavery and Abolition* 44(2).

Davies, N. (2014) *Hack Attack: How the Truth Caught Up with Rupert Murdoch.* London: Chatto & Windus.

Davies, W. (2014) *The Limits of Neoliberalism: Authority, Sovereignty and the Limits of Competition.* London: Sage.

Davis, A. (1983) *Women, Race and Class.* New York: Vintage.

Davis, A. (2002) *Public Relations Democracy.* Manchester: Manchester University Press.

Davis, J., Ossowski, R., Richardson, T. and Barnett, S. (2000) 'Fiscal and Macroeconomic Impact of Privatization', IMF Occasional Paper 194.

Davis, S. (2021) 'What Is Netflix Imperialism? Interrogating the Monopoly Aspirations of the "World's Largest Television Network"', *Information, Communication & Society* 26(6).

Dean, J. (2009) *Democracy and Other Neoliberal Fantasies: Communicative Capitalism and Left Politics.* Durham, NC: Duke University Press.

Dean, J. (2025) *Capital's Grave: Neofeudalism and the New Class Struggle.* London: Verso.

Dencik, L., Hintz, A., Redden, J. and Treré, E. (2022) *Data Justice.* London: Sage.

deWaard, A. (2024) *Derivative Media: How Wall Street Devours Culture.* Oakland: University of California Press.

DiMaggio, A. (2017) *The Politics of Persuasion: Economic Policy and Media Bias in the Modern Era.* Albany: SUNY Press.

Dorfman, A. and Mattelart, A. (2019 [1971]) *How to Read Donald Duck: Imperialist Ideology in the Disney Comic.* London: Pluto.

Dragomir, M. (2024) 'The Capture Effect: How Media Capture Affects Journalists, Markets and Audiences', *Central European Journal of Communication* 17(2).

Du Bois, W. E. B. (2007 [1903]) *The Souls of Black Folk.* Oxford: Oxford University Press.

Du Bois, W. E. B. (2013 [1935]) *Black Reconstruction in America.* London: Transaction.

Dyson, E. (1997) *Release 2.0: A Design for Living in the Digital Age.* New York: Broadway Books.

Eagleton, T. (1991) *Ideology: An Introduction.* London: Verso.

Edwards, D. and Cromwell, D. (2006) *Guardians of Power: The Myth of the Liberal Media.* London: Pluto.

Engels, F. (1947 [1878]) *Anti-Duhring.* Moscow: Progress.

Engels, F. (1972 [1884]) *The Origin of the Family, Private Property and the State.* London: Lawrence & Wishart.

Engels, F. (1972 [1890]) 'Letter to J. Bloch', 21 September 1890, in T. Borodulina (ed.), *K. Marx, F. Engels, V. Lenin on Historical Materialism.* Moscow: Progress Publishers.

Entman, R. (2004) *Projections of Power: Framing News, Public Opinion and US Foreign Policy.* Chicago: University of Chicago Press.

Entman, R. (2007) 'Framing Bias: Media in the Distribution of Power', *Journal of Communication* 57(1).

Entman, R. and Page, B. (1994) 'The News before the Storm', in W. L. Bennett and D. Paletz (eds), *Taken by Storm: The Media, Public Opinion, and US Foreign Policy in the Gulf War.* Chicago: University of Chicago Press.

Enzensberger, H. M. (1976) *Raids and Reconstructions: Essays in Politics and Culture.* London: Pluto.

Evans, H. (2017) *Do I Make Myself Clear? Why Writing Well Matters.* New York: Little Brown.

Fanon, F. (1965 [1959]) *A Dying Colonialism.* New York: Grove Press.

Fanon, F. (2004 [1963]) *The Wretched of the Earth.* New York: Grove Press.

Farkas, J. and Schou, J. (2024) *Post-Truth, Fake News and Democracy: Mapping the Politics of Falsehood.* New York: Routledge.

Farrow, R. (2022) 'A Hacked Newsroom Brings a Spyware Maker to U.S. Court', *New Yorker*, 30 November, https://www.newyorker.com/news/news-desk/a-hacked-newsroom-brings-a-spyware-maker-to-us-court-pegasus

Federici, S. (2004) *Caliban and the Witch.* London: Autonomedia.

Fenton, N. (2025) *Democratic Delusions: How the Media Hollows Out Democracy and What We Can Do about It.* Cambridge: Polity.

Fenton, N. and Freedman, D. (2018) 'Fake Democracy, Bad News', in L. Panitch and G. Albo (eds), *Rethinking Democracy: Socialist Register 2018.* London: Merlin Press.

Ferguson, S. and McNally, D. (2013) 'Introduction', in L. Vogel, *Marxism and the Oppression of Women: Toward a Unitary Theory.* Leiden, Netherlands: Brill.

Finnegan, W. (2002) 'Leasing the Rain', *New Yorker*, 31 March, https://www.newyorker.com/magazine/2002/04/08/leasing-the-rain

Fisher, M. (2009) *Capitalist Realism.* London: Zero.

Fletcher, R. and Neilsen, R. (2017) 'Are News Audiences Increasingly Fragmented? A Cross-National Comparative Analysis of Cross-Platform News Audience Fragmentation and Duplication', *Journal of Communication* 67.

Foot, P. (1982) 'Three Letters to a Bennite', 7 January, https://www.marxists.org/archive/foot-paul/1982/3letters/letter2.htm

Foot, P. (2024) *The Vote: How It Was Won and How It Was Undermined.* London: Verso.

Foster, J. B. (1999) 'Marx's Theory of Metabolic Rift: Classical Foundations for Environmental Sociology', *American Journal of Sociology* 105(2).

Fraser, N. (2014) 'Behind Marx's Hidden Abode: For an Expanded Conception of Capitalism', *New Left Review* 86 (March/April).

Fraser, N. (2022) *Cannibal Capitalism: How Our System Is Devouring Democracy, Care and the Planet – and What We Can Do about It.* London: Verso.

Freedman, D. (2008) *The Politics of Media Policy.* Cambridge: Polity.

Freedman, D. (2009) '"Smooth Operator"? The Propaganda Model and Moments of Crisis', *Westminster Papers in Communication and Culture* 6(2).

Freedman, D. (2014) *The Contradictions of Media Power*. London: Bloomsbury.

Freedman, D. (2016) 'The Internet of Capital: Concentration and Commodification in a World of Abundance', in J. Curran, N. Fenton and D. Freedman (eds), *Misunderstanding the Internet*, 2nd edn. London: Routledge.

Freedman, D. (2019) '"Public Service" and the Journalism Crisis: Is the BBC the Answer?' *Television & New Media* 20(3).

Freedman, D. (2020) 'The State of Political Communications', in A. Davis, N. Fenton, D. Freedman and G. Khiabany, *Media, Democracy and Social Change: Re-Imagining Political Communications*. London: Sage.

Freedman, D. (2024a) 'Media Shouldn't Be "Impartial" – but Fearless and Truthful', *Declassified UK*, 22 March, https://www.declassifieduk.org/uk -media-shouldnt-be-impartial-but-fearless-and-truthful/

Freedman, D. (2024b) 'Neither Private Property nor Public Service Media: Critical Reflections on the Concept of Public Service', *European Journal of Communications* 39(5).

Friedman, A. (2015) 'The Economics of the Podcast Boom', *Columbia Journalism Review*, 20 March, https://www.cjr.org/first_person/the_econo mics_of_the_podcast_boom.php

Friedman, M. (1990) 'Private Property', *National Review*, 5 November.

Friedman, M. (2002 [1962]) *Capitalism and Freedom*. Chicago: University of Chicago Press.

Friedman, T. (1996) 'Foreign Affairs Big Mac 1', *New York Times*, 8 December, https://www.nytimes.com/1996/12/08/opinion/foreign-affairs -big-mac-i.html

Friedman, T. (2000) *The Lexus and the Olive Tree*. London: Harper Collins.

Friedman, T. (2009) *Hot, Flat and Crowded: Why We Need a Green Revolution – and How It Can Renew America*, updated edn. New York: Picador.

Fryer, P. (1984) *Staying Power: The History of Black People in Britain*. London: Pluto.

FTC (2023) 'FTC Sues Amazon for Illegally Maintaining Monopoly', Federal Trade Commission, 26 September, https://www.ftc.gov/news -events/news/press-releases/2023/09/ftc-sues-amazon-illegally-maintai ning-monopoly-power

Fuchs, C. (2011) 'Web 2.0, Prosumption and Surveillance', *Surveillance & Society* 8(3).

Fuchs, C. (2019) 'Karl Marx in the Age of Big Data Capitalism', in D. Chandler and C. Fuchs (eds), *Digital Objects, Digital Subjects: Interdisciplinary Perspectives on Capitalism, Labour and Politics in the Age of Big Data*. London: University of Westminster Press.

Fulcher, J. (2015) *Capitalism: A Very Short Introduction*, 2nd edn. Oxford: Oxford University Press.

Gabrys, J. (2011) *Digital Rubbish: A Natural History of Electronics*. Ann Arbor: University of Michigan Press.

Garnham, N. (1990) *Capitalism and Communication: Global Culture and the Economics of Information*. London: Sage.

Giblin, R. and Doctorow, C. (2022) *Chokepoint Capitalism: How Big Tech and Big Content Captured Creative Labor Markets and How We'll Win Them Back*. Boston: Beacon Press.

Giddens, A. (1991) *The Consequences of Modernity*. Cambridge: Polity.

Giddens, A. (1999) 'Runaway World', BBC Reith Lecture, 7 April, https:// www.bbc.co.uk/radio4/reith1999/lecture1.shtml

Gilroy, P. (1987) *There Ain't No Black in the Union Jack*. London: Hutchinson.

Giroux, H. (2019) *Neoliberalism's War on Higher Education*. Chicago: Haymarket.

Gitlin, T. (1980) *The Whole World is Watching: Mass Media in the Making and Unmaking of the New Left*. Berkeley: University of California Press.

Glasgow University Media Group (1976) 'Bad News', *Theory and Society* 3(3).

Goclowski, M. (2016) 'Public Media Independence Undermined in Poland: OSCE', Reuters, 22 September, https://www.reuters.com/article/world /public-media-independence-undermined-in-poland-osce-idUSKCN11S 192/

Goffman, E. (1974) *Frame Analysis: An Essay on the Organization of Experience*. New York: Harper & Row.

Golding, P. and Murdock, G. (2000) 'Culture, Communications and Political Economy', in J. Curran and M. Gurevitch (eds), *Mass Media and Society*, 3rd edn. London: Arnold.

Goldman Sachs (2024) 'Gen AI: Too Much Spend, Too Little Benefit?' 25 June, https://www.goldmansachs.com/insights/top-of-mind/gen-ai-too -much-spend-too-little-benefit

Graeber, D. (2012) 'Of Flying Cars and the Declining Rate of Profit', *The Baffler*, https://thebaffler.com/salvos/of-flying-cars-and-the-declining-rate -of-profit

Graham, J. (2024) MacTaggart Lecture, Edinburgh International Television Festival, 21 August, https://www.televisual.com/news/james-grahams -mactaggart-the-full-lecture/

Gramsci, A. (1971) *Selections from the Prison Notebooks*, ed. and trans. by Q. Hoare and G. Nowell-Smith. New York: International Publishers.

Gray, H. (1940) 'The Passing of the Public Utility Concept', *Journal of Land & Public Utility Economics* 16(1).

Greenly (2025) 'The Carbon Cost of Streaming', https://greenly.earth/en-gb /leaf-media/data-stories/the-carbon-cost-of-streaming

Gross, A. and Murphy, H. (2023) 'Elon Musk Tells Rishi Sunak AI Will Render All Jobs Obsolete', *Financial Times*, 2 November, https://www.ft .com/content/3b3845b0-0102-47a0-ba58-03ef4d5b69da

Grostern, J. (2025) 'Climate Disinformation "Normalised" on French TV and Radio, Report Finds', *DeSmog*, 15 April, https://www.desmog.com/2025/04/15/climate-disinformation-normalised-on-french-tv-and-radio-report-finds/

Guidroz, K. and Berger, M. (2009) 'A Conversation with Founding Scholars of Intersectionality', in M. Berger and K. Guidroz (eds), *The Intersectional Approach: Transforming the Academy through Race, Class and Gender*. Chapel Hill: University of North Carolina Press.

Habermas, J. (1989 [1962]) *The Structural Transformation of the Public Sphere*. Cambridge: Polity Press.

Hall, S. (1997) *Race, the Floating Signifier*. Video. Northampton, MA: Media Education Foundation.

Hall, S. (2011) 'The Neo-Liberal Revolution', *Cultural Studies* 25(6).

Hall, S., Critcher, C., Jefferson, T., Clarke, J. and Roberts, B. (1978) *Policing the Crisis: Mugging, the State and Law and Order*. Basingstoke: Macmillan.

Hall, T. (2011) 'Justice and the Good Life in Lukács's *History and Class Consciousness*', in T. Bewes and T. Hall (eds), *Georg Lukács: The Fundamental Dissonance of Existence*. London: Bloomsbury.

Hallin, D. (1994) *We Keep America on Top of the World: Television Journalism and the Public Sphere*. London: Routledge.

Hanif, F. (2021) *British Media's Coverage of Muslims and Islam*, Centre for Media Monitoring, https://cfmm.org.uk/wp-content/uploads/2021/11/CfMM-Annual-Report-2018-2020-digital.pdf

Hanif, F. (2024) *Media Bias Gaza 23–24*, Centre for Media Monitoring, https://cfmm.org.uk/wp-content/uploads/2024/03/CfMM-Report-Final-MEDIA-BIAS-GAZA-2023-24-ePDF.pdf

Harari, Y. N. (2024) *Nexus: A Brief History of Information Networks from the Stone Age to AI*. New York: Random House.

Hardt, H. (2000) 'Communication is Freedom: Karl Marx on Press Freedom and Censorship', *Javnost – The Public* 7(4).

Harkness, T. (2024) *Technology Is Not the Problem*. London: Harper Collins.

Harrington, T. (2025) 'Netflix Q4 2024: More Subs, More Price Rises', Enders Analysis, 22 January.

Harrington, T. and Sutcliffe, G. (2024) 'Netflix Q4 2023: Big Strides as People Pay Up', Enders Analysis, 24 January.

Harris, M. (2022) 'Are We Living under "Technofeudalism"?' *New York* magazine, 28 October, https://nymag.com/intelligencer/2022/10/what-is-technofeudalism.html

Harvey, D. (2003) *The New Imperialism*. Oxford: Oxford University Press.

Harvey, D. (2005) *A Brief History of Neoliberalism*. Oxford: Oxford University Press.

Harvey, D. (2014) *Seventeen Contradictions and the End of Capitalism*. London: Profile.

Hayek, F. (1944) *The Road to Serfdom*. London: George Routledge & Sons.

Headrick, D. (1981) *The Tools of Empire: Technology and European Imperialism in the Nineteenth Century*. Oxford: Oxford University Press.

Heath, O. and Bennett, M. (2023) 'BSA 40: A Liberalisation in Attitudes'. London: National Centre for Social Research.

Hedges, C. (2009) 'With Gaza, Journalists Fail Again', *truthdig*, 26 January, https://www.truthdig.com/articles/with-gaza-journalists-fail-again/

Herman, E. and Chomsky, N. (1988) *Manufacturing Consent: The Political Economy of the Mass Media*. New York: Pantheon.

Hesmondhalgh, D. (2010) 'User-Generated Content, Free Labour and the Cultural Industries', *Ephemera* 10(3/4).

Hesmondhalgh, D. (2026) *The Cultural Industries*, 5th edn. London: Sage.

Hesmondhalgh, D., Valverde, R., Kaye, D. and Li, Z. (2023) 'Digital Platforms and Infrastructure in the Realm of Culture', *Media and Communication* 11(2).

Hilferding, R. (1981 [1910]) *Finance Capital: A Study of the Latest Phase of Development*. London: Routledge & Kegan Paul.

Hill, C. (1984) *The World Turned Upside Down: Radical Ideas during the English Revolution*. London: Penguin.

Hind, D. (2010) *The Return of the Public: Democracy, Power and the Case for Media Reform*. London: Verso.

Hobbes, T. (1991 [1651]) *Leviathan*. Cambridge: Cambridge University Press.

Hobsbawm, E. (1964) *The Age of Revolution: 1789–1848*. New York: Mentor.

Hobsbawm, E. (1989) *The Age of Empire: 1875–1914*. New York: Vintage.

Holland, S. and Singh, K. (2025) 'Biden Takes Aim at "Tech Industrial Complex", Echoing Eisenhower', Reuters, 16 January, https://www.reuters.com/world/us/biden-raises-alarm-about-dangerous-concentration-power-among-few-wealthy-people-2025-01-16/

Holt, J. (2024) *Cloud Policy: A History of Regulating Pipelines, Platforms and Data*. Cambridge, MA: MIT Press.

House, K. E. (2024) 'The World is Up for Grabs', *Wall Street Journal*, 15 December, https://www.wsj.com/opinion/the-middle-east-is-up-for-grabs-syria-collapse-iran-nuclear-race-israel-suadi-arabia-be43258f

Huber, M. (2022) *Climate Change as Class War*. London: Verso.

Human Rights Watch (2024) 'Hungary: Media Curbs Harm Rule of Law', 13 February, https://www.hrw.org/news/2024/02/13/hungary-media-curbs-harm-rule-law

Huws, U. (2013) 'The Underpinnings of Class in the Digital Age: Living, Labour and Value', in L. Panitch, G. Albo and V. Chibber (eds), *Registering Class: Socialist Register 2014*. London: Merlin Press.

Inman, P. (2024) 'Why Government Debt Is Not like Household Borrowing', *Guardian*, 13 June, https://www.theguardian.com/business/article/2024/jun/13/why-government-debt-is-not-like-household-borrowing

International Energy Agency (2025) *Energy and AI: World Energy Outlook Special Report*, https://iea.blob.core.windows.net/assets/601eaec9-ba91-4623-819b-4ded331ec9e8/EnergyandAI.pdf

International Federation of Journalists (2025) 'Palestine: At Least 156 Journalists and Media Workers Killed in Gaza', 9 April, https://www.ifj.org/media-centre/news/detail/category/press-releases/article/palestine-at-least-156-journalists-and-media-workers-killed-in-gaza

IPPR (2024) 'Transformed by AI: How Generative Artificial Intelligence Could Affect Work in the UK – and How to Manage It'. London: IPPR, https://www.ippr.org/articles/transformed-by-ai

Isaac, M. and Griffith, E. (2024) 'OpenAI is Growing Fast and Burning through Piles of Money', *New York Times*, 27 September, https://www.nytimes.com/2024/09/27/technology/openai-chatgpt-investors-funding.html

Jacobsen, K. (2025) 'Alarm Bells: Trump's First 100 Days Ramp up Fear for the Press, Democracy', Committee to Protect Journalists, 30 April, https://cpj.org/special-reports/alarm-bells-trumps-first-100-days-ramp-up-fear-for-the-press-democracy/

Jahan, S. and Mahmud, A. (2015) 'What is Capitalism?' *Finance & Development* 52(2).

Jakubowski, F. (1976) *Ideology and Superstructure in Historical Materialism*. London: Allison & Busby.

James, C. L. R. (1963) *The Black Jacobins*. New York: Vintage.

James, C. L. R. (2013) *Modern Politics*. Oakland: PM Press.

Jarvis, J. (2009) *What Would Google Do?* New York: Harper Collins.

Jessop, B. (2002) *The Future of the Capitalist State*. Cambridge: Polity.

Jin, D. Y. (2015) *Digital Platforms, Imperialism and Political Culture*. London: Routledge.

Johnson, A. and Ali, O. (2024) 'Coverage of Gaza War in the *New York Times* and Other Major Newspapers Heavily Favoured Israel, Analysis Shows', *Intercept*, 9 January, https://theintercept.com/2024/01/09/newspapers-israel-palestine-bias-new-york-times/

Jones, R. (2014) 'Intersectional Feminism, Class, and Austerity', *Velvet Coalmine*, 11 March, https://rhianejones.com/2014/03/11/rhian-e-jones-manchester-conference-intersectional-feminism-class-and-austerity/

Kay, J. (2024) *The Corporation in the Twenty-First Century: Why (Almost) Everything We Are Told about Business Is Wrong*. London: Profile.

Kelly, K. (2020) 'What "Capitalism" Is and How It Affects People', *Teen Vogue*, 25 August, https://www.teenvogue.com/story/what-capitalism-is

Kelly, M., Harb, H., Loveluck, L., Berger, M. and Brown, C. (2024) 'Palestinian Medics Said Israel Gave Them Safe Passage to Save a 6-year-old Girl in Gaza. They Were All Killed', *Washington Post*, 16 April, https://www.washingtonpost.com/world/interactive/2024/hind-rajab-israel-gaza-killing-timeline/

Kennard, M. (2019) 'How the UK Military and Intelligence Establishment Is Working to Stop Jeremy Corbyn Becoming Prime Minister', *Declassified UK*, 4 December, https://www.declassifieduk.org/how-the-uk-military-and-intelligence-establishment-is-working-to-stop-jeremy-corbyn-becoming-prime-minister/

Kennedy, M. (2025) 'America's AI Strategy: Playing Defence while China

Plays to Win', Wilson Center, 24 January, https://www.wilsoncenter.org
/article/americas-ai-strategy-playing-defense-while-china-plays-win

Keynes, J. M. (1936) *General Theory of Employment, Interest and Money.*
Cambridge: Cambridge University Press.

Khalili, L. (2025) *Extractive Capitalism: How Commodities and Cronyism
Drive the Global Economy.* London: Profile.

Khan, L. (2024) Remarks to FTC Tech Summit, 25 January, https://www
.ftc.gov/system/files/ftc_gov/pdf/2024.01.25-chair-khan-remarks-at-ot-te
ch-summit.pdf

Khiabany, G. (2020) 'The Violence of an Illiberal Liberalism', in A. Davis,
N. Fenton, D. Freedman and G. Khiabany (eds), *Media, Democracy and
Social Change.* London: Sage.

Kikeri, S., Nellis, J. and Shirley, M. (1992) *Privatization: The Lesson of
Experience.* Washington, DC: World Bank.

Klein, N. (2005 [1999]) *No Logo.* London: Harper Perennial.

Klein, N. (2014) *This Changes Everything: Capitalism vs the Climate.* London:
Penguin.

Klontzas, M. (2025) 'Public Service, Technology and Innovation', in
D. Freedman and M. Klontzas (eds), *Media Pasts and Futures: Critical
Reflections on 'Power Without Responsibility'.* London: University of
Westminster Press.

Kocka, J. (2016) *Capitalism: A Short History.* Princeton: Princeton University
Press.

Koehler, B. (2014) *Early Islam and the Birth of Capitalism.* New York:
Lexington Books.

Kollontai, A. (1977) *Selected Writings.* London: Allison & Busby.

Konrad, A. and Cai, K. (2023) Interview with Sam Altman, *Forbes,* 22
February, https://www.forbes.com/sites/alexkonrad/2023/02/03/exclusive
-openai-sam-altman-chatgpt-agi-google-search/

Kreps, D. (2015) 'Prince Warns Young Artists: Record Contracts Are
"Slavery"', *Rolling Stone,* 9 August, https://www.rollingstone.com/music
/music-news/prince-warns-young-artists-record-contracts-are-slavery-32
645/

Kumar, A. (2020) *Monopsony Capitalism: Power and Production in the Twilight
of the Sweatshop Age.* Cambridge: Cambridge University Press.

Kumar, A. (2024) 'When Monopsony Power Wanes', *Historical Materialism*
31(4).

Kurzweil, R. (2024) *The Singularity Is Nearer – When We Merge with AI.*
London: Bodley Head.

Laclau, E. and Mouffe, C. (2001) *Hegemony and Socialist Strategy,* 2nd edn.
London: Verso.

Lazzarato, M. (1976) 'Immaterial Labor', in P. Virno and M. Hardt (eds),
*Radical Thought in Italy: A Potential Politics.* Minneapolis: University of
Minnesota Press.

Leadbeater, C. (2009) *Living on Thin Air.* London: Viking.

Lefebvre, H. (1968) *The Sociology of Marx.* New York: Random House.

Lenin, V. (1933 [1917]) *Imperialism: The Highest Stage of Capitalism*. London: Martin Lawrence.

Lenin, V. (1977 [1917]) *The State and Revolution*. Moscow: Progress.

Levitsky, S. and Ziblatt, D. (2024) *The Tyranny of the Majority*. New York: Penguin Random House.

Lewis, J., Brookes, R., Mosdell, N. and Threadgold, T. (2006) *Shoot First and Ask Questions Later: Media Coverage of the 2003 Iraq War*. New York: Peter Lang.

Leys, C. (2001) *Market-Driven Politics: Neoliberal Democracy and the Public Interest*. London: Verso.

Liebling, A. J. (1960) 'The Wayward Press: Do You Belong in Journalism?', *New Yorker*, 14 May, https://www.newyorker.com/magazine/1960/05/14/do-you-belong-in-journalism

Lindgren, S. (2023) *Critical Theory of AI*. Cambridge: Polity.

Lindsey, R. and Dahlman, L. (2025) 'Climate Change: Global Temperature', Climate.gov, 29 May, https://www.climate.gov/news-features/understanding-climate/climate-change-global-temperature

Linebaugh, P. (2008) *Magna Carta Manifesto: Liberties and Commons for All*. Berkeley: University of California Press.

Lorenz, T. (2023a) *Extremely Online: The Untold Story of Fame, Influence and Power on the Internet*. London: W. H. Allen.

Lorenz, T. (2023b) '"The Internet is Vicious and Toxic, but I'd Never Go Back to the 90s": Taylor Lorenz talks to Monica Lewinsky', *Guardian*, 5 October, https://www.theguardian.com/media/2023/oct/05/monica-lewinsky-taylor-lorenz-social-media-interview

Losurdo, D. (2011) *Liberalism: A Counter-History*. London: Verso.

Lowenstein, R. (2004) *Origins of the Crash: The Great Bubble and Its Undoing*. New York: Penguin.

Lukács, G. (1971 [1923]) *History and Class Consciousness*. London: Merlin Press.

Luxemburg, R. (2003 [1913]) *The Accumulation of Capital*. London: Routledge.

Lyon, D. (2015) *Surveillance after Snowden*. Cambridge: Polity.

MacLeod, A. (ed.) (2019) *Propaganda in the Information Age: Still Manufacturing Consent*. London: Routledge.

Macpherson, C. B. (1978) 'The Meaning of Property', in C. B. Macpherson (ed.), *Property*. Toronto: University of Toronto Press.

Mair, P. (2013) *Ruling the Void: The Hollowing of Western Democracy*. London: Verso.

Malm, A. (2013) 'The Origins of Fossil Capital: From Water to Steam in the British Cotton Industry', *Historical Materialism* 21(1).

Marvin, C. (1988) *When Old Technologies Were New: Thinking About Electric Communication in the Late Nineteenth Century*. New York: Oxford University Press.

Marx, K. (1844) *A Contribution to the Critique of Hegel's Philosophy of Right*,

https://www.marxists.org/archive/marx/works/1843/critique-hpr/intro
.htm

Marx, K. (1870) 'Letter to Sigfrid Mayer and August Vogt in New York',
9 April, https://www.marxists.org/archive/marx/works/1870/letters/70_04
_09.htm

Marx, K. (1970 [1859]) *A Contribution to the Critique of Political Economy*.
New York: International Publishers.

Marx, K. (1971 [1894]) *Capital, Volume 3*. Moscow: Progress Publishers.

Marx, K. (1973 [1857–61]) *Grundrisse*. London: Penguin.

Marx, K. (1977 [1867]) *Capital, Volume 1*. New York: Vintage.

Marx, K. (1978 [1849]) *Wage Labour and Capital*. Beijing: Foreign
Languages Press.

Marx, K. (2009 [1844]) *Economic and Philosophic Manuscripts of 1844*.
Amherst, NY: Prometheus.

Marx, K. and Engels, F. (1973 [1848]) *Manifesto of the Communist Party*.
Beijing: Foreign Languages Press.

Marx, K. and Engels, F. (2022 [1846]) *The German Ideology*. Paris: Foreign
Languages Press.

Mattelart, A. (1979) 'For a Class Analysis of Communication', in
A. Mattelart and S. Siegelaub (eds), *Communication and Class Struggle,
Vol. 1: Capitalism, Imperialism*. New York: International General.

Mattelart, A. and Siegelaub, S. (eds) (1979) *Communication and Class
Struggle, Vol. 1: Capitalism, Imperialism*. New York: International General.

Mattelart, A. and Siegelaub, S. (eds) (1983) *Communication and Class
Struggle, Vol. 2: Liberation, Socialism*. New York: International General.

Maxwell, R. and Miller, T. (2012) *Greening the Media*. Oxford: Oxford
University Press.

Mazzucato, M. (2015) *The Entrepreneurial State: Debunking Public vs. Private
Sector Myths*. London: Anthem Press.

McCarrick, P. (2024) 'Here are All the Musicians Suing Donald Trump this
Year', *Dazed*, 30 August, https://www.dazeddigital.com/music/article/64
480/1/donald-trump-lawsuits-beyonce-jack-white-sinead-oconnor-celine
-dion-foo-fighters

McChesney, R. (2004) *The Problem of the Media: U.S. Communication Policies
in the 21st Century*. New York: Monthly Review Press.

McChesney, R. (2013) *Digital Disconnect: How Capitalism Is Turning the
Internet against Democracy*. New York: New Press.

McGreal, C. (2024) 'CNN Staff Say Network's Pro-Israel Slant Amounts
to "Journalistic Malpractice"', *Guardian*, 4 February, https://www.theguar
dian.com/media/2024/feb/04/cnn-staff-pro-israel-bias

McGuigan, J. (2009) *Cool Capitalism*. London: Pluto.

McKibben, B. (2008) 'The Greenback Effect', *Mother Jones*, May/June,
https://www.motherjones.com/environment/2008/05/greenback-effect/

McLuhan, M. (2001 [1964]) *Understanding Media*. London: Routledge.

Meszaros, I. (1975) *Marx's Theory of Alienation*. London: Merlin Press.

Metcalf, S. (2017) 'Neoliberalism: The Idea that Swallowed the World', *Guardian*, 18 August, https://www.theguardian.com/news/2017/aug/18/ne oliberalism-the-idea-that-changed-the-world

Meyrick, C. (2025) 'Why is the UK Film and Television Sector Struggling?' Economics Observatory, 16 January, https://economicsobservatory.com /why-is-the-uk-film-and-television-sector-struggling

Miles, R. and Brown, M. (2003) *Racism*, 2nd edn. London: Routledge.

Miliband, R. (1969) *The State in Capitalist Society*. London: Camelot.

Mill, J. S. (2016 [1859]) *On Liberty*. Los Angeles: Enhanced Media.

Miller, T. (2024) *Why Journalism? A Polemic*. London: Routledge.

Mills, C. W. (1970) *The Sociological Imagination*. London: Penguin.

Milmo, D. (2025) 'Meta to Stop Targeting UK Citizen with Personalised Ads after Settling Privacy Case', *Guardian*, 22 March, https://www.thegu ardian.com/technology/2025/mar/22/meta-confirms-it-is-considering-ch arging-uk-users-for-ad-free-version

Mirrlees, T. (2025) *Work in the Digital Media and Entertainment Industries: A Critical Introduction*. London: Routledge.

Mitchell, M. (2019) *Artificial Intelligence: A Guide for Thinking Humans*. London: Penguin.

Mitchell, B. and Fazi, T. (2017) *Reclaiming the State: A Progressive Vision of Sovereignty for a Post-Neoliberal World*. London: Pluto.

Monbiot, G. (2024) Thread on 'X', 23 September, https://threadreaderapp .com/thread/1838183112649425118.html

Mondon, A. and Winter, A. (2020) *Reactionary Democracy: How Racism and the Populist Far Right Became Mainstream*. London: Verso.

Moore, J. (2016) 'Introduction: Anthropocene or Capitalocene? Nature, History and the Crisis of Capitalism', in J. Moore (ed.), *Anthropocene or Capitalocene? Nature, History and the Crisis of Capitalism*. Oakland: PM Press.

Morozov, E. (2022) 'Critique of Techno-Feudal Reason', *New Left Review* 133/134 (January/April).

Morris, H. (2025) *Apocalyptic Authoritarianism: Climate Crisis, Media and Power*. Oxford: Oxford University Press.

Mosco, V. (2009) *The Political Economy of Communication*. London: Sage.

Moulier-Boutang, Y. (2011) *Cognitive Capitalism*. Cambridge: Polity.

Muldoon, J., Graham, M. and Cant, C. (2024) *Feeding the Machine: The Hidden Human Labour Powering AI*. Edinburgh: Canongate.

Murdock, G. and Golding, P. (1973) 'For a Political Economy of Mass Communications', in R. Miliband and J. Saville (eds), *Socialist Register 1973*. London: Merlin Press.

Negroponte, N. (1996) *Being Digital*. London: Coronet.

Newell, P. and Paterson, M. (2010) *Climate Capitalism: Global Warming and the Transformation of the Global Economy*. Cambridge: Cambridge University Press.

Nicolaou, A. (2024a) 'Spotify Hits Record Quarterly Profit as It Enters "New Phase"', *Financial Times*, 23 April, https://www.ft.com/content/b63 53fb2-a149-46ae-bb12-901e65d2c445

Nicolaou, A. (2024b) 'Streaming Model for Music Set for a Streamlining', *Financial Times*, 18 January, https://www.ft.com/content/78a7b1b8-20ae -4800-8a08-af2b5fc35d7b

Nicolaou, A. and Temple-West, P. (2024) 'Spotify Executives Cash in as Streaming Service Stock Price Soars', *Financial Times*, 22 December, https://www.ft.com/content/d7ecd25a-e827-49b0-b19a-fed96fe7e0b3

Nineham, C. (2023) *Radical Chains: Why Class Matters*. London: Zero.

Norberg, J. (2023) *The Capitalist Manifesto: Why the Global Free Market Will Save the World*. London: Atlantic Books.

Nye, J. (1990) 'Soft Power', *Foreign Policy* 80.

O'Brien, I. (2024) 'TikTok's Annual Carbon Footprint is Likely Bigger than Greece's, Study Finds', 12 December, https://www.theguardian.com/tech nology/2024/dec/12/tiktok-carbon-footprint

OECD (2023) 'OECD Employment Outlook 2023: Artificial Intelligence and the Labour Market', OECD Publishing, https://doi.org/10.1787/08 785bba-en

Ofcom (2023) 'BBC Audience Review: Understanding What Factors May Drive Lower Satisfaction Levels among D and E Socio-Economic Groups', 30 November, https://www.ofcom.org.uk/tv-radio-and-on-dema nd/bbc/bbc-audiences-review/

O'Hara, G. (2010) 'New Histories of British Imperial Communication and the "Networked World" of the 19th and Early 20th Centuries', *History Compass* 8(7).

O'Neill, O. (2004) *Rethinking Freedom of the Press*. Dublin: Royal Irish Academy.

Palma, S. and Acton, M. (2024) 'US Accuses Apple of Building Smartphone Monopoly in Antitrust Case', *Financial Times*, 21 March, https://www.ft .com/content/e3f83740-f44a-4e1d-9dec-0439ef2ebf58

Palma, S. and Murphy, H. (2025) '"We Had to Buy Them": Old Emails Prove Uncomfortable for Zuckerberg in High-Stakes Trial', *Financial Times*, 18 April, https://www.ft.com/content/931337f6-6fad-40b0-a8a5 -2fb78ba4976a

Palma, S., Acton, M. and Morris, S. (2025) 'Google Shares Jump after Judge Refrains from Ordering Break-up', *Financial Times*, 3 September, https://www.ft.com/content/25863491-1f19-4deb-95a2-fa18ee84eabb

Partington, R. (2024) 'AI "Apocalypse" Could Take Away almost 8m Jobs in UK, Says Report', *Guardian*, 27 March, https://www.theguardian.com /technology/2024/mar/27/ai-apocalypse-could-take-away-almost-8m-jobs -in-uk-says-report

Pasquale, F. (2015) *The Black Box Society*. Cambridge, MA: Harvard University Press.

Pedro-Carañana, J., Broudy, D. and Klaehn, J. (eds) (2018) *The Propaganda Model Today: Filtering Perception and Awareness*. London: University of Westminster Press.

Petre, C. (2021) *All the News that's Fit to Click: How Metrics Are Transforming the Work of Journalists*. Princeton: Princeton University Press.

Pew Research Center (2022) 'Modest Declines in Positive Views of "Socialism" and "Capitalism" in U.S.', 19 September, https://www.pew research.org/politics/2022/09/19/modest-declines-in-positive-views-of-so cialism-and-capitalism-in-u-s/

Philo, G. and Berry, M. (2011) *More Bad News from Israel.* London: Pluto.

Philo, G. and Berry, M. (2023) 'Media Research Shows BBC Is Far from "Biased against Israel"', 23 December, *openDemocracy*, https://www.open democracy.net/en/israel-palestine-bbc-news-coverage-bias-gaza-war/

Pickard, V. (2020) *Democracy without Journalism? Confronting the Misinformation Society.* Oxford: Oxford University Press.

Pickard, V. and Williams, A. (2014) 'Salvation or Folly: The Promises and Perils of Digital Paywalls', *Digital Journalism* 2(2).

Piechota, G. (2023) 'Which Paywall Models Are Most Popular and Most Effective?' International News Media Association blog, 5 February, https://www.inma.org/blogs/reader-revenue/post.cfm/which-paywall-mo dels-are-most-popular-and-which-are-most-effective

Piketty, T. (2014) *Capital in the Twenty-First Century.* London: Harvard University Press.

Piketty, T. (2020) *Capital and Ideology.* London: Harvard University Press.

Polanyi, K. (2001 [1944]) *The Great Transformation: The Political and Economic Origins of Our Time*, 2nd edn. Boston: Beacon Press.

Pollock, A. (2020) *NHS plc: The Privatisation of our Health Care.* London: Verso.

Pope, A. (2024) 'NYT v. OpenAI: The Times' About-Face', *Harvard Law Review*, 10 April, https://harvardlawreview.org/blog/2024/04/nyt-v-openai -the-timess-about-face/

Poulantzas, N. (1980) *State, Power, Socialism.* London: Verso.

Press, G. (2025) 'Are We at Peak AI Bubble and the Cusp of "AI Moment"?' *Forbes*, 30 March, https://www.forbes.com/sites/gilpress/2025/03/30/are -we-at-peak-ai-bubble-and-the-cusp-of-ai-moment/

Quinn, W. and Turner, J. (2020) *Boom and Bust: A Global History of Financial Bubbles.* Cambridge: Cambridge University Press.

Raihani, N. (2021) *The Social Instinct: What Nature Can Teach Us about Working Together.* London: Random House.

Rampton, S. and Stauber, J. (2003) *Weapons of Mass Deception: The Uses of Propaganda in Bush's War in Iraq.* London: Robinson.

Rees, J. (1998) *The Algebra of Revolution.* London: Routledge.

Reuters Institute (2025) *Digital News Report 2025.* Oxford: Reuters Institute for the Study of Journalism.

Ricci, A. (2018) 'French Opposition Parties Are Taking Macron's Anti-Misinformation Law to Court', Poynter, 4 December, https://www.poyn ter.org/fact-checking/2018/french-opposition-parties-are-taking-macrons -anti-misinformation-law-to-court/

Rifkin, J. (2011) *The Third Industrial Revolution: How Lateral Power is*

*Transforming Energy, the Economy, and the World.* New York: St Martin's Press.

Risen, J. (2016) 'If Donald Trump Targets Journalists, Thank Obama', *New York Times*, 30 December, https://www.nytimes.com/2016/12/30/opinion /sunday/if-donald-trump-targets-journalists-thank-obama.html

Ritman, A. (2025) 'How the UK Film and TV Industry is Juggling a Boom in Hollywood Production Like "Avengers" and "Harry Potter" and a Bust For Everything Else', *Variety*, 13 June, https://variety.com/2025/film/glo bal/uk-hollywood-boom-bust-local-film-tv-1236429372/

Robbins, D. (2015) 'Why the Media Doesn't Care about Climate Change', *Irish Times*, 26 November, https://www.irishtimes.com/opinion/why-the -media-doesn-t-care-about-climate-change-1.2443663

Robin, C. (2025) 'Waiting Game', *Sidecar*, 20 June, https://newleftreview .org/sidecar/posts/waiting-game

Robinson, C. (1983) *Black Marxism: The Making of the Black Radical Tradition.* Durham: University of North Carolina Press.

Robinson, J. (2013 [1956]) *The Accumulation of Capital.* Basingstoke: Palgrave Macmillan.

Rodney, W. (1982 [1972]) *How Europe Underdeveloped Africa.* Washington, DC: Howard University Press.

Rottenberg, C. (2018) *The Rise of Neoliberal Feminism.* Oxford: Oxford University Press.

Rousseau, J. J. (1987 [1755]) *Basic Political Writings*, trans. and ed. D. A. Cress. Indianapolis: Hackett.

Rowbotham, S. (1973) *Hidden from History: 300 Years of Women's Oppression and the Fight against It.* London: Pluto.

Rueckert, P. (2021) 'Pegasus: The New Global Weapon for Silencing Journalists', *Forbidden Stories*, 18 July, https://forbiddenstories.org/pegas us-the-new-global-weapon-for-silencing-journalists/

Russell, S. (2021) 'BBC Reith Lectures 2021 – Living with Artificial Intelligence', BBC Radio 4, http://downloads.bbc.co.uk/radio4/reith2021 /BBC_2021_Reith_Lecture_2021_1.pdf

Saha, A. (2018) *Race and the Cultural Industries.* Cambridge: Polity.

Said, E. (1979) *Orientalism.* New York: Vintage.

Said, E. (1997) *Covering Islam.* New York: Vintage.

Said, E. (2024 [1979]) *The Question of Palestine.* London: Fitzcarraldo.

Saito, K. (2023) *Marx in the Anthropocene: Towards the Idea of Degrowth Communism.* Cambridge: Cambridge University Press.

Sandhu, S. (2025) 'Humans Generate 62 Million Tonnes of E-Waste Each Year: Here's What Happens when It's Recycled', *The Conversation*, 19 February, https://theconversation.com/humans-generate-62-million-ton nes-of-e-waste-each-year-heres-what-happens-when-its-recycled-249842

Savage, M. (2015) *Social Class in the 21st Century.* London: Pelican.

Sawhney, H. (1996) 'Information Superhighway: Metaphors as Midwives', *Media, Culture & Society* 18(2).

Schiller, D. (2025) 'Baltic Blow-Up', *Information Observatory*, 31 January, https://informationobservatory.info/2025/01/31/baltic-blow-up/

Schiller, H. (1971) *Mass Communications and American Empire*. Boston: Beacon.

Schiller, H. (1976) *Communication and Cultural Domination*. White Plains, NY: M. E. Sharpe.

Schlosberg, J. (2013) *Power beyond Scrutiny: Media, Justice and Accountability*. London: Pluto.

Schumpeter, J. (2010 [1942]) *Capitalism, Socialism and Democracy*. London: Routledge.

Schwab, K. (2017) *The Fourth Industrial Revolution*. London: Portfolio Penguin.

Segura, M. and Waisbord, S. (2019) 'Between Data Capitalism and Data Citizenship', *Television & New Media* 20(4).

Shaw, L. (2022) 'The Age of Peak TV Is Ending. An Age of Austerity Is Beginning', Bloomberg UK, 4 July, https://www.bloomberg.com/news/newsletters/2022-07-04/the-age-of-peak-tv-is-ending-an-age-of-austerity-is-beginning

Sherif, A. (2024) 'Operating Systems Market Share of Desktop PCs 2013–2024, by Month', 5 March, https://www.statista.com/statistics/218089/global-market-share-of-windows-7/

Siebert, F., Peterson, T. and Schramm, W. (1956) *Four Theories of the Press*. Champaign: University of Illinois Press.

Silke, H. and Graham, C. (2017) 'Framing Privatisation: The Domination of Neoliberal Discourse and the Death of the Public Good', *Triple C* 15(2).

Skocpol, T. (1979) *States and Social Revolutions*. New York: Cambridge University Press.

Smith, A. (2012 [1776]) *The Wealth of Nations*. Ware, UK: Wordsworth Editions.

Smythe, D. (1977) 'Communications: Blindspot of Western Marxism', *Canadian Journal of Political and Social Theory* 1(3).

Sodergren, D. (2023) *Intelligence: The Fifth Industrial Revolution*, https://www.thefifthindustrialrevolution.co.uk/

Sparks, C. (1986) 'The Media and the State', in J. Curran, J. Ecclestone, G. Oakley and A. Richardson (eds), *Bending Reality: The State of the Media*. London: Pluto.

Sparks, C. (1998) *Communism, Capitalism and the Mass Media*. London: Sage.

Sparks, C. (2007) 'Extending and Refining the Propaganda Model', *Westminster Papers in Communication and Culture* 4(2).

Spilsbury, M. (2024) *Journalists at Work*, National Council for the Training of Journalists, https://www.nctj.com/wp-content/uploads/2024/09/Journalists-at-Work-2024-1.pdf

Srnicek, N. (2016) *Platform Capitalism*. Cambridge: Polity.

Standage, T. (1998) *The Victorian Internet*. London: Weidenfeld and Nicolson.

Standing, G. (2011) *The Precariat: The New Dangerous Class*. London: Bloomsbury.

Starr, P. (2004) *The Creation of the Media*. New York: Basic Books.

Ste Croix, G. (1981) *The Class Struggle in the Ancient Greek World: From the Archaic Age to the Arab Conquests*. London: Duckworth.

Stepansky, J. and Kestler-D'Amours, J. (2024) '"Strategic Interests" and Lobby Power: The Influences behind Biden's Support for Israel', Al Jazeera, 30 January, https://www.aljazeera.com/news/longform/2024/1/30/strategic-interests-lobby-power-what-influences-bidens-israel-support

Stoller, M. (2020) *Goliath: The 100-Year War between Monopoly Power and Democracy*. New York: Simon & Schuster.

Strange, S. (1996) *The Retreat of the State*. Cambridge: Cambridge University Press.

Streeck, W. (2011) 'The Crises of Democratic Capitalism', *New Left Review* 71 (September/October).

Streeck, W. (2014) 'How Will Capitalism End?' *New Left Review* 87 (May/June).

Streeck, W. (2024) *Taking Back Control? States and State Systems after Globalism*. London: Verso.

Suleyman, M. (2023) *The Coming Wave: AI, Power and the 21st Century's Greatest Dilemma*. London: Bodley Head.

Suroyo, G. and Sulaiman, S. (2024) 'Indonesia's Presumed President Prabowo Vows Smooth Transition, Pushes Privatisation', Reuters, 5 March, https://www.reuters.com/world/asia-pacific/presumed-president-prabowo-says-indonesia-democracy-messy-should-be-proud-2024-03-05/

Susca, M. (2024) *Hedged: How Private Investment Funds Helped Destroy American Newspapers and Undermine Democracy*. Urbana: University of Illinois Press.

Sutton Trust (2019) *Elitist Britain 2019: The Educational Backgrounds of Britain's Leading People*. London: Sutton Trust.

Sykes, S. and Hopner, V. (2024) 'Tradwives: Right-Wing Social Media Influencers', *Journal of Contemporary Ethnography* 53(4).

Syme, R. (2023) 'How Much Netflix Can the World Absorb?' *New Yorker*, 9 January, https://www.newyorker.com/magazine/2023/01/16/how-much-more-netflix-can-the-world-absorb-bela-bajaria

Syvertsen, T., Enli, G., Mjos, O. and Moe, H. (2014) *The Media Welfare State: Nordic Media in the Digital Era*. Ann Arbor: University of Michigan Press.

Tambini, D. (2021) *Media Freedom*. Cambridge: Polity.

Tapscott, D. and Williams, A. (2008) *Wikinomics: How Mass Collaboration Changes Everything*. London: Atlantic Books.

Taussig, M. (1980) *The Devil and Commodity Fetishism in South America*. Chapel Hill: University of North Carolina Press.

Tavlin, W. (2025) 'Casual Viewing: Why Netflix Looks Like That', *n +1* 49, https://www.nplusonemag.com/issue-49/essays/casual-viewing/

Tencer, D. (2024) 'Major Record Companies Sue AI Music Generators Suno, Udio for "Mass Infringement" of Copyright', 24 June, https://www.musicbusinessworldwide.com/major-record-companies-sue-ai-music-generators-suno-udio-for-mass-infringement-of-copyright/

Terranova, T. (2000) 'Free Labor: Producing Culture for the Digital Economy', *Social Text* 63, 18(2).

Tett, G. (2025) 'America's New "Patriotic" Capitalism', *Financial Times*, 30–31 August, https://www.ft.com/content/830ee74d-6a6f-4c30-adda-38 97750b015c

Theine, H. and Sevignani, S. (2024) 'Media Property: Mapping the Field and Future Trajectories in the Digital Age', *European Journal of Communication* 39(5).

Thiel, P. (2009) 'The Education of a Libertarian', *Cato Unbound*, 13 April, https://www.cato-unbound.org/2009/04/13/peter-thiel/education-libertarian/

Thiel, P. (2014) 'Competition Is for Losers', *Wall Street Journal*, 12 September, https://www.wsj.com/articles/peter-thiel-competition-is-for-losers-1410535536

Thompson, E. P. (1963) *The Making of the English Working Class*. London: Victor Gollancz.

Thompson, J. (1995) *The Media and Modernity*. Stanford: Stanford University Press.

Thussu, D. (ed.) (2007) *Media on the Move: Global Flow and Contra-Flow*. London: Routledge.

*Times* (2008) 'Crisis and Capitalism', leader column, *Times*, 17 September, https://www.thetimes.com/business-money/companies/article/crisis-and-capitalism-9nq2vs7ccvl

Titley, G. (2020) *Is Free Speech Racist?* Cambridge: Polity.

Tobitt, C. (2024) 'Subscription Giants News Corp and New York Times Buck the Trend of Revenue Decline', *Press Gazette*, 8 February, https://pressgazette.co.uk/media_business/news-corp-subscriptions-new-york-times/

Tomlinson, J. (1991) *Cultural Imperialism*. London: Continuum.

Toon, N. (2024) *How AI Thinks*. London: Transworld.

Traverso, E. (2021) *Revolution: An Intellectual History*. London: Verso.

Trotsky, L. (1973) *The First Five Years of the Communist International, Vol. 1*. London: New Park.

Trotsky, L. (1977) *Collected Works, Vol. 8*. New York: Pathfinder Press.

Tuchman, G. (1972) 'Objectivity as Strategic Ritual: An Examination of Newsmen's Notions of Objectivity', *American Journal of Sociology* 77(4).

Tunstall, J. (1977) *The Media Are American*. London: Constable.

Vanatta, S. (2024) *Plastic Capitalism*. New Haven: Yale University Press.

Varoufakis, Y. (2023) *Technofeudalism: What Killed Capitalism*. London: Bodley Head.

Vogel, L. (2013) *Marxism and the Oppression of Women: Toward a Unitary Theory*. Leiden, Netherlands: Brill.

Voltaire (2003 [1733]) *Philosophical Letters: Or, Letters Regarding the English Nation*. Indianapolis: Hackett.

Wallerstein, E. (1974) *The Modern World System*. London: Academic Press.

Wang, W. and Downey, J. (2024) 'Have We Reached a "Tipping Point" in Climate Change Reporting? How Mainstream Newspapers Cover Heatwaves', *Journalism Practice*, https://doi.org/10.1080/17512786.2024.2409840

Wark, M. (2019) *Capital Is Dead: Is This Something Worse?* London: Verso.

Watercutter, A. (2023) 'The Hollywood Strikes Stopped AI from Taking Your Job. But for How Long?' *Wired*, 25 December, https://www.wired.com/story/hollywood-saved-your-job-from-ai-2023-will-it-last/

Watson, E., Dalrymple, A. and Harrington, T. (2024) 'Pressure on to Deliver Profits', Enders Analysis, 14 March.

Weber, M. (2001 [1930]) *The Protestant Ethic and the Spirit of Capitalism*. London: Routledge.

Weber, M. (2013) *From Max Weber: Essays in Sociology*. London: Routledge.

Welsh, B. and Randewich, N. (2024) 'The Magnificent Seven Monitor', Reuters, 30 October, https://www.reuters.com/data/magnificent-seven-monitor-2024-10-30/

Wheeler, K. (2024) 'How NVidia's AI Made It the World's Most Valuable Firm', 8 November, *Technology Magazine*, https://technologymagazine.com/articles/how-nvidias-ai-made-it-the-worlds-most-valuable-firm

White Jr, L. (1964) *Medieval Technology and Social Change*. Oxford: Oxford University Press.

Williams, A., Miceli, M. and Gebru, T. (2022) 'The Exploited Labour behind Artificial Intelligence', 13 October, *Noema*, https://www.noemamag.com/the-exploited-labor-behind-artificial-intelligence/

Williams, E. (1964 [1944]) *Capitalism and Slavery*. London: Andre Deutsch.

Williams, R. (1968 [1962]) *Communications*. London: Penguin.

Williams, R. (1974) *Television: Technology and Cultural Form*. London: Fontana.

Williams, R. (1980) *Problems in Materialism and Culture*. London: Verso.

Williams, R. (1981) 'Communication Technologies and Social Institutions', in R. Williams (ed.), *Contact: Human Communication and Its History*. London: Thames & Hudson.

Williams, R. (1982) 'Democracy and Parliament', *Marxism Today*, June.

Williams, R. (1983) *Keywords: A Vocabulary of Culture and Society*. New York: Oxford University Press.

Williams, R. (1985) *Towards 2000*. London: Penguin.

Williamson, M. (2016) *Celebrity and Capitalism*. Cambridge: Polity Press.

Winseck, D. and Pike, R. (2007) *Communication and Empire: Media, Markets and Globalization, 1860–1930*. Durham, NC: Duke University Press.

Wiseman, J., Panyi, S., Maltepioti, K. and Chondrogiannos, T. (2024) 'Watching the Watchdogs: Spyware Surveillance of Journalists in Europe and the Ongoing Fight for Accountability', International Press Institute, https://ipi.media/wp-content/uploads/2024/03/Watching-the-watchdogs _ENG_online.pdf

Wollstonecraft, M. (1995 [1792]) *A Vindication of the Rights of Men with A Vindication of the Rights of Woman*, ed. S. Tomaselli. Cambridge: Cambridge University Press.

Wood, E. (1995) *Democracy against Capitalism: Renewing Historical Materialism*. Cambridge: Cambridge University Press.

Wood, E. (2002a) *The Origin of Capitalism*. London: Verso.

Wood, E. (2002b) 'Contradictions: Only in Capitalism?', in L. Panitch and C. Leys (eds), *Socialist Register*. London: Merlin Press.

Wright, E. O. (1997) *Class Counts: Comparative Studies in Class Analysis*. Cambridge: Cambridge University Press.

Wright, E. O. (2010) *Envisioning Real Utopias*. London: Verso.

Wright, E. O. (2021) *How to Be an Anticapitalist*. London: Verso.

Wright, K., Scott, M. and Bunce, M. (2024) *Capturing News, Capturing Democracy: Trump and the Voice of America*. New York: Oxford University Press.

Wu, T. (2017) *The Attention Merchants: The Epic Struggle to Get Inside Our Heads*. London: Atlantic Books.

Yeo, S. and Schiller, D. (2024) 'A Paradox: Corporate Power Increases as Corporate Competition Grows', *Information Observatory*, 13 August, https://informationobservatory.info/2024/08/13/a-paradox-corporate-po wer-increases-as-corporate-competition-grows/

Young, R. (2016) *Postcolonialism: An Historical Introduction*. Oxford: Wiley.

Zakaria, F. (2009) 'The Return of Capitalism', *Washington Post*, 15 June, https://www.washingtonpost.com/archive/opinions/2009/06/16/the-return -of-capitalism/7ff02983-fed8-4b6f-a305-2531ab57c106/

Zitelmann, R. (2023) 'Attitudes towards Capitalism in 34 Countries on Five Continents', *Economic Affairs* 43.

Zittrain, J. (2009) *The Future of the Internet*. London: Penguin.

Zuboff, S. (2019) *The Age of Surveillance Capitalism: The Fight for a Human Future at the New Frontier of Power*. New York: Public Affairs.

# Index